TRUE CRIME CHRONICLES

Volume Two

SERIAL KILLERS, OUTLAWS, AND JUSTICE
REAL CRIME STORIES FROM THE 1800s

Commentary by New York Times
Bestselling Author & former Detective

MIKE ROTHMILLER

WILDBLUE PRESS

WildBluePress.com

TRUE CRIME CHRONICLES Volume Two published by:
WILDBLUE PRESS
P.O. Box 102440
Denver, Colorado 80250

Publisher Disclaimer: Any opinions, statements of fact or fiction, descriptions, dialogue, and citations found in this book were provided by the author, and are solely those of the author. The publisher makes no claim as to their veracity or accuracy, and assumes no liability for the content.

Copyright 2020 by Mike Rothmiller

All rights reserved. No part of this book may be reproduced in any form or by any means without the prior written consent of the Publisher, excepting brief quotes used in reviews.

WILDBLUE PRESS is registered at the U.S. Patent and Trademark Offices.

ISBN 978-1-952225-42-0 Trade Paperback

ISBN 978-1-952225-41-3 eBook

Cover design © 2020 WildBlue Press. All rights reserved.

Interior Formatting/Book Cover Design by Elijah Toten www.totencreative.com

TRUE CRIME
CHRONICLES

INTRODUCTION

Welcome to Vol. 2 of the True Crime Chronicles. You will not be disappointed. While researching these books, I learned new details about various criminals, crimes, justice, and punishment during the 1800s. I am positive you had the same experience. I have repeated some of the introduction from Vol. 1 since it is relevant in Vol. 2. It will serve as a quick refresher before the start of your journey into these fascinating stories.

As a former detective of the Los Angeles Police Department, I witnessed the death and destruction caused by criminals of all races, ages, and religions. I saw good families in both the ghetto and upscale neighborhoods torn apart when facing the harsh reality that one of their children engaged in horrendous criminal activity or became a murder victim. Many times, a desperate parent struggling to find an answer as to their child's commission of a serious crime or, as a victim, asked, "Officer, do you know why he (or she) would do that?" Or, "Officer, do you know why they killed my child?" Sadly, my answer was nearly always the same, "I don't know."

During my research, it became abundantly clear some people then, as today, will readily engage in criminal activity and extinguish a human life as quickly as crushing a cockroach underfoot. The propensity for violence among some will never change.

Vol. 2 presents more of the best crime reporting during the 1800s. You will recognize many of the people and gangs mentioned, such as Billy the Kid, John Wilkes Booth, and Butch Cassidy and the Sundance Kid. However, there are hundreds of hideous criminals' time has forgotten. Do you know the story of; Anna Maria Zwanziger, who had a passion for employing poison? Or, the infamous "Jack the Ripper" or Lizzie Halliday? These criminals were the vilest of society. Many of their lives ended with a hangman's noose or by a bullet. Some managed to escape justice for the remainder of their lives.

These original newspaper stories represent the most accurate and colorful true crime stories of the day. It was a time when criminals were viewed criminals, and in most cases, justice was swift and unforgiving.

Much of the gruesome details in these articles could not, and would not be printed today. Political correctness, overzealous attorneys, and current police investigation techniques would not allow the finer details of the crimes to be released. Some will find the terms used to describe various races and individuals shocking and racist by today's standards. Yet, there was a time when the words and phrases used were considered ordinary language. The masses understood the terms, and rarely was an eyebrow raised in righteous indignation.

These reporters were extremely graphic when describing crime scenes and victims' injuries because that is what sold newspapers. People then, like today, are drawn to tragedy. We have all witnessed a traffic accident causing a massive slow down as gawkers strain their necks to view the carnage. Or reflect on the popularity of true crime magazines, television, and books.

Remember the first commandment of news reporting; *if it bleeds, it leads*. All forms of media understand people are fascinated by tragic events—be it accidental or by evil intentions. That is why these early crime stories are dramatic, graphic, and compelling. The better the story, the more newspapers sold.

In many cases, these stories shed new light on the dramatic effect the passage of time has on the truth.

With the retelling of an event or an individual's life over generations, accurate history invariably transforms into what people know today. With the invention of television and movies, tales of the old west nearly always stereotyped Native Americans as ruthless, uncivilized killers, while glorifying the white "Indian" fighters and cowboys. That wasn't always the case.

As a historian, in some instances, I have combined articles to tell as much of a complete story as possible, and I added my commentary as needed to bring more factual details to the story. In other cases, one article told the entire story.

I have not altered the context of these stories. The punctuation remains 99% untouched, except when I added a comma for easier reading. In a few instances, I corrected misspellings. I did this sparingly. When I grouped articles mentioning the same individual, there are times when names are spelled differently. That was not an uncommon error during those times. A reporter heard the name and spelled it according to the best of their ability, or the typesetter erred.

Also, the formatting of the story remains untouched. To make such unnecessary changes would be to alter history and do a disservice to these early crime reporters and the record.

As you experienced in Vol. 1, these books resurrect astonishing accounts of true crime and will take you on a journey to when these stories captivated a nation. Imagine yourself accompanying these reporters at the crime scenes, interviewing witnesses, and composing the stories. These are their firsthand experiences.

Unfortunately, newspapers at the time rarely listed a reporter's name. As with lengthy and detailed accounts of today, I believe more than one person contributed to some of these stories. I would have acknowledged the reporters if known.

As I pondered the crimes and punishment of the 1800s, it was abundantly clear human nature has not changed. Money, love, hatred, religious beliefs, disrespect, and insanity are all motivators for committing a crime.

Dedicated to Nancy

TABLE OF CONTENTS

SERIAL KILLERS   13
"Jack the Ripper." The Whitechapel Murders
Lizzie Halliday
The Texas Servant Girl Annihilator
Anna Maria Zwanziger
The Nebraska Murderer
The Atlanta Ripper
The New York Ripper

THE OTHER "JACKS"   105
Jack the Haircutter
Jack the Kisser
Jack the Hugger
Jack the Cutter

THE OLD WEST   127
Butch Cassidy and the Sundance Kid
Billy the Kid
Jesse James
Tribucio Vasques the California Bandido

THE ASSASSINATION OF PRESIDENT LINCOLN   241
The Shooting of the President
The Trial of the Conspirators
The Execution of the Conspirators

SHORT CRIME STORIES   269
The Negro Rapist
She Kills her Lover and Rival
Joe Taylor is Hung
Deadly Blue Gum Negro
Two Crooks and a Gold Brick
Father and Son Avenge Girls Wrong
Practical Joke or Murder
Effects of Murder
Beechers Burglary
The Defense Attorney and the Washington, D.C. Mistress

PHOTOS   283

SERIAL KILLERS

"JACK THE RIPPER"
The Whitechapel Murders
London

AUTHOR'S COMMENTARY

In 1888, a serial killer nicknamed "Jack the Ripper" terrorized the districts of Whitechapel, Spitalfields, and Aldgate on London's East Side. Whitechapel was considered "an undesirable district" by the refined, upper-class Londoners. It was an area where prostitutes and other dubious individuals lived, worked, and engaged in criminal enterprises. In America, Whitechapel would be considered a slum or ghetto.

During a few weeks in 1888, several female prostitutes were brutally murdered and their bodies mutilated. Some were disemboweled, some had their breast cut off, and some were nearly decapitated from a deep gash to their throats. If time permitted, the "Ripper" would skillfully employ a knife to mutilate the victim's face and other parts of the body. Some speculated his keen ability to mutilate the body proved he had anatomical knowledge, perhaps medical training. Others believed his skill with a knife was the result of working in a "slaughterhouse" killing and dissecting animals for consumption. And some speculated the "Ripper" was part of the United Kingdom's royal family, which accounted for no person charged with the crimes.

The killings caused widespread panic among Whitechapel's prostitutes and residents. Every man was suspect as the police quickly widened their dragnet as the body tally increased. At first, the media labeled the killer the "Leather Apron" since some women in the area saw a strange man who wore a leather apron. When a leather apron was found at a crime scene, speculation intensified; he was indeed the killer. In the end, the police determined he was not the "Ripper." Then the nickname evolved to what is commonly known today as "Jack the Ripper." Police detained and interrogated scores of men, but the identity of the "Ripper" remained a mystery.

Then, for reasons unknown to this day, the murders stopped. The terrified citizens and the police speculated that the "Ripper" might have died. Or was imprisoned on other charges. And finally, if alive, they hoped he left England. Or, was the "Ripper" a woman? Those are unanswerable questions.

However, according to Sir Robert Anderson, Chief of the Detective Bureau of Scotland Yard, who headed the "Ripper" investigation, they did identify the killer. But, did not have sufficient evidence to charge him. So, they used the power of the crown and quickly placed him in custody by order of the sovereign. Sir Anderson was perhaps the most knowledgeable officer involved in the case. As a result, his opinion as to the "Ripper's" identity is still the most likely, until proven otherwise.

Anderson's revelations are in the second story I've included. The first story depicts one of the murders and the anxiety and fear exhibited by the people of Whitechapel.

The viciousness of the murders engrossed the world then and still elicits conjecture. The story of England's "Jack the Ripper" is now folklore and will be studied and speculated upon for centuries. Despite Sir Anderson's revelations, it is doubtful the "Ripper's" true identity will ever be known, and that is what keeps the mystery alive, and people craving to know more.

A final thought, there are people with underlying mental conditions who seek notoriety, whether it's positive or negative. They desire to have their name known today and remembered over time. Unfortunately, these people rarely, if ever, attain such status by doing good. They achieve it by committing evil. Was that the motivation of "Jack the Ripper?"

Since the case of "Jack the Ripper," there have been people craving his infamy and unquestionably looked to him as an example of achieving their horrendous goal.

Birmingham Daily Post

Monday, September 10, 1888

ANOTHER BRUTAL MURDER IN WHITECHAPEL

MUTILATION OF THE VICTIM.

On Saturday morning, at quarter past six, the neighborhood of Whitechapel was horrified to a degree bordering on panic by the discovery of another barbarous murder of a woman at 29, Hanbury Street (late Brown Lane, Spitalfields). Hanbury Street is a thoroughfare running between Commercial Street and Whitechapel Road, the occupants of which are poor and for the most part of Jewish extraction. The circumstances of the murder are of such a revolting character as to point to the conclusion that it has been perpetrated by the same hand as committed that in Buck's Row and the two previous murders, of which have occurred within a stone's throw of each other. The murdered woman, who appears to have been regrettably connected, was known in the neighborhood by others of the unfortunate class as Annie Sivvy, but her real name was

Annie Chapman. She is described by those who knew her best as a decent although poor liking woman, about 5'2" or 5'3" high, with long brown wavy hair, blue eyes, large flat nose; and, strange to say, she had two of her front teeth missing, as did Mary Ann Nicholls, who was murdered in Buck's Row.

When her body was found on Saturday morning, it was respectably clad. She wore no head covering, but simply attired with bodice and two light petticoats. A search being made in her pockets, nothing was found, but an envelope stamped "The Sussex Regiment."

The house on Hanbury Street, in the yard of which the crime was committed, is occupied by a woman named Richardson, who employ several men in the rough packing line. There is a small shop in front at the basement of the house, which is utilized for the purpose of a cats-meat shop. From the upper end of the house, there is a passage of the door at either end leading to a small yard, some 13 feet or 14 ft. square, separated from the adjoining houses by a slight wooden fence. There is no outlet at the back, and any person who gains access must of necessity make his exit from the same and as his entry. In the yard, there were recently some packing cases, which had been sent up from the basement of the dwelling, but just behind the lower door, there was a clear space left, wherein the murder was undoubtedly committed.

The theory primarily formed was that the unfortunate victim had been first murdered, and there afterward dragged through the entry into the backyard; but from an inspection made later in the day, it appears that the murder was actually committed in the corner of the yard. Which the back door, when open, places in obscurity. There was on Saturday some marks of blood observable in the passage, but it is now known that these were caused during the work of removal of some packing cases, the edges of which accidentally came in contact with the blood which remained upon the spot from which the unhappy victim was removed.

The evidence which has been collected up to the present shows that the murder was committed shortly before half-past five o'clock in the morning. Albert Cadoach, who lodges next door, had occasion to go into the adjoining yard at the back at 5:25, and states that he heard a conversation on the other side of the piling as it between two people. He caught the word "No," and fancied he subsequently heard a slight scuffle, with the noise of a falling against the pilings, but thinking that his neighbor might potentially be out in the yard, he took no further notice and went to his work.

Nothing further can be traced of the dreadful tragedy, until shortly after 6 o'clock, when the man Davies passing into the yard at the back of 29 Hanbury Street, observed a mutilated mass which caused him to go shrieking in forthright into the street. In the house the back premise of which happened to become the scene of this hideous crime no fewer than six separate families reside, some people who live on the ground floor and are credited with being "light sleepers" stated emphatically that during the night and morning they heard no sound of a suspicious nature, which is likely enough in view of the fact that the passage from the front to the back of the house has been invariably left open for the convenience of dwellers in the building, the traffic being constant.

One of the occupants of the house is a man named John Davies, a porter in the Spitalfields Market. When he discovered the body in the yard, he made no attempt to ascertain the condition of deceased, but immediately alarm the other inmates of the house, and then proceeded to acquaint the police at the Commercial Street Station of what occurred. In the meantime, Mrs. Richardson, the principal occupier of the premises, together with a young woman named Eliza Cooksley, sleeping on the second floor, were aroused, and under the notion that the building was on fire ran to the back bedroom window, whence they in abled to the murdered woman lying on the paved yard, her clothes strewn about her waist, and her person horribly mutilated.

When the police arrived, they found that the woman had been murdered in a terribly brutal fashion. It was obvious, both from the marks upon the body and of the splashes of blood upon the pilings which separate dwellings one from the other, that the woman while lying down, had her throat first cut, and then was ripped open and disemboweled. The perpetrator of the ghastly deed undoubtedly occupied some considerable time in doing his victim to death, inasmuch as it appears that he, with fiendish resolve, not only killed the object of his caprice or passion, but afterward mutilated her body in a terrible manner, leaving the heart and liver lying by the shoulder.

There is, on every hand, the one opinion prevailing that the Whitechapel murders have been all enacted by the same person.

The mortuary in which the body of the murdered woman lies is situated at the corner of Eagle Street, a cul-de-sac ending in a pair of green doors, within which several officers of the police guard the remains of the dead. The lady is already in shell, and the autopsy having been made by Dr. Phillips and assistants, the portions of flesh and entrails removed by the fiendish hands of the murderer have been so far as possible replaced in their natural positions, and there is little else observable beyond the usual postmortem indicators. The body is that of a fairly nourished woman with bear traces of rough usage. The corpse is covered by a wrap, and those in custody of it are charged by the police authorities that it shall neither be shown to any person nor disturbed in any way. The district coroner visited the mortuary on Saturday afternoon and made arrangements for holding an inquest this morning.

Mrs. Richardson, the landlady at 29 Hanbury Street, the house from the body of deceased, was found, in an interview, said: "I have lived at this house 15 years, and my lodgers are poor but hard-working people. Some have lodged with me as long as 12 years. They mostly work at the fish market or the Spitalfields Market. Some of the men in the fish market go out to work as early as 1 AM, while others go out at four and five, so that the place is open all night, and anyone can get in.

It is certain that the deceased came voluntarily into the yard, as if there had been any struggle it must have been heard. Several lodgers sleep at the back of the house, and some had their windows open, but no noise was heard from the yard. One of my lodgers, a Carman, named Thompson, employed at Goodson's, in Brick Lane, went out at 4 o'clock in the morning. He did not go into the yard, but he did not notice anything particular in the passage as he went out. My son John came in ten minutes to five, and he gave a look around before he went to the market. He went through the yard, but no one was there, and everything was right.

Just before 6 o'clock, when Mr. Davis, another of my lodgers, came down, he found the deceased lying in the corner of the yard, close to the house, and by the side of the step. The lower part of her body was uncovered. There was not the slightest sign of a struggle, and the pool of blood which flowed from the throat after it was cut close to the step where she lay. She does not appear to have moved an inch after the fiend struck her with the knife. She must have died instantly. The murderer must have gone away from the spot covered with blood. There was an earthenware pan containing water in the yard: but this was not discolored, and could not, therefore, have been used by the murderer. The only possible clue that I can think of is that Mr. Thompson's wife met a man about a month ago lying on the stairs. This is about 4 o'clock in the morning. He looks like a Jew and spoke with a foreign accent. When asked what he was doing there, he replied he was waiting to do a 'doss' before the market opened. He slept on the stairs that night, and I believe he has slept on the stairs on other nights. Mrs. Thompson is certain she could recognize the man again both by his personal appearance and his peculiar voice. Police have taken a full and careful description of this man."

The deputy of a lodging house at 30 Dorset Street, states that Annie Chapman used to lodge there about two years ago with a man called Jack Sivvy, a sieve maker, hence her nickname Annie Sivvy. She appeared to be a quiet woman, and not given to drinking; in fact, he was quite surprised to hear that she had been seen drinking the night before the murder. The woman had two children to his knowledge – a boy who was a cripple, and who he believed was at the same charitable school, and a daughter who was somewhere in France.

Timothy Donovan, the deputy at the lodging house, 35 Dorset Street, where the deceased frequently stayed, states that the deceased stayed there on Sunday night last. She had been in the habit of coming there for the past four months. She was a quiet woman, and gave no trouble. He had heard her say she wished she was as well-off as her relations, but she never told him who her friends or where they live. A pensioner or a soldier usually came to the lodging house with her on Saturday nights, and generally stayed until Monday morning. He would be able to identify *the man instantly if he saw him. After the man left on Monday, the deceased would usually keep in the room for some days longer, the charge being eight pence per night. This man stayed at the house from Saturday to Monday last, and when he went, the deceased went with him. She was not seen at the house again until Friday night, about half-past eleven o'clock, when she passed the doorway, and Donovan, calling out, asked her where she had been since Monday, and why she had not slept there, and she replied: "I have been in the infirmary."*

Then she went on her way in the direction of Bishopsgate Street. About 1:40 on Saturday morning, she came again to the lodging house, and asked for a bed. The message was brought upstairs to him, and he sent downstairs to ask for the money.

The woman replied, "I haven't enough now, but keep my bed for me. I shan't belong."

Then as she was going the way, she said to John Evans, the watchman, "Bummy, I won't belong. See that Jim keeps my bed for me." She was the worst for drink at the time, and was eating some baked potatoes. He said nothing to her again until he was called to the mortuary on Saturday morning when he identified the deceased by her features and her wavy hair, which was turning gray.

After the deceased left on Monday last, he found two large bottles in the room, one containing medicine, and labeled as follows: "St. Bartholomew's Hospital. Take two spoonful's three times a day." The other bottle containing a milky solution, and was labeled, "St. Bartholomew's Hospital. The lotion. Poison." This confirmed her statement that she had been under medical treatment. On being asked whether he knew a man called "Leather Apron," whom common rumor in the neighborhood has pointed at him as the murderer,

Donovan said he knew him well. He came to the lodging-house about 12 months ago, a woman being his companion. In the early hours of the morning, the woman commenced screaming murder, and it seems that "Leather Apron" had knocked her down and tore her hair and clothes.

"Leather Apron," said the woman was trying to rob him, but he (Donovan) did not believe him, and turned him out of the house. The man had come there several times since for a lodging, but they would not admit him. One of the assistants, George Sole, of the Ten Bells public house, owned by Mr. E. Waldron, situated at the corner Spitalfields Market, in commercial Street, on hearing of the murder, gave information of a woman as he thought answering to the description of Annie Chapman. A woman had called there about 5 o'clock. She was poorly dressed, having no bodice to her skirt. She appeared to be middle age. On the point of having something to drink, a man thrust his head into the door and angrily asked her to come out, retiring immediately afterward. He had on a skullcap, and was, as far as he, the assistant, could see, without a coat. He thought that he would know the faces of both the man and woman again. On being contacted by the police last night, at about 8 o'clock, to the mortuary to see the remains of the murdered woman, he merely stated that she was not the woman he had seen in the morning.

At about 10 o'clock on Saturday morning a woman, named Amelia Farmer, gave important information that she had been a fellow lodger with the deceased, and had known her for some considerable time. She stated that the deceased woman was Annie Chapman, the wife of a veterinary surgeon, who had died at Windsor about 18 months ago. She was accordingly taken to the mortuary at 11:30 o'clock, and immediately recognized her friend, apparently being much touched at the dreadful spectacle.

Later on, she made a statement of what she knew of the history of the murdered woman. Annie Chapman had, for a long time been separated from her husband, a veterinary surgeon at Windsor, by mutual agreement, and had been allowed 10 schilling a week by him for her maintenance. The money had been sent by post office order, made payable at the Commercial Street post office, and had always come regularly. About 18 months ago, the installments suddenly ceased, and, upon inquiry being made, it was found that the husband had died.

Annie Chapman had two children, but where they were, she could not say. The deceased had a mother and sister, who were living in the neighborhood of Brompton of Fulham. Farmer had been in the habit of writing letters for her friend, but could not remember the exact address of the mother or sister, but thought it was near the Brompton Hospital. Last Monday, Chapman had intimated her intention of communicating with her sister, saying, "If I can get a pair of boots from my sister, I shall go hoppicking." Another relation, a brother-in-law of the deceased, lives somewhere in or near Oxford Street. Farmer asserted that her murdered friend was apparently a sober, steady-going sort of woman, and one who seldom took any drink. For some time, past she had been living occasionally with a man named Ted Stonley, who had been in the militia, but was now working at some neighboring brewery. Ted Stonley was a good-tempered man, rather tall, about 5'10", fair, and a florid complexion. He was the last man in the world to have quarreled with Chapman, nor would he have injured her in any way.

At the beginning of the week, the deceased had been rather severely knocked about in the breast and faced by another woman of the locality through jealousy in connection with Ted Stonley, and had been obliged to go to the casual ward.

As a regular means of livelihood, she had not been in the habit of frequenting the streets, but had made antimacassars for sale. Sometimes she would buy flowers or matches, with which to pick up a living. Farmer was perfectly certain that on Friday night, the murdered woman had worn three rings, which were not genuine, but were imitations, otherwise, she would not have troubled to go out and find money for her lodgings.

The place on the statement of farmer, made a vigilant search for the mother, sister, and brother-in-law, but without success. A man named Chapman, from Oxford Street, was found, but proved to be no relation.

Great weight is attached to the statement as to the rings which were on the murdered woman's hand before the murder was committed, but which had been wrenched off by the wretch before he made his escape. Another clue which may prove of value was furnished by Mrs. Fiddymont, wife of the proprietor of the Prince Albert public house, better known as the "Clean House," at the corner of Brush Field and Stored Streets, as a mile from the scene of the murder.

Mrs. Fiddymont states that at 7 o'clock on Saturday morning, she was standing in the bar talking with another woman, a friend, in the first compartment. Suddenly there came into the middle compartment a man whose rough appearance frightened her. He had on a brown stiff hat, a dark coat, and no waistcoat. He came in with his hat drawn over his eyes, and, with his face partly concealed; and asked for half a pint of ale. She drew the ale, and meanwhile looked at him through the mirror at the back of the bar. As soon as he saw the woman and the other compartment watching him, he turned his back, and got the partition between himself and her. The thing that struck Mrs. Fiddymont particularly was a fact that there were blood spots on the back of his right hand. This, taken in connection with his appearance, caused her uneasiness. She also noticed that his shirt was torn. As soon as he had drunk the ale, which he swallowed at a gulp, he went out. Her friends went out also to watch him.

Her friend is Mrs. Mary Chappell, who lives at 28 Stuart Street, nearby. Her story corroborates Mrs. Fiddymont's and is more particular. When the man came in, the expression of his eyes caught her attention; his look was so startling and terrifying. It frightened Mrs. Fiddymont so that she requested her to stay. He wore a light blue checked shirt, which was torn badly, into rags in fact, on the right shoulder. There was a narrow streak of blood under his right ear, parallel with the edge of his shirt. There was also dried blood between the fingers of his hand. When he went out, she slipped out at the other door, and watched him as he went towards Bishopsgate Street. She called Joseph Taylor's attention to him, and Joseph Taylor followed him. Joseph Taylor is a builder at 22 Seward Street. He states that as soon as his attention was attracted to the man, he followed him. He walked rapidly, and came alongside him, but did not speak to him. The man was rather thin, 5'8" high, and appeared between 40 and 50 years of age. He had a shabby-genteel look, pepper and salt trousers, which fitted badly, and dark coat. When Taylor came alongside him, the man glanced at him, and Taylor's description of the look was, "His eyes were as wild as a hawks." Taylor is a perfectly reliable man, well known throughout the neighborhood. The man walked, he says, holding his coat together at the top. He had a nervous and frightened way about him. He wore a ginger-colored mustache and had short sandy hair. Taylor ceased to follow him, watched him as far as "Dirty Dick's," in Half Moon Street, where he became lost to view.

Mrs. Elizabeth Bell, of Hanbury Street, states: – I have been living here for some time, and I wish I had never come. Such a terrible site is enough to shock any woman with the hardest heart. The house is open all night next door, and the poor creature was taken into the yard and butchered, no doubt, by the same man who committed the others. We were all roused at 6 o'clock by Adam Osborne, calling out, "For God's sake, get up: here's a woman murdered." We all got up and hurried on our clothes, and I'm going into the yard, so the poor creature lying by the steps in the next yard, with her clothes torn and her body gashed in a dreadful manner. The people in the house next door were all asleep, I believe, and knew nothing of the matter until the police came and roused them up. I cannot be sure if anybody in the house knew of the murder, or took part in it, but I believe not. The passage is open all night, and anyone can get in, and no doubt that is what happened. All the other tenants of the house gave the same opinion, and those in the house of Mr. Richardson, at 29, where the murder occurred, state that they heard no cries of "Murder" or "Help," nor anything unusual during the night.

John Davis, who was the first to make the shocking discovery, says: having a cup of tea on Saturday morning at about 6 o'clock, I went downstairs. When I got to the end of the passage, I saw a female lying down, her clothing up to her knees, and her face covered with blood. What was lying beside her, I cannot describe – it was part of her body. I heard no noise, nor had my missus. I saw Mr. Bailey's men waiting at the back of the Black Swan ready to go into their work – making packing cases. I said to them, "Here's a site; a woman must have been murdered." I then ran to the police station in Commercial Road, and I told them there what I had seen, and some constables came back with me. I did not examine the woman when I saw her – I was too frightened at the dreadful sight. Our front door at 29 Hanbury Street, *is never bolted, and anyone has only to push it open and walked through the gate at the backyard. Immoral women have at times gone there, and Miss Mrs. Richardson, our landlady, had occasion to keep a closet lock there, but no lock has ever been placed on the front door; at least, I have never seen one: but it is only a fortnight ago that I came to lodge there. I have known people open the passage door and walk through into the yard when they have had no right there. There are about 15 altogether living in the house.*

Mrs. Davis has made the following statement: – "The bell was ringing for 6 o'clock, and that is how I know the time that my husband went downstairs. He then said to me, 'Old woman, I must now go down, for it is time I was off to my work.' He went down, but did not return, as he tells me that when he saw the deceased, in the shocking state in which she was, he at once ran off for the police. We never heard any screams, either in the night or this morning. I went down myself shortly after; I nearly fainted away at what I saw. The poor woman's throat was cut, and the inside of her body was lying beside her. Someone beside me then remarked that the murder was just like the one committed in Buck's Row. The other one could not have been such a dreadful sight as this, for the poor woman found this morning was quite ripped open. She was lying in a corner of the yard, on her back, with her legs drawn up. It was just in such a spot that no one could see from the outside, and thus the dead creature might have been lying there for some time.

Two young men named Simpson and Stevens, living in Dorset Street, who knew the deceased is residing at that address, state that her name is Annie Chapman. She returned thither about 11 o'clock, stating that she had been to see some friends at Vauxhall. It is also stated that the murdered woman had two children – one of them, a girl age

14, is at present performing in a circus traveling in France. The other is a boy between four and five years of age. He is now at school at Windsor, the native place of the woman Chapman.

Reference is made to a mysterious being bearing the name of "Leather Apron," concerning whom a number of stories have for a week or more been current in Whitechapel. The following is a description of the man: – he is 5 feet four or 5 inches in height and wears a dark, close-fitting cap. He is thickset, and has an unusually thick neck. His hair is black, and closely clipped, his age about 38 or 40. He has a small black mustache. The distinguishing feature of costume is a Leather Apron, which he always wears, and from which he gets his nickname. His expression is sinister, and seems to be full of terror for the women who described it. His eyes are small and glittering. His lips are usually parted in a grin, which is not only not reassuring, but excessively repellent. He is a slipper-maker by trade, but does not work. His business is blackmailing women late at night. A number of men in Whitechapel follow this interesting profession.

He has never cut anybody so far as I know, but always carries a leather knife, presumably as sharp as other knives are want to be. This knife a number of the women have seen. His name nobody knows, but all are united in the belief that he is a Jew or of Jewish parentage, his face being of a marked Hebrew type. But the most singular characteristic of the man is the universal statement that in moving about, he never makes any noise. What he wears on his feet the women do not know, but they agree that he moves noiselessly. His uncanny peculiarity to them is that they never see him or know of his presence till he is close by them. "Leather Apron" never by any chance attacks a man. He runs away on the slightest appearance of rescue. One woman who he assailed some time ago boldly prosecuted him for it, and he was sent up for seven days. He has no settled place of residence, but has slept oftenest in a fourpenny lodging house of the lowest kind in a disreputable lane leading from Brick Lane. The people at this lodging house denied that he had been there, and appeared disposed to shield him.

"Leather Apron's" pal, "Mickeldy Joe," was in the house at the time, and his presence had doubtless something to do with the unwillingness to give information. "Leather Apron" was last at this house some weeks ago, though his account may be untrue. He ranges all over London and rarely assails the same woman twice. He has lately been seen in Leather Lane, which is in the Holborn district.

LATEST PARTICULARS.

THE SEARCH FOR THE MURDERER.

The Central News says although the police have made the most diligent inquiry after the murderer of the woman Chapman they had, up to last night, failed to secure the slightest clue to his whereabouts. As a matter of fact, says one correspondent, they are in the dark as to the personal appearance of the man for whom they are looking.

It is true that they possess the description of a man who was known as "Leather Apron," and will arrest him if he can be found: but their theory is that "Leather Apron" is "more or less a mythical personage," and that he is consequently not responsible for the terrible crimes with which his name has been associated. All the same, the details of his appearance have been widely circulated with a view to his early apprehension, and all the police in the vicinity are on the lookout for him.

On Saturday night, a large force of police constables and detectives closely watched the neighborhood. Men were posted at all the entrances and exits of the numerous alleys *and passages in the neighborhood, and every few minutes they made a thorough examination of the places under their surveillance, and from time to time these are visited by the inspectors on duty, with the view of ascertaining whether any suspicious character had been observed.*

From 10 o'clock at night until late in the morning, a large crowd occupied Hanbury Street, in the vicinity of the notorious house No. 29. When the public houses emptied, their occupants swarmed into the street and caused a good deal of trouble to the police by their behavior. The people living in the adjoining houses had no rest until four or 5 o'clock, when the crowd gradually melted away, only, however, to reassemble in greater force so soon as daylight appeared.

In the course of Saturday night and Sunday morning, the police arrested two men on suspicion of being concerned in the crime. One man, whose appearance left little doubt in the minds of his captors that he was a Hanbury Street murderer, was found by an officer in Buck's Row, shortly after 1 o'clock on Sunday morning. A murder was, it will be remembered, committed in this neighborhood but a short time since the police have since that and constantly pursuing their investigations in that quarter. The man upon whom suspicion rested had a most forbidding air. He appeared to be hiding in the street, and when accosted by the officers rushed off at the top of his speed. An alarm was raised, and after a sharp race, the man was arrested. He is described as "a villainous-looking fellow with long hair and a shaggy beard," and he was dressed only in a pair of ragged blue serge trousers and an old dirty shirt. He resisted his captors, but was secured and conveyed to Bethnal Green Police Station. It was said at the time that he was carrying a long knife concealed in the sleeve of his shirt, but no weapon was found upon him. He gave an account of himself, which was in the first instance considered unsatisfactory, but inquiries being set on foot, the man, who appears to be a common vagrant, was released from custody.

The second arrest was affected in Gloucester Street, and a man, aged about 40, having the look of a seafarer, was a suspected person. It was pretty obvious, however, from the replies which he gave, and, indeed, from his general appearance, that he was not the man sought for, and after he had spent some time in Commercial Street Police Station, he was also set at liberty.

It is suggested that the first-mentioned man is the person who has been spoken of by Mrs. Fiddymont has stated to the police that at 7 o'clock on Saturday morning, a rough-looking man came into the house, and got some ale. He presented an excited appearance, and some blood spots were said to have been observed on his right hand. This man, however, had a coat and hat on.

The police, who give information very unwillingly, and who, as already stated, do not accept the theory that the crime has been committed by the man designated "Leather Apron," are indisposed to believe that the person seen by Mrs. Fiddymont had any connection with the crime. They are not desirous indeed to accept assistance or suggestions from any private source, and work upon a plan of their own, which consist of frequent visits to the common lodging houses of the neighborhood, and of a strict watch at night and all the streets in the vicinity.

All-day yesterday five policemen guarded the scene of the crime in Hanbury Street, and no one was admitted unless he resided in the house. In the street, half a dozen costermongers took up their stand and did a brisk business in fruit and refreshments. Thousands of respectably dressed persons visited the scene, and occasionally the road became *so crowded that the constables had to clear it by making a series of raids upon the spectators. The windows of the adjoining houses were full of persons watching the crowd below. A number of people also visited the house in Dorset Street, where the murdered woman lodged.*

It was ascertained yesterday that the soldier who had frequently slept with the woman at this place did not return to the house on Saturday night. The police, however, attach no importance to this circumstance. Inquiries have been made at Vauxball and at Windsor, where Chapman or "Sivvy," as she was more generally called, is said to have relatives, but so far without any fresh information being obtained as to her antecedents. The deceased has been identified by persons who have known her since she has lived in London, but her relatives, if she possesses any, have not yet communicated with the police.

The small portion of writing on the envelope found upon the body bearing the stamp of the Essex Regiment has not been identified or traced. The authorities of St. Bartholomew's Hospital, where the woman spent some time, have been communicated with, but they have not been able to afford any information of a useful character. The usually lively condition of Whitechapel and Spitalfields on a Sunday was considerably heightened yesterday by reason of the excitement aroused by the murder.

In the course of the day nearly a dozen, persons were arrested on everyday charges, and conveyed to the Commercial Street Police Station. In the afternoon, a vast crowd had collected about the streets, and as each apprehension was made, they rushed pell-mell towards the station, obviously under the idea that the murderer of the woman had been caught.

Shortly before 5 o'clock a man was arrested in Dal Street, after a long chase, on a charge of assault, and the constable who took him proceeded with his prisoner by way of an Barry Street to the police station, and so was obliged to make his way through the crowd outside the house. His prisoner stood in some danger of being mobbed, but the people eventually gave way, and the prisoner was safely lodged in the station. A few minutes later, two men were arrested in Wentworth Street. As soon as the crowd saw them in the hands of the police, there were loud cries of "Leather Apron!" And thereupon, hundreds of people turned out from the side streets and followed the officers in a tumultuous throng to the station.

Not five minutes later, a woman was apprehended on some small charge, and the excitement became so intense that a posse of officers was sent out from the building to preserve order. They marched three and four abreast up and down the pavement, and while they were so engaged, yet another prisoner was brought in. There was a good deal of shouting in the mob, which surged about in a dangerous fashion, but by and by a diversion was caused by the rapid passage along Hanbury Street of three men, who were supposed to be two detectives and their prisoner. The centerman wore a strong resemblance to "Leather Apron," and the cry of "That's him!" Having been raised, a rush was made at him; but the little party immediately turned down a side street, and the police prevented the crowd from proceeding further.

In the neighborhood of the mortuary, which is situated in Eagle Place, at the Whitechapel, and of Hanbury Street, all was quiet during the day. The green doors open now and again to admit some inspectors of police and several medical gentlemen, but all others were rigidly excluded. The inquest on the body will be held today by Dr. MacDonald, the coroner for the district. Dr. Phillips, the surgeon, and the witnesses who first discovered the body, will be called, and the police will also give certain evidence. Dr. Phillips believes that the woman had been dead for about two hours or more when she was discovered. It is a remarkable fact, however, that the man Richardson, who first went into the yard where the corpse was discovered, says that he actually sat down on the step of the passage to cut a piece of leather off his shoe, and yet did not see the body. This, however, may be explained by the circumstances that the passage door opens outwards and towards the left, and so would conceal the body behind it. It is the custom to leave both of the passage doors open at night, and although they were found shut on the morning of the murder, no suspicion was excited on that account.

The advisability of employing bloodhounds to trace the perpetrator of the crime has been eagerly discussed by the inhabitants of the district. It is considered, however, by experts that the time has gone by for such an experiment in the present instance, and it is pointed out also that in the case of the Blackburn murder, who was discovered by this means, the circumstances were different, and that the present case does not admit of the test. Last night the police were posted in strong force throughout the neighborhood. Their precautions are such that they consider impossible that any further outrage can be perpetrated. Inhabitants of the place, however, although by day regarding the matter as one for discussion and excitement rather than serious regard, profess to fear that the miscreant will soon be at his dark work again, and that if he be captured at all, he will be taken red-handed in the commission of another horrible crime.

The Press Association says: – the police are fully conscious of the difficulty of connecting any prisoner they may make with the series of appalling crimes. "God knows," said an officer to our reporter, "but we may have another tonight, though we have been patrolling the whole region of Whitechapel and Spitalfields." That the police are putting forth every possible effort, there can be no doubt. There is a large force on duty. One-third of the men are in plainclothes, and even those entitled to leave of absence are retained. That the public is anxious to second their efforts is testified by the presence of the record at Commercial Street of no fewer than 50 personal statements, made with the object of assisting in the work of identification.

One officer has been occupied many consecutive hours in writing the statements, and up to 9 o'clock last night, they were being supplemented by others. The police are not permitted to make public the written evidence, if evidence it can be called. It is doubtful if it will ultimately prove of much value, but our representative, pursuing his investigations, heard in the presence of the police a statement which, perhaps, but not to be altogether dismissed as unworthy of notice.

The informant was a young woman named Lyons, of the class commonly known as unfortunates. She stated that at 3 o'clock yesterday afternoon, she met a strange man in Flower and Dean Street, one of the worst streets in the East End of London. He asked her to go to the Queens Head public house at 6:30, and drink with him. Having obtained from the young woman a promise that she would do so, he disappeared. She was at the house at the appointed time, and while they were conversing, Lyons noticed a large knife in the man's right-hand trousers pocket, and called another woman's attention to the fact.

A moment later, Lyons was startled by the remark which the stranger addressed to her: "You are about the same style of woman as the one that's murdered." She said, "What do you know about her?"

To which question, the man replied, "You're beginning to smell a rat. Foxes hunt geese, but they don't always find them." Having uttered these words, the man hurriedly left.

Lyons followed until near Spitalfields Church. Turning around at the spot, and noticing that the woman was behind him, the stranger ran at a swift pace into Church Street, and was at once lost to view. One noteworthy fact in this story is that the description of the man's appearance is in all material points identical with the published description of the unknown, and up to the present undiscovered, wearer of the Leather Apron.

Over 200 common lodging-houses have been visited by the police in the hopes of finding some trace of this mysterious and much talk of person, but he has succeeded in evading arrest. The police have reason for suspecting he is employed in one of the London sweating-dens as a slipper-maker: and that, as it is usual to supply food and lodging in many of these houses, he is virtually in hiding. Though "Leather Apron" was a figure well known to many policemen in the Whitechapel district, prior to the murder of Mrs. Nicholls, in Buck's Row, the man has kept himself out of the way since, and this is regarded as a significant circumstance.

Telegraphing at midnight the Press Association says the man arrested at Deptford has not up to the present been brought to Commercial Street Police Station for the purpose of identification, and no further particulars concerning him can be obtained. Inspector Chandler has been to Deptford to see the prisoner, but what the result of his inquiries is kept secret, but it is understood that not so much importance is attached to the arrest as with a case in the first instance.

The Inter Ocean

Sunday, May 27, 1910

JACK THE RIPPER IN INSANE ASYLUM

FORMER CHIEF OF SCOTLAND YARD TELLS TRUTH AT

LAST ABOUT FAMOUS WHITECHAPEL MURDERER

The truth about Jack the Ripper has been told at last. The fiendish perpetrator of the murders in the Whitechapel district of London in the early 90s is an inmate of Broadmoor Asylum for the Criminal Insane in England.

The revelation of his identity sets at rest the stories ascribing the outrages of an English nobleman, now dead, who, despite his great wealth, had rendered himself an outcast by his vices and eccentricities, or to an Englishman, untitled, but of birth and breeding, who, after manifesting unmistakable signs of mental disorder, disappeared from his accustom haunts in London to die in a madhouse.

Jack the Ripper, at whose hands 14 women of the unfortunate class lost their lives successively within a circumscribed district of the East End of the English metropolis, was a poll of the lower, though educated, class, and a maniac of the most virulent and homicidal type – a type that is known to science as a sadist.

These facts have just been given to the world by Sir Robert Anderson, for more than 30 years Chief of the Criminal Investigation Department of the British government and head of the Detective Bureau at Scotland Yard.

Sir Robert's disclosures were made in one of the London reviews for March, and were supplemented by a letter from him printed in the London Times.

He describes in his written statement the house to house search for the murderer in the district in which the atrocities were committed. He declares the police investigated every man in Whitechapel whose circumstances were such that he could go and come and get rid of bloodstains in secret. In this dragnet, he says, Jack the Ripper was enmeshed.

But, he declares, though the police authorities were able to establish the fiends identity beyond doubt, they were unable to secure sufficient legal evidence upon which to convict him.

Sir Robert says that once the criminal investigation department was sure it had the real perpetrator of the mysterious murders in the tolls it procured from the Secretary of State of the Home Department a warrant committing the man for detention "during the sovereign's pleasure," to the great asylum for the criminal insane at Broadmoor.

Committed to Asylum

The Ripper was not committed by means of any judicial process, but was consigned to the assignment by virtue of a warrant of the Home Secretary acting for the sovereign. Sir Robert makes this clear.

The power of committal is a prerogative of the crown. But the preparation of any abuse of these royal "lettres de cachet" (such as was in vogue in the days of the court of Versailles. When the Kings of France were able to consign to lifelong captivity in the Bastille nobles guilty of no other offense than that of having spoken slightly of the monarchs fair favorite of the hour,) is guarded against by the fact that it is the Secretary of State for the Home Department who signs the warrant of committal, and that he is responsible in this, as for all his other official acts, to parliament.

Jack the Ripper's crimes, shocked the civilized world and constituted the greatest criminal mystery of the last quarter of a century. For his field of operations, the maniac chose the Whitechapel district, then the most squalid in disreputable of the slums of London. He committed his murders only at night, and his victims were wholly women of the underworld.

The First Murder

The first murder convinced the police that they had an extraordinary criminal to deal with. A woman was found murdered in the doorway of a populace street. When she was struck down, it was evident that pedestrians must have been passing only a few feet away. She had been horribly mutilated. The murderer had escaped, leaving behind no clue to his identity. On the dust-begrimed door above the victim, he had left a message scrawled with a piece of chalk, addressed to the police, and declaring he would murder another woman on a certain night. This strange note was signed "Jack the Ripper" – a name that at once rang around the world.

On the night set for his second murder by the mysterious murderer, the police swarmed in Whitechapel. There were plainclothesmen disguised as workmen slouching about on every block. But Jack, the Ripper kept his word. About midnight, a great hue and cry was raised when the body of another mutilated woman was found stretched on the sidewalk of an ill-lighted side street. In all essential details, the murder was similar to the first. Again, a message from the Ripper was scrawled upon a dead wall above the victim.

More police were thrown into the district. They were powerless. Murder followed murder. Within a few weeks, 14 women had fallen beneath the butcher's knife.

The mysterious murders struck the district with terror. There was a panic-stricken exodus of unfortunate women to other parts of the city. In Whitechapel, they lived in nightly fear being struck down by the cunning assassin. Fourteen women had been slashed to death in the boldest fashion, but not the faintest clue had been obtained to the murderer. The women looked with suspicious dread upon all men. They were not sure that even their most intimate man friend was not the murderous "terror that walked in darkness."

The murders were all committed within a period of a few weeks. Some of the Rippers victims were slain within the light of streetlamps. Others were killed in lonely lanes and areaways. Some were murdered in their rooms. But the method was always the same. The mutilation of the body of one of Jack the Ripper's victims was described by a London newspaper in this way:

Mutilated the Body

"The miserable woman's body was literally scattered all over her little room. Almost every conceivable mutilation had been practiced on the body. The woman's nose was cut off, and the face gashed. She had been completely disemboweled, as had been all the murderer's former victims, and all the intestines had been placed upon a small table, which, with a chair and a bed, constituted all the furniture in the room. Both the woman's breast had been removed and placed upon the table. Large portions of the thighs had been cut away, and the head almost severed from the body. One leg also was almost completely cut off. The mutilation was so frightful that more than an hour was spent by the doctors in endeavoring to reconstruct the woman's body from the pieces so as to place it in a coffin and have it photographed. It was found that portions of certain organs had been carried away by the murderer."

The London police have never had been called upon to solve such a puzzling mystery. They throughout what is technically known as the "dragnet." All suspicion characters in the Whitechapel district and all men who could not give a good account of themselves were taken in custody and put through a strenuous "sweating" process such as has since been given the name of the "third degree." Manhunters took the trail. The best detectives in Europe are called to London. All were baffled. Jack the Ripper continued to advertise the date upon which he would slaughter his next victim, but the police could not catch him. Such boldness such cunning and such murderous ferocity were unprecedented in the history of crime.

England is the home of the bloodhound, a dog's nose is the keenest among all domesticated animals, if not the keenest among all beast. Dogs of this ancient breed with the most sensitive noses and the best training in England were taken to the scene of a Jack the Ripper crime with the blood of the victim was fresh upon the paving stones. One of the hounds, sniffing at the spot where the murderer had stood when he struck his victim down, followed a trail through the crowded London streets to the Liverpool dock on the Thames. It was supposed by many this indicated that Jack the Ripper was perhaps sailor and had taken ship for some foreign shore.

Suddenly the murders ceased. The reign of terror ended. Whitechapel and the East End breathed again.

Theories Advanced.

When the police left off, the theorists began. How to account for this terrible murderer who killed seemingly without *provocation, and as if to satisfy a lust for blood, became the question. Many theories were advanced. Among them was one by Archibald Forbes, the famous war correspondent, who advanced the idea that the Ripper had once suffered an injury from women of the street and had become inspired with an insane desire to avenge himself upon the class.*

Other more scientific men set the Ripper down as the most violent type of sadist known to history. The name sadist is applied to a certain class of degenerates who indulge in violence against the opposite sex. Krafft-Ebing, in his authoritative work on "Psychopathia Sexualis," treats this form of insanity exclusively.

If many theories were advanced to explain the crimes, many theories also were promulgated as to the identity of Jack the Ripper. When the murder suddenly ceased, it was generally believed that the police had, at last, solved the mystery and had arrested the murderer. Nothing about any arrest, however, was made public. It came gradually to believe that the Ripper was a member of the nobility, addicted to sadistic practices. It was supposed that he had been caught and committed to a private insane asylum and that the news of his arrest and incarceration had been hushed up later these rumors became more definite and fastened the long list of murders upon a certain nobleman who has since died.

Dr. G. Frank Lydston of Chicago, and his work, "Disease of Society and a Degeneracy," cites the case of Nicholas Wassilyi is illustrating the growth and development of peculiar mania from which Jack the Ripper suffered. The Wassilyi case shows the genesis of the mania, and it is possible that it parallels Jack the Ripper's case and more than the mere violence of the murders.

"A series of murders identical with those of Whitechapel occurred in Paris in 1872," Says Dr. Lydston. "They were

perpetrated by a religious fanatic, Nicholas Wassilyi, called by the Parisians' La Saveur des Ames Perdues' – 'The Savior of lost souls.'

"In the year mentioned there was a movement in the Orthodox Church of Russia against some sectarians. Some of the people, menaced because of their religion, fled from the country. Most of them were peasants, but Wassilyi left a good home. His parents were quite wealthy, and he had been educated at the College of Odessa. But Nicholas was a fanatic sectarian and soon became a leader among them. The chief belief of his sect was in the renunciation of earthly joys to secure and moral life in paradise. Wassilyi fled to Paris.

Life in Paris

"He was an excellent type of Russian. He had a tall, elastic figure, a regular manly physiognomy, burning, languishing eyes, and a pale complexion. He avoided his countrymen, taking a small lodging in the Quartier Mouffetard, where the poor and miserable live.

"He became a riddle to his neighbors. He used to stay all day in his room studying books. At night he wandered through the streets until morning. He was often seen talking with abandon women, and it soon became known that he followed a secret mission in doing so. First, he tried mild persuasion on the poor creatures, telling them to return to the path of virtue. When words failed, he put premiums on virtue and gave large sums to the cocottes conditioned that they commence a new life.

"Some of the women were really touched by his earnestness and promised to follow his advice. He could often be seen on the street corners preaching to gaudy nymphs who bitterly shed repentant tears.

"His mission, however, was not crowned with much success. He often met girls who had broken an oath that they would sin no more. Then there was a change. He would approach the woman, speak to her kindly, and follow her home. When alone with her, he would take out a butcher knife, kneel on her prostrate body and force her to swear not to sin again in the same manner. He seemed to believe in these forced oaths and went away happy.

"One evening in the Due de Richelieu, he met another woman. She had an elegant figure and beautiful blue eyes. This girl seemed to make a great impression on him. He spoke to her – she was a lost one, too – but not brutally. She told him the story of her life – the story of a poor, parentless girl, who had been torn from happiness and cast into misery and shame.

"Wassilyi, for the first time, fell in love. He procured a place for the woman in a business house and paid liberally for her support, although he made her believe she was supporting herself. For several weeks the girl was straight. But one day when Wassilyi visited her home – a thing he seldom did, and then only when an Old Guardian of hers was present – he found that she was gone. She had left a letter to him in which she said that, though thankful to him for all his kindness, her life was now to monotonous for her, and she preferred to be left alone.

"Wassilyi was in a fearful mood after this. He wanders so restlessly through the streets as to attract attention of the constables. Eight weeks afterward, he disappeared. At the same time, Madeline, the woman he had supported, was found murdered in the quarter where she had formally led a life of shame. Two days afterward, in a quiet street of the Faubourg St. Germain, the corpse of another murdered woman was found. Three days afterward, a Phryne of the Quartier Mouffe was butchered at night. All the murders were perpetrated in the same horrible way as those in Whitechapel. Jewels and everything of value on the corpses remained untouched.

"Five more victims were found butchered in the Arrondissement du Pantheon between the boulevards St. Michel and De L'Hopital. Finally, in the Rue de Lyon, an attack was made upon a girl who had a chance to cry for help before she was strangled. The would-be murderer was captured, he was Nicholas Wassilyi. At his trial, his lawyer claimed that his client was insane. The jury decided that such was the case, and Wassilyi was sent back to Russia after a short stay in a private asylum at Bayonne.

"In the case of Wassilyi, the transition from religious psychic erethism to perverted sexuality was brought about by his love affair in the psychic shock of the discovery of the woman's duplicity."

There have been many sadistic murders in the United States in recent years. Several murders of this type terrorized Cincinnati a few years ago. Girls were waylaid in a lonely Lane of a sparsely settled suburb and choked to death. One who was attacked fought desperately and screamed, and frightened away her assailant. She described him as a man of middle-age, whose appearance was quite genteel. As he sauntered toward her in the twilight, she took him for some prosperous businessman, and he caused her no alarm. He made no suspicious movement until he came abreast of her and then suddenly ceased her by the throat and attempted to drag her into the bushes that flanked the road. The man ran away with great fleetness when she screamed.

A long time after the murders ceased, a man name Hoag was arrested in Dayton, Ohio, for murdering his father and mother and burning their home. Before his execution, he confessed to having committed the Cincinnati murders.

An Ohio Case.

Dr. Lydston, in his work already quoted from cities another recent American case of the kind.

"A recent case occurring in Ohio," says Dr. Lydstron, "is a graphic illustration of the sadistic form of murder. The subject who was executed for the murder of a woman confessed that she was the fifth one he had murdered, three of the women having been his wives. His confession was not attended by the slightest emotion or expression of the danger and the moral responsibility involved in his acts. He himself attributed his murders to the domination of a homicidal mania, which irresistibly impelled him to shed the blood of women.

A fourth wife, to whom he was recently married, narrowly escaped death at his hands. With reference to the escape of his last wife from death at his hands, the murderer said in his confession: "I know that she has waked up several times since we were married and found my hands grasping her neck while I was asleep. She would wake when I grabbed her and asked what I meant by taking hold of her neck in that way, and I could not tell her why, because I was asleep and did not know that I had done it. Just last week, she woke up just in time, or she might never have waked at all. I had grabbed her so tight and was choking her that she was nearly gone when she came to and woke me up."

If the murderer's statement is to be believed, it affords the unique case of a murder almost accomplished in sleep.

"The explanation the murderer gave of his case," continues Dr. Lydston, "is the ordinary medical and also the popular one. It is, however, fallacious. The restriction of his homicidal impulses to the female sex is in itself suspicious. His many marriages are still more suggestive. His portrait shows a degenerate of a decidedly common type."

There was a startling sadistic murder in Chicago only last January, when Annie Cleghorn, an unfortunate woman, was killed in her room at 17th and Dearborn streets. Her assailant entered her room in the small hours of the night, murdered her, mutilated her body in horrible fashion, cut off her head, and carried it away, rolled up in some towels. The head afterwards was recovered on a commons a few blocks from the scene of the crime. The murderer has not been captured.

"Jack the Hugger," Jack the Kisser," "Jack the Hair Clipper," and the miscreants who bother women pedestrians and various other ways and about his freakish doings there is much in the newspapers from time to time or psychopathic kinsman of Jack the Ripper. They are maniacs, and their insanity is only a milder type of the mania, which impelled Jack the Ripper to commit the most atrocious, the most mysterious, the most cunning devised and adroitly executed murders in the history of civilization.

Lizzie Halliday

AUTHOR'S COMMENTARY

In the history of crime, women serial and mass murderers are not the standard; they are exceedingly rare. White, young men predominantly dominate this class of killers.

Yet, some women are as proficient and devious as men when it comes to multiple killing. Their motives are generally the same as in men. In serial killings, love, hate, jealousy, and revenge rarely play a pivotal role since, in most cases, the victims are unknown to the killer before being selected for death.

There will always be serial killers. We can only hope law enforcement identifies and capturers them before the body count mounts.

Lizzie was a fascinating killer, and without question, mental illness was her driving force.

The Courier News

Monday, September 11, 1893

A MURDEROUS MANIAC

The Many Crimes Charged Against Lizzie Halliday

A MANIA LIKE JACK THE RIPPER

She Killed and Mutilated Her First Husband in the Same Manner as Her Second—The McQuillan Women Murdered Through Thirst for Blood.

MIDDLETOWN, N.Y., Sept. 11.

The solution of the mystery surrounding Lizzie Halliday's awful crimes will be found in the history of her previous life and her relations with her husband.

Young Paul and Robert Halliday have told their stories, and when all this new and old information is put together, there is produced a story of very unusual, but not of unprecedented criminality.

Lizzie Halliday, herself a type of low humanity, was merely an ignorant, mean, cunning and revengeful woman, with the belief that she possessed the power to deceive everybody she chose.

This appears to have been her character under ordinary circumstances, but at certain periods she appears to have become possessed of a mania. On each occasion, when she was in this wild mental condition, she was expecting to become a mother.

She never did, however, so far as is known, give birth to a living child. This mania, which is not without numerous precedents, assumed in Lizzie Halliday's case a phase almost unbelievably shocking.

In fact, there is excellent reason to assume that her case and that of the mysterious London assassin, known as "Jack the Ripper," are very similar.

In both the mania appears to have developed crimes of a similar nature, the difference being chiefly that in one developed in a man and in this last case in a woman.

Lizzie Halliday has killed two men in her life, both of them husbands, and she mutilated both.

It has just come out, through the stories told by Paul Halliday's two sons, that the woman confessed to old Paul soon after her marriage to him that she had been married before and had killed and then hacked her husband.

Old Paul professed not to believe the story and undoubtedly did not. But it now appears that she treated his body after she had killed him as she had that of her first husband.

Her two subsequent crimes, the killing of the McQuillan women, must have been committed in the pure thirst for blood, induced by her mania and probably whetted by her fearful crime of a few days before.

She did not mutilate the bodies of the women, which shows that it must have been merely a thirst for blood which prompted her to the deed.

In a protracted interview with Robert Halliday, the eldest son of the murdered man, he made the following statement: "This woman came from the same county in Ireland as my father. He told me this himself. He first met her in an intelligence office in Newburg, where he secured her services as housekeeper. Sometime after, he married her. None of the family liked the woman. Her appearance was against her. She did not conduct yourself as a wife should. My father, however, was infatuated with her. She held a peculiar influence over him, which nothing could shake. Soon after his marriage to the woman, who gave her name as Lizzie Brown, there began a peculiar succession of crimes which finally led to her being committed to the insane asylum.

"First, there was the burning of the house. Then the burning of the barn, and finally the burning of the Old Mill where my father, his wife, and my brother John lived, in which fire my brother lost his life.

"Following this at a stated period came her theft of the team of a Newburg liveryman. She hired a horse and buggy in Newburg on the statement that she was a poor Irish servant who wanted to visit her sick mother. The man let her have a horse and buggy. She drove out of town, got an old man to go with her as she did not know the country, and within 24 hours, had sold the rig and horse to some Gypsies.

"She was arrested, tried, and found not guilty on the ground of insanity.

"Two fires in my father's place occurred in quick succession. After a long period came the conflagration in which my young brother perished. For this crime, she was arrested, but on the ground of insanity was remanded to the insane asylum at Middletown. She remained there a while, was then sent to another asylum, and finally was released as cured at my father's request.

"My father told me subsequently to these affairs that his wife, at the time of their commission, was in a condition peculiar to women. That when in that condition, she was subject to spells of insanity. With the disappearance of the physical condition, there was a disappearance of the criminal tendencies. I begged my father to leave the woman, but he would not listen to me."

After a great deal of deliberation, the coroner's jury arrived at its verdict: "We do say upon our oath that Margaret J. McQuillan and Sarah J. McQuillan came to their deaths from bullets fired from a pistol in the hands of Lizzie Halliday. That said, Margaret was killed on or about August 30, and Sarah J. McQuillan on or about September 2."

The inquest on the body of Paul Halliday was resumed at 9 o'clock this morning, but nothing new, it is believed, will be elicited. After that, the case will sink out of sight until Mrs. Halliday's call to answer at court sometime next month.

The Press

Friday, June 22, 1894

IS FACING THE JURY

LIZZIE HALLIDAY AND HER MANY CRIMES

HER LIFE IS HANGING IN THE BALANCE

The Most Inhuman Woman Fiend of the Century—Murder Seems to Have Been Her Diversion—Some of Her Deeds.

THE TRIAL OF Lizzie Halliday for murder, which is now in progress in the pretty village of Monticello, New York, is attracting the attention of the whole country thereabout, such as known the trial has done before it. For almost a year she has languished in the jail awaiting trial for three murders – those of her husband, Paul Halliday, and of Mrs. Margaret McQuillan and Sarah J., her daughter – between the 30th of last August and 2nd of last September.

The accompanying portrait shows a far more human-looking thing than that which the dwellers in Walker Valley wanted to hang last year when they found her dead husband's body under his own cabin floor, after having found those of the McQuillan's in the barn. Her stock of coarse hair has grown long enough to be gathered in a neat wavy knot. The faded and dirty calico wrapper has been replaced by a quite coquettish blouse and tie.

But however she has improved in appearance, Lizzie Halliday has turned since she has been in jail and even more abnormal monstrosity than the country people who got the rope out at Bennett's Hotel to hang her though she was. She has made disclosures since she was shut up *here that make one pause to wonder whether this is the 19th century or the 16th, New York State, or the Scotch border about the time of the Regent Murray. Bigamy has been her past time, murder her diversion, arson the serious business of her life for ten years. She is only 28. Yet, until her arrest for these crimes, she has never been punished for any offense saved by a short two-year term in the Eastern penitentiary at Philadelphia. Then she had burned up, not only her own little house on Kensington Avenue, but those of two neighbors on either side at midnight and during the blizzard of March, 1888.*

Aside from the light that they have thrown on her own character, who disclosures are mainly interesting and the suggestion that the summer borders of Orange and Sullivan counties have been living for years in the neighborhood of a nest of murderous banditti, who could do business in Sicily as competition with the Mala Vita. One of her statements, which seemed at the time mere raving, was that she had not murdered the McQuillan's and her husband, but had seen them murdered by a band of brigands who made a practice of doing away with people, generally peddlers with packs and desolate women with stolen money or jewelry in their possession.

The bodies, she said, were thrown into the "old lead mines." The "old lead mines" are some disused workings about 10 miles from Paul Halliday's house. A very brief inquiry showed that no longer ago than the summer of 1890, Samuel Hatch, a peddler, was found murdered in that very place. The suggestion, of course, arises that Lizzie Halliday had heard of this murder, and the same kind of low cunning that led her to "play crazy" last fall, inspired, the thought of putting her own murders upon the unknown assassins of Hutch. But the reference is not at all a strained one that she may have become, upon marrying

Paul Halliday, a decoy for a band who did all the murders. On them, too, if there are any such, she puts the murder on John Halliday, her worthless stepson, who was burned to death in the incendiary fire, which destroyed the original Halliday house in May, 1891. It was murder as well it as arson, for she or they knew that the imbecile and crippled man was in the house when it was fired and permissively, if not actively, kept him there.

Five husbands may certainly be credited to Mrs. Lizzie Halliday and a companion who is probably the sixth. With one or possibly two exceptions, these were all men of the Paul Halliday type – old men who with senile fancies were captivated by the attribute which he who runs may read in the nose and mouth and chin shown in this photograph. She only murdered one as far as known – Paul Halliday.

Her first, "Ketspool" Brown, otherwise known as Hopkins, whom she married ten years ago, died a natural death in Vermont soon after she married him and had her only child. Poor old Artemus Brewer, a broken-down veteran of Greenwich Village, Washington County, whence her first husband had also come, was her second, and he died in a year, glad to escape from her beatings and hair-pulling. His old army comrade, George Smith, saw him die and knew what a life he had led, and still, he married the widow. She gave him a cup of poison tea a few months afterward and laughingly left him withering on the floor. When the doctors brought him around, he was glad to know that she had fled with another old man, Hiram Parkinson. It is not known that she married Parkinson at all. A little while afterward, she did marry Charlie Playstel in Bellows Falls, Vermont, the only man on her list who could be called younger.

It will be seen that this she Henry VIII went to the altar, or rather, to a justice of the peace. This may have been due to her County Antrim antecedents. Her people, the McNally's, came from Ireland to Newburgh in 1867. Or it may have been a discrete regard for the stern self-protected moral sense of rural communities. Couples who have "forgotten to go to church" are in the country liable to midnight visitations of buckets of tar and bundles of feathers.

It is interesting to know that when she decoyed the McQuillan's, mother and daughter, from Newburgh over to their deaths in Walker Valley, she knew that she was dealing with old friends of her family. The McQuillan's and McNally's were neighbors, both in the old country and the new. When she turned up in Philadelphia in the winter of 1888, she first went to John McQuillan's saloon and home at 1218 N. Front St., and waited to stay there on the old family friendship plea. She had her boy, Charlie Hopkins, with her then, and money enough to come in a cab and then hire a little shop at 2840 Kensington Ave., which she ensured on the "ten cent a week" installment premium plan, and then set fire to it.

Springville Journal

Thursday, June 28, 1894

LIZZIE HALLIDAY CONVICTED

The Verdict Says Guilty of Murder in the First Degree

MONTICELLO, N.Y., June 22

The jury in the trial of Lizzie Halliday came in at 5 o'clock. Foreman George W. Decker announced that Lizzie Halliday was found guilty of murder in the first degree of Sarah J.

McQuillan and Ella McQuillan. The vote stood 11 to 1 in the first ballot.

Lizzie Halliday was held in a standing position by two constables while the verdict was given. She had covered her face with her handkerchief and betrayed no emotion when the verdict was rendered.

MONTICELLO, N.Y., June 22-- The trial of Mrs. Lizzie Halliday, the murderess, was concluded at Monticello in the sentence of death by electrocution was pronounced upon her by Judge Samuel Edwards. The prisoner was the first woman ever sentenced to electrocution, took the sentence stolidly, keeping up very bravely her show of insanity. She will die between August 6 and 14th.

The New York Times

Saturday, June 29, 1918

<h2 align="center">LIZZIE HALLIDAY DEAD.</h2>

Guilty of Five Murders and Described as "Worst Woman on Earth"

Special to the New York Times

BEACON, N.Y., June 28

Lizzie Halliday, described as the "worst woman on earth" after she had killed five persons, her husband, a stepson, two women friends, and then a nurse who attended her in Matteawan asylum, died at the state hospital today. She was convicted and then adjudged insane, but there was a strong suspicion that she had murdered several others, including a former husband and an itinerant peddler.

She was said to have been a member of a wandering Gypsy band when she married Paul Halliday, an aged farmer of Burlingham, Sullivan County. The New York authorities first heard of her when her first husband disappeared in 1893. The mountains near Burlingham were searched, and the bodies of two women, buried at the bottom of the haymow, were found. When arrested, she confessed to the murders.

In 1894 she was sentenced to die in the electric chair, but her conduct under imprisonment led to the appointment of a commission to investigate her sanity. Gov. Flower commuted her sentence, and she was sent to Matteawan, from which she tried to escape several times. Then she tried to murder her nurse, Miss Catherine Ward. Of all the attendants, Nelly Wickes was the one who best had control over Lizzie, and the insane woman became attached to the nurse, who had planned to leave the asylum for other work. When she told her plans to Lizzie, the latter seized a pair of scissors and cut the nurse's throat. At the time of her death, Lizzie Halliday was in her 58th year.

The Texas Servant Girl Annihilator

AUTHOR'S COMMENTARY

In 1884, Austin, Texas, experienced the first in a series of brutal murders. The city was in a state of panic, and all women and girls employed as servants dreaded nightfall for fear of becoming the next victim. Roughly one year later, on Christmas Eve, the last known murder occurred. Seven women (possibly more) were murdered by this serial killer using an ax and knife. The majority of victims were African Americans, working as live-in cooks and maids for well-to-do families. The women and girls lived on the premises where they were murdered. The killer's method of operation was always the same. Late at night, the killer silently crept into the bedroom while the women slept and delivered a quick, forceful strike with an ax to their heads. In most cases, the attack crushed their skulls and inflicted massive brain damage. However, he did not stop there. He applied multiple strikes with an ax, causing blood and brains to splatter from the skull, engulfing the room in a bloody shower. The vicious attacks left a gruesome crime scene with the bed and walls saturated with blood and brain material. Fortunately, some victims died instantly, while others struggled to live while he completed his grisly work.

As quickly as the attacks began, they mysteriously ceased. Why? Speculation has continued to this day as to the motive(s) of the killer. Why were the majority of victims' black servants? Was the killer black, white, or Hispanic? These are questions no one can answer. What we do know is the following murders are the work of this killer.

> December 30, 1884, Mollie Smith, 25, murdered, and her lover, Walter Spencer, attacked, as they slept. Mollie worked as a cook and maid. She died and Walter was seriously wounded.

> March 19, 1885, Clara Strand and Christine Martenson, both Swedish girls employed as servants, were attacked and seriously wounded.

> May 6, 1885, Eliza Shelly was murdered.

> May 22, 1885, Irene Cross was murdered.

> August 1885, Clara Dick was seriously wounded.

> August 30, 1885, eleven-year-old Mary Ramey was murdered, and her mother Rebecca critically wounded.

> September 28, 1885, Gracie Vance was murdered.

December 24, 1885, Susan Hancock was murdered.

December 24, 1885, Eula Phillips was murdered. James Philips, her spouse, was seriously wounded.

As a former detective, I understand people kill for a variety of reasons. I also know that serial killers have a deep-seated psychological need to kill, and, in many cases, they'll target a particular sex, age group, or physical characteristics such as blond hair. At other times, they simply select victims randomly. In this case, the killer primarily chose black servant girls. Why? No one knows.

The following stories are excellent representations of the reporting of this crime spree.

Austin American Statesman

Thursday, January 1, 1885

BLOODY WORK.

A FEARFUL MIDNIGHT MURDER ON WEST PECAN—

MYSTERY AND CRIME.

A Colored Woman Killed Outright, and Her Lover Almost Done for.

No Clue to the Perpetrator of the Bloody Deed—Details of the Crime.

At a late hour Tuesday night, there occurred one of the most horrible murders that ever a reporter was called on to chronicle – a deed almost unparalleled in the atrocity of its execution. It happened on the premises of Mr. W. K. Hall, an insurance man lately from Galveston, residing at 901, West Pecan, about a block beyond the iron bridge that spans Shoal Creek.

A colored woman named Mollie Smith had been in the service of the family as a cook for little over a month. A young colored fellow named Walter Spencer, has been coming to see her for some months, and the couple, though not married, were lately living in the relation of man and wife. Between three and 4 o'clock Wednesday morning, Mr. Thomas Chalmers, a brother of Mrs. Hall, was aroused from sleep by the entrance of Spencer. He was bleeding freely from several wounds on the head, and said, "Mr. Tom, for God's sake, do something to help me; somebody has nearly killed me."

Young Chalmers at once sprung up, and striking a light, saw that the negro was badly hurt. He could tell nothing of the occurrence and did not know who hit him. He and the woman above mentioned have been occupying a small apartment in the rear of the house, just back of the kitchen. He remarked that Mollie was gone. Chalmers told him to go to the doctors and get his wounds dressed. He could not leave the house to go with him, owing to the sickness of one of the inmates. Spencer then went away. At breakfast time yesterday morning, Mollie was missing, but even then, nobody was aware of her terrible fate. It was perhaps about 9:00 AM when a neighbor servant in the employ of a neighbor observed a strange-looking object in the backyard of the Hall residence. He had once reported the matter, and several hurried to the spot. They laid the woman, stark dead, a ghastly object to behold.

A horrible hole on the side of her head told the tale. The reason she had not been discovered earlier was that she lay immediately behind a small outhouse, and no one thought of looking for her there. From the outhouse to the room where she slept was about 50 steps, so the unfortunate victim of the brutal attack had been dragged to the spot where her dead body was found. All the circumstances go to show that the murder was committed in the room where the two were sleeping.

Later in the day, a Statesman man repaired to the scene of the tragedy. He was first shown the woman still lying in the yard, but a brief glance at the sickening sight was sufficient. She was a light-colored mulatto, apparently about 25 years of age. A distinct trail on the ground leading to her door showed where the inhuman fiend had dragged her. She was nearly nude when first discovered. Inside the room, there was evidences of a desperate struggle. A broken looking glass, disarranged furniture, and bloodied finger marks on the door showed that a fight for life, silent, and unseen saved by principals, but obstinate to the end, had taken place. The pillows and sheets were bathed in blood, and sanguinary stains were all over the floor.

Beside the foot of the bed lay an ax, beyond doubt the instrument of the crime, as it, too, was bloodstained. Who used it? There lies the mystery. Did the man and woman engage in a fight between themselves, and did he slay her? That is one theory. It is only a theory. There is nothing particular to make it plausible. The kindest relations had previously existed between them. No difficulty had occurred to break off an intimacy that had lasted four months. Why should either want to murder the other? The other theory hinges on the arrest of William Brooks, a young colored man employed as a bartender in the Barrel House alone on East Pecan. Brooks was a former lover of Mollie, had known her in Waco before she came to Austin. The other theory supposes jealousy on his part. He was put in the county jail in the forenoon on suspicion. Late in the afternoon, when called on by a reporter, he made the following statement: "I know both the woman Mollie Smith and Walter Spencer. I liked them both, and never had any falling out with either. I knew her in Waco, and have had nothing to do with her here. I am innocent of the murder, and can prove by any number of witnesses that I was at a ball on Sandhill (near Tillotson Institute) till 4 o'clock in the morning, and was the prompter. They have got hold of the wrong man sure.

Going to the house where Brooks said he went after leaving the ball, in an alley back of Dr. Wright's church, the reporter asked of the colored woman living there and what hour Brooks came in. Between two and 3 o'clock in the night, she answered. Are you certain of that was asked, "Yes sir, I am, because after he had come in and slept a while, I woke up and happening to look at the clock noticed it was just three." It will be remembered that Brooks said it was 4 o'clock when he left the ball, and as the place was fully a mile and half distant, it would have been at least 4:20 ere he got to his room, had he gone directly home. A number of negroes, however, stated that he stayed through the dance, and it may be the colored woman was mistaken about the hour.

The wounded man was next called on. He was in a pitiful plight, but was able to speak, though with a somewhat indistinct utterance. There were five facial hurts – the most serious one being a puncture under the eye, fracturing the orbital bone. Dr. Bath, city physician, had found a part of the bone pressed back into the cavity against the eyeball, and had pulled it forward into place. Though badly hurt, the doctor thinks the chances of recovery are favorable. His statement was made in a clear way as follows;

"It was sometime between nine and ten o'clock Tuesday night that I went to Mollie's room. She complained of being sick, and asked me if I wasn't sorry for her. She also told me to wake her up early the next morning. I don't remember anything else that happened until I woke and found myself hurt. I don't know who did it, but it wasn't Mollie. I thought somebody had killed me. Mollie was not in the room, and I never saw her anymore. When I rounded front of the house, woke Mr. Chalmers, and told him what had happened. He told me to go to the doctor. I went out the back way and noticed that the gate was wide open, the wire I recollected having fastened. I first went to the house of a colored man living near, and he gave me a coat. Then I went to see Dr. Ralph Steiner, who washed and dressed my wound. I then went back to Mr. Hall's, and found the front gate open; then I started uptown but was weak that I fell down several times before getting to my brothers' restaurant on Brazos Street near Newton saloon. It was about 6 o'clock in the morning when I got there, and he had me taken home in a back. I have not quarreled with anybody but Brooks. Some three months ago, he wanted to fight me. He had stayed with Mollie in Waco. But I don't say that he was the one. I don't know who did it, but anybody could have got into the room easily through the door connecting it with the kitchen.

These are about the facts, and the reader is left to draw his own conclusions. Whether slain by her lover or some party from the outside is as yet a mystery and envelops as foul a deed as ever done in Austin.

AUTHOR'S COMMENTARY

Roughly two years later, a murderous assault in Gainesville brought the Austin murders to the forefront. Was it the same killer who moved to another city or a copycat? It is unknown.

St. Louis Post Dispatch

Friday, July 22, 1887

IS IT A TEXAN MR. HYDE?

AN AWFUL SUSPICION AS TO THE ASSAILANT OF THE TWO YOUNG GIRLS

No Explanation Except That the Butchery Was the Work of a Maniac—The

Crime Was Terribly Similar in Every Detail to the Successive

Murders of Nine Women at Austin— Has That Assassin Just Begun

Another Series in the Neighboring City? His Extraordinary Immunity From

Capture, Although Repeatedly Trace by Bloodhounds—The Human, as Well as

The Brute Detectives Absolutely Baffled.

New York World Special.

GAINSVILLE, Tex. July 18.

Yesterday was a sorrowing day for Gainesville. The memory of one young girl murdered and another still hanging between life and death, acted like a pall on the city. At all churches, the services partook of a funeral character.

People in assembling seem to tread more softly and whisper words of sympathy and sorrow for the hearts today bowed down in suffering. The firm tones of men and talking over the blood and double butchery show that the fire of human vengeance still burns, and seems to be fed by time.

An investigation, after five days analysis of every circumstance attending the murder, utterly fails to find the slightest reasonable clue, hushed conjecture, and beginning to connect the assault upon these two girls with the horrible series of murders in Austin two years ago. Nine women were killed in just 12 months' time, and that neighboring city, and almost every incident in each of those murders, was duplicated in last Wednesday night tragedy here. There was never a clue found to the perpetrator of the Austin murders. There was never an explanation to them, except that they were the work of one man, and he a maniac. The horrible fear is beginning to spread that he has begun his work here.

The Austin series started on one Christmas Eve and closed with a double tragedy on the eve of the next sacred natal day.

The first victim of the bloodied line was Mary Smith, a colored servant woman. Her body was found in the yard attached to her house on Christmas morning, 1884. There had been frightful mutilation gashes and cuts so vigorously made that the body fell apart when the neighbors came to lift it into a coffin. It was a bright moonlight night when the murder was committed, and the assassin seem to take abundance of time for his work. His footsteps were traced here and there around the yard, as though he had lingered long about the spot. There was deliberation marked at every point, and with no slight effort at concealment. It seems incredible that no clue was left leading up to the assassin. Explanation came readily enough. It was a discarded lover, the general opinion agreed, who had done the deed, and there was much talk over it.

REPEATING THE CRIME.

But on the night of May 7, 1885, Lizzie Shelley, another colored servant, was killed in precisely the same fashion. It was a bright moonlight night, as before. There was the same dragging out the victim from her bed to the open air; then the hacking and slashing with some instrument of the hatchet type – not a mere killing or forcing into insensibility, but a repeated use of the weapon, as though the ruffian found the light and hearing the thud upon the bone and flesh of his victim. The same explanation came readily enough – jealousy and the gratification of love turned to hate.

In June came the third on the list. She, too, was a colored servant girl, Irene Cross. There was the hacking and mutilation, the same seeming fiendish delight in mangling the body. In this case, it was not dragged out to the open air, but the victim's room shown that the ruffian had been hurried away by an alarm which he imagined have been directed at him.

This crime stirred the community. The negroes were certain that some terrible voodoo was working out an evil charm, and there was a great sale of all manner of nostrums and queer combinations to fight off the evil one. The white population began to put out some efforts, but the culmination and not yet been reached, and the unknown fiend felt emboldened in his work.

THE TERRIBLE RECORD CONTINUED.

On August 30 of that year, the same assassin, it now seems clear, visited the cabin on the place of Mr. V. O. Weed, a nephew of the late Thurlow Weed. In the cabin were two colored servants, mother, and daughter – Rebecca Ramey, aged 40, Mary Ramey, aged 12. It was 4 o'clock in the morning when Mr. Weed heard groans in this cabin. He found the mother bleeding from a gash in the head and the daughter missing. The trail was a hot one, for fresh blood spots led to a stable half a mile away where the body of the girl was found, assaulted and beaten on the head with that same hatchet before. There was not the usual scene of butchery, but there were evidences of haste in the work. The excitement ran up to fever heat, and then bloodhounds are put on the scent, and a 10 miles track was made in and out of the city streets, then out into the country and back until the scent was lost in the streets again.

The use of the hounds convinced many that the murderer was a negro, for the hounds are thrown off the scent by the old slave methods of baffling the dogs. Others pointed out that the great unknown may have been a white man, thoroughly familiar with negro lore on hounds in the best methods of throwing them off the scent. There were many traces that would seem to lead direct to certain individuals, but in each case, innocence was proven. The negroes abandon their notion that witches were doing the bloodied work and insisted that a white man was the wrongdoer, as the whole campaign showed too much method and purpose for black brain to compose.

Another month swung by, and people had ceased to sleep with a rifle in hand behind double bar doors. September 29 was the date of the next bloodied act. Again the scene was a negro cabin, this time occupied by four people – Mrs. Gracie Vance, Orange Washington, Lucinda Boddy, and Patsey Gibson, two mulatto girls. There were two apartments. And when the murderer beat the girls into insensibility, apparently with a sand club. The man was hammered into insensibility and died the next morning, while Mrs. Vance was dragged out of the cabin through a window, taken along the road some 80 yards and there, after so, had her brains beaten out.

A stone club was the weapon of murder in this case, and the hatchet or heavy cleaver seem to have been left at home. In the lifeless fingers of Gracie Vance was a bit of watch chain with broken crystal, but even this carelessly left piece of evidence did not serve to lead to the detection of the criminal.

October brought the next one on the list. It was another colored woman, Alice Davis, and she, too, was dragged from her bed in a cabin, taken some distance away, assaulted, and then hacked up far past the limit of ordinary killing. A whirlwind of doubt and dread swept over the city. Whites and blacks alike were in terror, but especially the latter, the superstitious fear was, at times, most pitiful to see.

TWO MORE MURDERS TO CLOSE THE YEAR.

The last and bloodiest of the awful series was on Christmas Eve, 1885. Mrs. Hancock and her husband lived in a pretty cottage in the older quiet streets of Austin. He was a mechanic of good standing, a white man. Hearing a slight noise on that night, he went to his wife's apartment. He found the bed empty and gory. The trail of blood was short and fresh. It ran to the yard, and there on the ground, weltering in her blood and gasping, lay the wife, with two hatchet wounds in the head, not yet dead, but beaten into insensibility; she died the next morning.

There was the bright moonlight as before, the apparent invitation to detection, and yet the old-time immunity from detection. But the murder of one white woman was not the whole record of that Christmas Eve. After midnight Mr. James Phillip heard groaning in the lower room of his house. The room whence the sound came was occupied by *a married son, together with his wife and infant son. The young man lay groaning on the bed, gashed into the brain above the right ear with the familiar hatchet mark. The sleeping child had its garment saturated with the blood of its parents. The mother was absent, there was the open, telltale trail leading out to the yard and there the nude body of Mrs. Phillips lay, assaulted, with the skull cleft almost in two by a blow dealt upon the forehead. A log had been lifted and flung across the chest. There had been no outcry, not the least sound or appeal for help, nothing until the quickly awaken father heard the groaning of his son and hurried down to the ghastly spectacle.*

The bloodhounds came in on Christmas morning, took up both trails only to follow them away, and then to bay and acknowledgment of defeat.

ABSOLUTELY NO CLUE.

Not alone was the instinct of the brut called in to find the criminal, but the best detective talent which money could secure was brought to bear on the case, but today they are as much shrouded in mystery as they were a year and a half ago. The husband of the murdered Eula Phillips was tried for her murder, as was the husband of Mrs. Hancock. In each case, long and exhaustive trials were had, but nothing was brought out of an incriminating character. The Pinkertons are called upon to aid in unraveling the crime, and given carte blanche as to time and money. Other detectives, too, were employed, but so far, not even remote clue has been unearthed.

Everyone in Austin has read Stevenson's extraordinary novel with the intensity of interest known in no other community. Was there a Dr. Jekyll and Mr. Hyde living there – one who could in a twinkling of an eye change his identity? If so, even how was it that there never was a discovery? Why did not someone meet the assassin, bloodied hands, and saturated with blood, as he must have been from head to foot? He took no special pains for concealment. He never made a failure. Was it a conspiracy for murder, or was someone playing a lone hand in the fearful game? There was no seeming purpose in some of the murders. Not a penny of gain by the slaughter, no grudge to gratify, no feud to fight out. He defied alike the Bhut and the human detective.

HAS HE APPEARED IN GAINESVILLE?

And the terrible similarity of his methods to the tragedy here, of which these dispatches have given the readers of the world full account. Miss Genie Watkins, the daughter of the hotel keeper in Dallas, has been on a visit to Miss Mamie Bostwick, the daughter of a rich cattle dealer in the city. They were aged 19 and 20 years, respectively. The house was a single-story one and, after the Texas fashion, spreading over a good deal of ground. The two young ladies occupied separate beds in the front room. It was about 3 o'clock last Wednesday morning when Mrs. Bostwick heard a slight scuffle in the girl's room. It was just on the first edge of daylight, and when she entered the apartment, her glance fell first upon the figure of a man sitting near the window with his feet up on the sill, as though taking a rest after a difficult job. He was thoroughly at ease, and, without extra haste, placed his hand upon the sill, vaulted lightly out and disappeared, leaving only the imprint of his bloodied palm upon the woodwork. Mrs. Bostwick turned to the beds for the girls were moaning and insensibility. Mrs. Bostwick screamed and fainted away, but aid came at once. The household was aroused, and all that could be done by medical skill was done for the two young ladies.

They were both fearfully gashed, and the blood flowing turned the room to the appearance of a slaughterhouse. There had been struggles of youth and vigor against the assailant, but in each instance, the hatchet had been used to give the quietus to the victim. Miss Watkins had received two blows. One had cut through the bones of the forehead from the right temple across to the left. It was given with force, and from the gaping opening, the brains were pouring out upon the clotted blood. Another blow had fallen upon the right temple and had forced in the bones of the skull in such a way as to force the eye from its socket. There were bruises upon the arm, as though the assailant had clutched her in a strong grip against her struggles to free herself from his hold.

THE SURVIVING GIRL'S STORY.

Miss Bostwick was three times struck with that active hatchet. One blow on the left temple fracture of the skull, another cut was a deep triangular gash on the right cheek, the third opened the face from the corner of the nose to the center of the upper lip. Two upper teeth are broken out, and to lower ones were broken. The wounds were terrible, and the pain from them was excruciating. Yet the victim lived, and her first inquiry upon becoming conscious was about Genie.

She was evidently not aware of what had taken place. From such questions, as could be put to the wounded girl, it was inferred that the assailant was a white man with a black mustache, but with such wounds, it is not surprising that the mind wandered, little weight can be placed upon such information. Here was her almost an articulate story: When asked if she saw her assailant, she said, "yes."

"Was he colored?"

"No."

"White?"

"Yes, and had a black mustache."

"Where did you see him first?"

"In the yard."

"With what were you struck?"

She returned no answer.

"With a stick?"

"No."

"With a hatchet?"

"Yes."

"Did the man enter at the window?"

"No."

"At the door?"

"Yes."

"Did he go out through the window?"

"Yes."

She saw him first "in the yard." Did this murderer, as his Austin prototype, drag his victim out of doors after beating her into insensibility, and then perhaps return her mangled body to the bed? Several of the Austin victims must have been beaten into unconsciousness while asleep and then taken away, for their outcry would have alarmed others in the house. The deliberation of the Gainesville murderer makes it possible that he did so drag the helpless body out and back again. But if so, he must be a maniac.

THE BLOODHOUNDS AGAIN BAFFLED.

It was a bright moonlight the night before – as on each night of the nine Austin murders – and an examination showed that the hard soil outside the windows had failed to take the impress of the assassins foot. But when daylight came, tracks were found in the plowed ground among the growing corn, in which a large portion of the vacant lot adjoining is planted. Still, there was little to indicate that the tracks belonged to the murderer save the fact of there being found near the scene of the assault. The tracks were evidently made by feet encased in socks only and were of gigantic size. Measuring over 12 inches in length. Another track of different size and shape was also found leading towards the house, but neither could be found near the window at which the fiend made egress.

A meeting of citizens raised $2,000 for use in ferreting out the criminal. Immediately upon being informed of the bloodied affair officers telegraphed to several towns for bloodhounds, and a train arrived bringing the trailers. They were taken to the house and given the scent, so great was a crowd about the lot that they failed to strike a trail. The dogs were taken away, and the crowd asked to disperse, which it did. Later on, the dogs were again given the scent, and, striking the trail, they followed it in a northerly direction to the creek bottom, where it was lost. Once more, the dogs were taken back to the house. This time they were kept for some time in the room where the deed was committed, were shown the spots of blood upon the windowsill left by the hand of the assassin, and the track found in the garden. Again they gave a cry and followed the trail over the same course as formally, losing it again at the same place. A third time they were taken back in, and a third time they went over the same ground and gave up the chase at the same point. The great heat and extreme dryness seem to have destroyed the scent, and the dogs were unable to accomplish anything more.

In the meantime, at least 500 men, divided in 20 or more posses, mounted on horseback, scoured the country in all directions. As they went along, they aroused the farmers, who joined in the pursuit. Nine arrests were made, and the suspected parties were put under guard to await examination. They were doubly protected by resolute man for fear that the enraged populace would tear them limb from limb even on a slight suspicion of guilt.

YOUNG NORWOOD'S QUEER SUGGESTION.

The arrested men one by one easily succeeded in proving their innocence, and then came an astonishing suggestion from young Able Norwood of Dallas, who was the affianced lover of Miss Watkins and who came here at once after the murder. Perhaps the young man is somewhat unbalanced by his grief, but here is his story: he met in Dallas some time ago a young lady, whose name he declines to give, who fell in love with him.

At first, he thought that the murder was the work of a discarded suitor of Miss Watkins, but now he believes it was instigated by the infatuated young woman referred to. After meeting this person, he says, he did not call on her until invited by letter to do so, and "then did not make any advances to indicate that he regarded her in any but the light of a mere friend." She told him that "she had understood that he was engaged to Miss Watkins and vowed she did not wish to come between them, but declared that she loved him and that "she could work harder and make more sacrifices for his happiness than Miss Watkins could."

He repelled her advances gently but firmly, telling her that Genie loved him and that he loved Genie and must be true to her. The young lady sent for him several times, so he avers and never worried of telling him of her devotion, though she saw her case was hopeless. He gave the place of her residence, which is a small Texas city, he said. She never was in Gainesville that he knew of, but he seemed to think, in spite of his disclaimer, that someone might have hired someone to be a representative here.

FRUITLESS CLUES.

In fact, there are all manner of reports, besides a conjecture that the murder was the work of a maniac. It is asserted, and the report seems to come from a reliable source, that Capt. Watkins stated in an interview that Mrs. Genie Watkins was a very important witness in a case several years ago wherein a man was sent to the penitentiary for robbery, and that man sentence was out a few days before this murder was committed. The man was heard to vow vengeance at the time of his conviction, and it is possible he may be the guilty party, having committed the crime at the first opportunity he had to secure the vengeance he vowed long ago.

But so strong is the belief here that the murder was the work of a maniac that grave suspicions rested upon the brother of Mrs. Bostwick, a young man some 21 or 22 years old, who is afflicted with epilepsy. Persons, however, well acquainted with the family, and knowing the young man's condition express emphatic disbelief in the theory. His physical condition, they said, was such that he could not fly in and out the window without assistance. Others expatiated on the case with which he could have jumped from the window, could have run around the house, throwing the hatchet in the well as he passed, climbed in a back window, and crawled into bed. It was even rumored that the bloodhounds ran around the house from the last window to a back window and tried to climb in the boy's room. This story on investigation proved to be false. A close examination was made of the well, parties going down into it twice, and nothing could be found. The boy's room was carefully searched, and no marks of blood or other traces could be found, which would connect him with the awful crime. Besides, some of those who were present early after the alarm was given are clear that he came into the room almost immediately with unmistakable signs upon his face having just waked up and that his frown and fright were such as could not be simulated. In short, the matter has been thoroughly sifted, and his connection with the assault seems to be clearly shown to be impossible.

BIG REWARD OFFERED.

The officers who held the inquest on Miss Watkins admit that they have found absolutely no clues. R. V. Bell, ex-district attorney, said: "It is a horrible thought, for we cannot tell where he may strike next, but it looks like the work of a maniac, a man who considers himself commissioned to kill certain persons, whose diseased mind is unable to resist what he considers his call to duty and who is yet possessed of that subtle coming which enables him to cover up his tracks successfully. As to the identity of the maniac, I have no theory and no clue from which to weave one."

Hon. J. A. Garnett, one of the leading criminal lawyers at this bar, was found in his office and said in reply to a question: "I think the assassin must have entered the house with the intention of committing an outrage, and that, discovered in his attempt, or else frightened by the presence of two young ladies, when he thought to find but one, he struck his murderous blows to enable him to make his escape. It is impossible to conceive of anybody committing such a deed without a motive, and whatever the motive could there be except that a satisfying a brutal lust?"

Gov. Ross has offered a reward of $1,000 for the capture of the murderer. Citizens of Gainesville have raised $2,500 altogether for the same purpose, and the Dallas News has offered its columns for a popular subscription fund to secure the best detective ability to work up the case. J. Marks, a banker at Texarkana, has sent a check for $250 and is the first to respond to the call for a popular subscription.

Mrs. Bostwick is slowly recovering. Much hope is express that with returning strength, her mind will become clearer and that she will remember something so conclusive of the terrible ordeal through which she passed as will aid the detectives to trace the assassin.

ANNA MARIA ZWANZIGER

AUTHOR'S COMMENTARY

Anna was born on August 7, 1760, and beheaded on September 17, 1811, for murder. She worked in several German homes as a housekeeper and cook. Her preference was working for judges whom she poisoned with arsenic. When her victims became extremely ill, Anna would nurse them back to health, hoping to gain their gratitude. Unfortunately, at least four times, she administered an overdose of arsenic, causing their deaths. Of the four, one was a baby.

It is unknown how many she poisoned during her life of crime. Just before being beheaded, it was reported she made a statement comparable to, "It is a good thing I'm being executed because I don't think I would stop."

The Washington Bee

A FAMOUS POISON CASE

Anna Maria Zwanziger is a

Name of Unpleasant Prominence in Crime

SHE LIVED IN GERMANY

Had a Reputation for Honesty and Probity Which Enabled Her

To Secure Victims Very Easily

Mental Constitution Peculiar—Had Passion for Poisoning—Her Crimes Only "Slight

Errors"—Never Expressed Remorse or Repentance—Fortunate She was Discovered as She Could Not Control Passion.

In the so-called renaissance period of European civilization, poison served many a purpose of political intrigue and personal vengeance. The demise of a victim was rarely followed by a judicial investigation save in instances where the ecclesiastical authorities found an opportunity to intervene.

In the early part of the nineteenth century, there was a series of murders committed in Germany, which have given to the name of Anna Maria Zwanziger an unpleasant prominence in the annals of crime. Anna Maria Zwanziger, or Anna Schouleben, as she called herself, was living in 1807 in Baireuth, supporting herself by knitting. Her reputation for probity and her exemplary mode of live induced Justice Glaser, who was at that time separated from his wife, to take her as his housekeeper in 1808. In July of that year, Glaser was reconciled to his wife, through the efforts, it seems, Anna Schouleben, but within a month after the wife's return, she was suddenly taken sick, though a strong and healthy woman, and died in a few days.

Anna now left Glaser's service and went to live as a housekeeper with Justice Grohmann. He was a sufferer *from gout and was confined to his bed. In May, 1809 after an illness of eleven days, accompanied by strange symptoms, he died, and his housekeeper appeared inconsolable. Her good name and her skill as a nurse soon procured her another place, this time at magistrate Gebhard's house, as a nurse for his wife. Soon after her advent, Mme. Gebhard was seized with a violent illness and died in great agony. At different times within the next few months curious and suspicious symptoms—vomiting, spasms, etc.—visited several persons in the house, guests as well as members of the household.*

Then a superstitious fear of the woman's unlucky presence, gradually deepening into distrust and suspicion, spread in the neighborhood, and Gebhard was induced to dismiss Anna from his service. He gave her, however, a written character for honesty and fidelity.

But it was at her departure the strangest occurrences were noticed. On the morning of that day, it was afterward remembered, she had exceeded the usual limits of her duties: she had filled the kitchen saltbox from the barrel and had taken pains to make for the two maids some coffee, which they drank. Leaving the house with every sign of cheerfulness and affection, she took Gebhard's child in her arms as she said farewell and gave it a biscuit soaked in milk. Scarcely half an hour had elapsed since her departure when the child became alarmingly ill; in a few hours, the maids were attacked in a similar way, and the kitchen saltbox, with the barrel, proved, upon examination, to contain a quantity of arsenic. When she was apprehended shortly afterward, a packet of arsenic was found in her pocket, and upon exhuming the bodies of Glaser, Grohmann and Gebhard distinct traces of arsenic were discovered in two of the three corpses. She was taken before a magistrate, and here the peculiar features of continental criminal procedure were strikingly brought out.

The circumstantial evident of murder against her was, in reality, not strong. Now, the favorite German mode of obtaining results in a criminal case is by some means or other to extract a confession, and here, evidently, only a confession could furnish the necessary evidence.

According to the most approved methods; therefore, she was subjected to a long series of rigid examinations alone in the presence of the judge and notary. All the cunning and adroitness of the judge were brought to bear, in order to entrap her into a confession, but nearly six months, from October 19, 1809, until April 16, 1810, she absolutely denied every form of the charge against her. The fact that poison had been found in the two corpses was not announced to Anna Zwanziger until April 16. This produced the desired effect, for, after two hours of stubborn composure, she broke down, wept, wrung her hands, and at length confessed to all the charges against her, and to several other murders that had passed for natural deaths. On September 11, 1811, she suffered death at the block, and her name is celebrated throughout Germany as the most infamous poisoner ever known.

There can be no doubt that her mental constitution was peculiar. She had a passion for poisoning and spoke of her deeds as only "slight errors" and "trifling offenses," never expressing any remorse or repentance. It was indeed fortunate for mankind, as she said, that she was to die, for she never could have ceased to poison.

The Nebraska Killer

AUTHOR'S COMMENTARY

Perhaps the most notable characteristic of this murderer was his coolness and indifference to his pending execution. And his thought-provoking desire that the news media reported his crimes accurately. No spinning, embellishment, and no fake news. Just the facts.

The Omaha (Neb.) Republican

Dec. 29, 1879

THE NEBRASKA MURDERER

A COOL CONFESSION OF HIS MANY CRIMES

THE PERPETRATOR OF SIX BRUTAL MURDERS

HIS INDIFFERENCE TO THE THREATS OF LYNCHING

Stephen D. Richards, the murderer, who has gained notoriety since the discovery of his diabolical crimes, three weeks ago, passed through Omaha yesterday morning, in route to Kearny Junction, in charge of Sheriff Anderson, of Buffalo County, and Sheriff Martin of Adams County.

A two hours' conversation with the man, as the Union Pacific train carried him and the writer to Valley Station, developed a tale of wickedness that sounds more like the stories of bloodthirsty pirates of the days of long ago than anything that could be dreamed of in this nineteenth century. Imagine a man 24 years old, well brought up, tolerably educated, with a pair of eyes that generally gaze from under his eyebrows peacefully and gently, but which at times flash spitefully, and you have Richards as he was yesterday. Throw in any amount of profanity and sangfroid,

TRUE CRIME CHRONICLES | 83

and you also have him, only more so. And yet he rode out over the road yesterday afternoon in a car which contained a number of gentle ladies and rough and gentlemen, and was more an object of pity and wonder than he was of contempt and disgust.

Getting into the passenger coach while it remained in the depot here, the writer found the aisle blocked with a crowd that jammed and jostled each other and craned their necks to get a better view of Richards and to better hear the words he voluminously spoke to a reporter in the seat beside him.

It was impossible to get close enough to speak to the brute, and we waited till the trains were about ready to start. Sheriffs Anderson and Martin were just finishing a hasty lunch as we left them and entered the car and took a seat just made vacant by the side of Richards.

Constable Frank Hanlon occupied the seat opposite and spoke formal words that broke the ice for the shake of hands and what followed. And bout then Conductor Kelly shouted his "all aboard," and Hanlon's seat was taken by Sheriff Anderson.

Yes, Richards was the one who committed the murders. How did he feel about it? "Bully." What had he got to say for himself, anyhow? "A ____ big pile." And with a jerky introduction of this sort of torture began. Richards didn't care much about being interviewed. He had met no one but reporters, it seemed, since his arrest, and whenever he told them anything, they deliberately garbled it. He wrote two articles himself for the Steubenville papers, but they mixed in a lot of slush and lied about him. He didn't want any great notoriety, but he wanted the papers to tell the truth, and it was only on a solemn promise to stick to the truth that Richards consented to answer questions, which resulted substantially in the following story:

He was born in Wheeling, West Va., and is 24 years old. He was brought up a Quaker, and stayed at home in Jefferson County, Ohio, where his father lives, till about three years ago. Then the desire to come West took possession of him, and he went to Iowa, where he got a situation in the insane asylum at Mt. Pleasant. His occupation there was 'Handling stiffs," he called it—that is, attending to the burial of patients and other work of an easy character. Here it was that he became accustomed to the dead bodies and had his finer senses blunted. He remained at the asylum about a year, and then went to Kansas, where he got work of various kinds, having no regular occupation. In this state, he committed his first murder.

He got into a dispute with a man whose name he did not recollect—in fact, never troubled himself to learn—and "got the drop on him," killing him instantly, and going off and leaving the corpse lying in the sand-hills where the fracas occurred. He was never troubled by any pursuit for his crime. The thought of having committed murder didn't bother him. He had no conscience, or if he had, he didn't know where it was.

He left Kansas and roamed through Colorado, finally bringing up at Kearney Junction in February last, where he first made himself famous as a desperate character by his general desperate bearing. About the 1st of March, he committed some crime that landed him in the Kearney Jail. That was when Sheriff Anderson made his acquaintance. In the jail, a short time before were the train-robbers, Underwood and Nixon, brought to Nebraska from Texas just a year ago last night, and Harolson, the horse-thief, husband of the woman Richards killed. One night these two worthies broke jail and escaped to Texas. Mrs. Harolson was suspected of complicity in the delivery and was arrested and jailed. While she was in custody, Richards was arrested, and there he made her acquaintance. When, in a short time, the woman was released, she invited all the boys to visit her at her home in Kearney County. The first thing Richards did when he got out was to go there. His next visit was two weeks later, and after that, he got to going frequently.

Well, one day, he made up his mind to kill the whole family. He was undecided as to the time, but when Mrs. Harolson expressed a desire to sell out and remove to Texas, where he husband was, he was sure the time had come. About the 1st of November last, the woman was to go. Richards was assiduous in his attentions, and did all in his power ostensibly to hasten her departure, but thought it not strange. The night of Oct. 31, Mrs. Harolson and Richards worked all night in their preparations, continuing them during the next day. On the night of Nov. 1, Mrs. Harolson, intending to leave the next day, put the children to bed early, and along toward midnight, threw herself on the bed without undressing, to obtain a few hours rest. Then it was that Richards looked upon the sleeping woman and went outside and deliberately dug the trench for the bodies of his intended victims, carefully lining the bottom and side of the cavity with hay. This job done, he entered the house, seized a flatiron, and with a couple of blows, smashed in the poor woman's skull. She died with only a low moan. Still holding his bloody weapon in his hand, he advanced to the bed in which the two little girls were sleeping, and, with a single blow for each, he crushed their little skulls. The baby awoke and began to cry, and, with the devil's own deliberation, did this fiend incarnate then walk to the bed in which the dead mother and living babe were lying, and, grasping the poor little innocent child by a leg, he swung him high overhead and brought the little boy's skull down against the floor with a crash that completely destroyed all vestige of human resemblance, and covered himself and all the surroundings with a spray of brain and blood.

"And when you took that poor little creature's life in that manner, didn't you have a spark of pity for it?"

"Pit be ____." Was the reply. "The brat was making too much noise to suit me." Then, with no living witness to his foul crime, did this brute drag the four bodies to the sepulcher he had provided, and placed them in the resting-place. A grim sense of something for which we can find no name impelled him to go to the house and get a couple of sheets, which he spread over the bodies. Then to pile a stack of straw into a mound was but short and easy for the monster, and his night's work was over. Before daylight, he hitched up the Harolson team of mules, loaded the wagon with whatever he thought of value, and was off to Hastings.

In a few days, he returned with a team of horses and a new wagon. To the neighbors, he brought kind messages from Mrs. Harolson, and to a few, he paid some of the murdered woman's minor debts. On the day of the murder, he persuaded the woman to sign a voluntary relinquishment of her homestead in blank to leave it with him to negotiate. On his return from Hastings, he filled this blank out in his own name, and in a day or two, went to Bloomington, presented the paper, and filed his claim for the homestead. Everything was now looking exceedingly well for the fiend. Possession of the homestead gave him the dignity of a citizen, and he was on the road to prosperity.

A few miles away lived a bachelor Swede named Peter Anderson, with whom Richards had become intimate. The latter proposed to the Swede that they live together during the Winter, and the unfortunate man consented. One of the arrangements was that Richards should be a cook for the establishment. On the 8th of this month, he told the Swede *that he would get up an extra good dinner. He did so, using poison for seasoning. Anderson, in the afternoon, felt sick and went to a neighbor and said he believed Richards was trying to kill him with poison. The neighbor doctored him, and when he returned, he told Richards of his suspicions. A quarrel ensued, and during it, Richards killed Anderson by crushing his skull with a hatchet. That evening a party of neighbors came up to inquire for Anderson, and found Richards hitching up the Swede's team. He told them to go into the house and see, and then three off the harness from one of the animals, mounted him, and made for Bloomington.*

In the sandhills on the southern edge of the divide, the horse gave out, and Richards left him there to die, going to Bloomington on foot. There he procured a conveyance to take him to Riverton, where he arrived near daylight Monday morning. He could not gain admission to the Riverton House, so he again hired a team to take him to Red Cloud. As that place, he remained all day Monday, the 9th. The next morning, he took the train to Hastings, where he arrived safely and remained until the morning of Friday, the 13th when he boarded the Burlington and Missouri River train for Omaha.

He says he reached this city that afternoon, lounged around the depot platform while waiting for the Union Pacific to take him over the river, and freely conversed with our officers and others concerning the very crime for which he was fleeing. The next afternoon he reached Chicago, bought a through ticket to Baltimore, but got off at Wheeling Sunday night and walked over to Bridgeport, Ohio, remaining there till the next day, when he went to mount pleasant, and remained in that neighborhood till he was arrested.

This is the story he tells in a disconnected way. At one time in the interview, Richards said he did not care to make any more statements. When he reached his destination, he said, he would make a general statement.

"But suppose you don't have a chance to do so---you know what I mean!"

"Well, I don't give a ____."

In answer to a request for the names of the women with whom he has been connected, he refused to divulge. He didn't want them to become known. "They are married women, though," *said he, with an air of pride.*

"If Anderson hadn't been so quick in coming," said Richards, "he wouldn't have got me. The day I was caught, I was going to start back for Nebraska. Why? Because they never would think of me coming West again, and would have gone on East, while I would have passed by here and gone to the mountains. But I went to a ball the night before I was caught, and if it had not been for that---but, anyhow, if I hadn't had the two girls with me, I guess the constable, McGrew, who arrested him, would have been a dead man— either of us would, for I'd have shot." *Richards denies the report that he has confessed to three more murders, as well as that which says he threatened vengeance on the man who arrested him.*

Sheriffs Anderson and Marin have had a lively time in the pursuit, and were almost worn out. To Anderson, by reason of his long experience belongs a great deal of the credit for the capture. The two officers paid over the reward to the Ohio constable, and the own expense have been over $500.

St. Joseph Gazette Herald

Sunday, April 27, 1879

Richards, who was hung at Minden yesterday, has since his conviction been confined in the penitentiary at Lincoln. The day of his being hung is Saturday, and not on a Friday, the usual hangman's day, was that the law requires 101 days at least to be given to a prisoner under sentence of death, and yesterday was the first day after the 101 days.

Judge Gaslin didn't want to give the brute a day more than was necessary. Richards, it is said, during the latter part of his confinement weakened terribly in his nerve. He became religiously inclined, and read the Bible considerably. He, at last, realized his fate and the enormity of his crimes.

Since Monday, he ate hardly anything, and the thoughts of his impending fate made him so weak that he was confined to his bed for the last few days.

THE MURDERER'S LADY FRIENDS

Up to Friday night, Richards, the murderer who was hung yesterday, was confined in the Lincoln penitentiary.

On Monday last, two well-dressed ladies, closely veiled, called at the penitentiary and asked to see Richards. They stated that they were acquaintances, lived near his old home, and were just returning from the West. They wished to learn if he had any message to send back. They were shown to the prison reception room, and Richards was asked in. One of the ladies asked with some feeling if he wished to send any message back. At the sound of the voice, Richards started, and his feelings almost overcame him as he shook hands with them.

"Mr. Nobes, I would like to see you alone for a moment."

Mr. Nobes went inside the door with him, and he said with great emotion, "I would like to have a private interview with these ladies."

"That will be impossible," said Mr. Nobes. "I must be present."

"I would rather have seen anybody in the world," said Richards; "they are nearer to me than my own folks. I want a word with them."

He argued and begged, but under the circumstances such an interview was impossible, and Mr. Nobes told him so.

Then Richards burst into a flood of tears and wept like a child. He returned to the room, talked quietly with his visitors for some time, and they departed toward the town, as they had come, on foot, and without having once removed their veils. One was below middle height and appeared young.

During the past week, he has been telling a story about the murders entirely different from the first version, and has even gone so far as to lay the murder of the Harolson family on an imaginary "Gillis, whose real name is Brown."

The Atlanta Ripper

AUTHOR'S COMMENTARY

Just a few decades after the devastation of the Civil War ravaged Atlanta, a harvester of death silently preyed upon black women during the night. Nineteen eleven marked the beginning of a murder spree matched by few serial killers. His chosen methods reflected the murderous work of London's notorious "Jack the Ripper." As a result, this

TRUE CRIME CHRONICLES | 91

killer became known as "The Atlanta Ripper." His female victims ranged from prostitutes, mothers, and working-class women. And all the victims were black.

He employed a unique method of operation. He silently stalked the deserted streets and alleys during darkness, waiting to ambush his unsuspecting victims. Police believe all his victims met their death in the same fashion. First, he inflicted a disabling strike with a hard object to the head—possibly a hammer or hand ax. With the massive cutting of the throat or beheading followed. The murders always occurred on Saturday night, with the bodies discovered Sunday morning. The police believe the killings ended in 1915.

Scores of men were arrested but never charged with the crime. Why the murder spree ended remains unknown, as does the identity of the killer or killers.

St Louis Dispatch

Sunday, May 12, 1912

18 GIRLS VICTIMS OF CRUEL RIPPER

ATLANTA, Ga., May 11.

More than a year ago, April 30, 1911, to be exact, a milkman driving his wagon through a suburban street at dawn found the body of a negro girl lying by the roadside. The head was almost severed from the body, the shoes had been removed from the feet and were missing, the torso bore the bruises of a heavy club.

That was the first of the "Jack the Ripper" crimes, which have kept the police of Atlanta awake at night for a year. A few days ago, the body of a negro girl, her throat cut and her shoes missing, was found floating down the Chattahoochee River below the city.

She was the 18th victim of "Jack the Ripper," if there really is such a criminal. Police and court officials and amateur detectives who have investigated the various crimes differ on this point. The police insist that the murders are not those of one person but the work of probably 18 criminals; the closer students believe one man slew every one of the 18 women. This is certain; the slayer has never been caught. One murderer of a negro woman has confessed to his crime and has been sentenced to prison for life, but his victim bore none of the marks characteristic of the "Ripper's" work, and he proved that he could not have committed the others.

"Only a Negro Girl."

If white women had been the victim of the mysterious murderer, the city would have been stirred to its depths, and the succession of crimes would have awaken interest as wide as the Whitechapel murders, which made London's "Jack the Ripper" a household bogey. But the death of a negro attracts bypassing notice; the police make a desultory effort at tracing down the slayer, and then something new arises to divert their attention.

The first girl killed was named Clara Millender. Then followed, in May, Maggie Brooks. A few days later, Estelle Johnson was found slain in Jackson Street. June brought the deaths of Rosa Trice and Addie Watts. In July Lizzie Watts, not related to Addie, was found with the "Ripper's" marks upon her. August brought the murder of Lena Sharpe, and a girl known only as Emma Lou. In September, the body of a woman was found but never identified. November's toll was Eva Florence. December brought death to Mary Kate Sledge. Then followed a succession of unidentified women, evidently newcomers to Atlanta. These, with the girl, found floating in the Chattahoochee brought the list to 18.

Victims of All Classes.

The "Ripper" has not chosen his victims from one class of women. There had been hard-working servants; dissolute women, aged and infirmed women; comely young girls in their teens, and married women with numerous children. There has been no evidence to connect any one of the women with a stranger; not one of the crimes has taken place in the victim's home.

They have all fallen by the roadside, some on well-known streets, some in suburban fields, and one on a railway embankment just outside the city limits.

That the crimes are the work of one man, a maniac with a murderous tendency and weird ingenuity in concealing his tracks, as evidenced by the details of the crimes themselves. Each has been marked by the sign of the "Ripper."

In every instance, the head of the victim has been nearly or entirely severed from the body, not hacked or bruised, but cut as though a surgeon had worked at leisure. In every case, the shoes of the victim have been removed, and none of these has been found. In no instance has the victim been robbed. In no instance have there been signs of assault with intent other than murder.

Women Frantic With Fear.

Atlanta servants have been frantic with fear for the past year. Housewives cannot engage a cook or maid without a promise to keep her on the premises or release her in time to reach her home before dark. One woman's cry that "Jack the Ripper" was following her resulted in a man chased by a mob of blacks, and the victim escaped death only by taking refuge in a white residence house and proving his good reputation. No negro woman feels safe; none knows who will be the next victim.

And the police, though they investigate each individual crime, have not found one clue which appears likely to run down the most mysterious criminal and Atlanta's history, the "Black Jack Ripper."

THE NEW YORK RIPPER
AUTHOR'S COMMENTARY

As you read, "Jack the Ripper" terrorized London's prostitutes; and the London Ripper was never positively identified or formally charged. The fear of the Ripper leaving London and traveling to other parts of the world came to life in New York City.

Around 1890 and 1891, several New York prostitutes were murdered in a nearly identical fashion as London's "Jack the Ripper." As word spread and newspapers ran significant stories of the killings, panic began to raise its ugly head. Overnight, the fear within New Yorkers grew exponentially with the realization that London's "Jack the Ripper" may be applying his deadly trade in the city.

New York's mayor and police commissioner were under enormous pressure to bring these murders to an end, capture the guilty party, and ensure justice was done. Political and police management pressure of this nature always cascades downward and only comes to rest on the shoulders of the detectives handling the investigation. It is unknown if that pressure impacted the detective's decisions, but it appears it did.

In this case, the worst possible police conduct occurred. Was it merely a corrupt cop employing tactics used in other cases, or did he accede to pressure applied by the police commissioner and mayor to make a speedy arrest? We will never know. In simplest terms, the detective leading the investigation framed an innocent man, Ameer Ben Ali, also known as "Frenchy."

Unfortunately, "Frenchy" was middle eastern and was not fluent in English. Adding to his misfortune, he happened to be staying in a boarding house room directly across the hallway from the murder victim, Carrie Brown.

Mary Miniter was the only person who saw the man accompanying Carrie Brown to her room. She described him as approximately 30 years of age, average height, and build with a long sharp nose and light-colored mustache. She added he appeared to be European, light-skinned, perhaps German.

Ameer Ben Ali was dark-skinned and middle eastern. The difference in appearance did not alter the detective's assumptions or zeal for charging him. Whatever his reasons were, he decided Ali was the murderer and was determined to prove it. Unfortunately for Ali, the detective required more evidence and did not hesitate to manufacture it. The detective spread blood from Carrie Brown's room across the hallway to Ali's room. He placed blood on the doorknob and inside of Ali's room. That was enough for the jury to convict Ali for second-degree murder, and the judge sentenced him to life in prison. If the jury found him guilty of first-degree murder, he would have faced execution.

Fortunately for Ali, several honest reporters inspected the crime scene shortly after the murder and knew the blood trail the detective claimed to have found was not there. It would take over a decade before the truth would emerge, and the Governor of New York would pardon Ali.

This case represents the worst conduct committed by a police officer. The detective decided Ali was guilty and elected to frame him by falsifying evidence. Unfortunately, the behavior of that detective is alive and well today. Every year we learn of innocent people released from prison. At times, it's due to DNA testing, while in other cases, it is a matter of the false evidence being uncovered. As a cop, I saw this occur in Los Angeles. Fortunately, it was infrequent, but once is too often. I have never understood why an officer would falsify evidence to send a person they know is innocent to prison.

The Sheffield and Rotherham Independent

Saturday, April 25, 1891

JACK THE RIPPER IN AMERICA

SHOCKING MURDER AND MUTILATION OF A WOMAN

(FROM OUR CORRESPONDENT)

New York, Friday

A terrible murder was committed here last night, at East River Hotel, a low resort in the east end of this city. The victim being a woman of the most degraded class. It appears that a man and woman, in the course of the evening, arrived at the hotel, and having registered themselves, under the name of Knicloi, as man and wife, were assigned a room on an upper floor. Nothing more was seen of either of them during the night, nor was any cry or other disturbance heard.

This morning, however, when an attendant knocked at the door, he received no reply, and on the door being broken, an awful spectacle presented itself. The woman was lying on the bed, drenched with blood, and mutilated in a shocking manner. The abdomen had been ripped open evidently with a table knife, which lay dulled and broken on the floor. The internal organs had been cut out, and portions of them apparently are missing. The head was wrapped in a bandage, and a cloth had been tied around the neck and face.

The name of the unhappy victim has not yet been ascertained, but it is known that she was one of a number of abandoned women who infest the most disreputable quarters of the city.

The manner in which the crime was perpetrated, as well as the circumstance that the woman was an unfortunate of the lowest description, seem to afford ground for the belief that Jack the Ripper has transferred his operations to New York. Captain O'Connor, one of Inspector Byrne's sharpest detectives, has emphatically expressed this opinion. To quote his own words on viewing the body—"It is Jack's work to a dot."

The police are actively engaged in investigating the affair, and several detectives have been specially told to track the murderer.

The Wichita Daily Eagle

Friday, May 1, 1891

THE NEW YORK RIPPER

NEW YORK, April 30.

Inspector Byrnes this morning made a public statement to the effect that the man known as "Frenchy No. 1" was ascertained to have slept in the East River Hotel on the night of the murder. The murdered woman, Carrie Brown, occupied room 31, while "Frenchy No.1" slept in 33. On the evening of the night of the murder, Carrie Brown was seen going into the hotel with a strange man. This man left the place about midnight. It is believed that "Frenchy No.

I" then went to Carrie Brown's room; that they quarreled, and that the result of the row was the murder of the woman.

The belief that the murderer has been found is substantiated by the following facts: when he completed his murderous work, he recrossed the hall and reentered room 33. In that room, he left evidences of his guilt. Traces of blood were found on every side. The chair was smeared with blood where he sat down; the bedclothes were found to be covered with blood: his stockings (he having removed his shoes) were soaked with blood, and his clothes were bloodied. When he was arrested, his hands and fingernails were examined. The latter were carefully scraped, and distinct traces of human blood were found. The dirt under his fingernails was submitted to a chemical test. The very statements made by the man are very contradicting.

The Boston Globe

Monday, April 27, 1891

"FRENCHY NO. 2 NOT FOUND."

He is Suspected of the Murder of

Carrie Brown—His Cousin Under Arrest in New York

NEW YORK, April 27.

After three days and nights of unremitting search on the part of the shrewdest and most experienced detectives of Inspector Byrnes staff, aided by the entire force of Captain Connor's precinct, the fiend who butchered Carrie Brown, alias Shakespeare, in the East River Hotel last week, is still at large.

Inspector Byrnes has stated that all the evidence in his possession points to the fact that the brutal crime was committed by "Frenchy No. 2," the cousin of the man who was arrested the day after the murder and is known by the same name.

Except for the fact that the "Frenchy" now under arrest has dark hair and a swarthy complexion. Mary Miniter, who saw "Shakespeare" and her companion go to the room on the top floor of the hotel late Thursday night, says that the resemblance between the two-man is very strong.

The "Frenchy" who is now wanted by the police has a light mustache and long nose described by Mary Miniter, and he is known to be one of the most desperate characters in the neighborhood.

Several additional arrests were made today of men with light mustaches and long noses, but they were, in all cases, discharged.

Pittsburgh Dispatch

Saturday, July 4, 1891

FRENCHY FOUND GUILTY.

BUT IT IS ONLY FOR MURDER

IN THE SECOND DEGREE

The Peculiar Verdict Returned by the Jury in the Alleged Jack the Ripper Case

The Closing Scenes of the Remarkable Trial.
(SPECIAL TELEGRAM TO THE DISPATCH.)

NEW YORK, July 3.

Tonight the jury in the case of the people against Ameer Ben Ali, George Frank, or Frenchy, returned to the courtroom after an absence of two hours with a verdict of murder in the second degree. It fastened the butchery of Old Shakespeare upon the prisoner, and doomed him to imprisonment for life. The jury came in at 7:15 o'clock, and were followed by inspector Byrnes and Mr. Nicolls.

"Gentlemen," said the clerk, "have you agreed upon a verdict?"

"Yes, sir," said foreman Joseph Bartels.

"Do you find the defendant guilty or –"

"Guilty of murder in the second degree," said the foreman before the clerk of court had time to finish.

The faces of the Inspector and District Attorney, the lawyers for the defense, all expressed disappointment. Frenchy looked inquiringly, but not eagerly about and seemed puzzled. He continued to look from the silent attorney at his side to the faces of the jurors while the jury was polled. The recorder Smyth said: "The thanks of the court and of the community are due to you, gentlemen of the jury, for the part you have performed in this trial. You have been intelligent, faithful, and I believe have rendered a verdict in a satisfactory manner. You have discharged your duty, I think, with justice. You are discharged."

Although court had not adjourned all crowded around Frenchy and his lawyers. "Mr. Sultan, have you told him?"

"I told him he was guilty," said Sultan.

"You had better wait a while before you tell him the full verdict," said Friend. That Sultan said to him, "you are guilty in the second degree."

"Will they hang me?" Asked Frenchy.

"No, you will go to prison for a long time."

He seemed neither elated nor cast down, and when his guard touched him on the shoulder, he shambled toward the back of the room with no change of face or gait. At the far end of the room, he turned, looked toward the judge, who was still sitting on the bench, then looked up toward the ceiling and extending his right-hand palm up and arm stiff; he muttered something about "Allah." Whether it was a curse or a prayer, no one knows. Lawyer Friend asked that he be remanded until Friday next for sentence, and the recorder so remanded him.

Inspector Byrnes expressed disappointment at first. He said in the courtroom: "The man deserved to die, and has escaped his deserts."

"Do you think Frenchy in the London Ripper are the same person?"

"I must hesitate to express an opinion on that point, but I had considerable documentary evidence, which it was not necessary to introduce on the trial, tending to show the movements of Frenchy since he left Algiers. I have a statement proving that he was in London when some of the Ripper murders were committed. I do not say that he is the London Ripper, but this has a tendency to indicate that he may be."

The Selinsgrove Times Tribune

Thursday, April 24, 1902

"FRENCHY IS PARDONED"

He Was Convicted of "Old Shakespeare's" Murder,

Governor Odell Thinks there was Grave Doubts of His Guilt—New Evidence Which Indicates His Innocence.

Albany, N.Y. – Governor Odell has pardoned Amer Ben Ali, better known as "Frenchy," who has been serving a life sentence in the Matteawan State Hospital for Insane Criminals for the murder of a woman called "Old Shakespeare," in New York City in 1891. The pardon was granted by the governor because he believes there are grave doubts of the prisoner's guilt, much of the testimony being of a peculiar character, and "Frenchy," being placed at a disadvantage, being unable to speak English. The pardon was asked for by several influential and prominent men, including the Hon. Jules Cambon, the French ambassador: Frederic R. Coudert, J. B. Martin, and others.

"Frenchy" was convicted of murder in the second degree in 1891. He is an Algerian, and it is said he will go back to Algiers.

New York City. – About 12 years ago, the world was astir over atrocious murders committed by a "Jack the Ripper" in London. The press at that time printed interviews with police chiefs and famous detectives on the possibilities of such a crime being committed in this country.

Superintendent Thomas Byrnes, in an interview, said that a crime of that sort being committed in the city was out of the question. A few days after the White Chapel murder in London, however, a woman, known as "Old Shakespeare," was discovered murdered, George Frank, a sailor, known as "Frenchy," who had been stopping at the Fourth Ward hotel, was arrested and charged with committing the crime.

"Frenchy," being an Algerian, at the time, he could speak no English. He steadfastly maintained his innocence, but he was indicted and placed on trial. The jury returned a verdict of murder in the second degree, and "Frenchy" was sentenced to life imprisonment.

At the time of the murder, a peculiar key which "Old Shakespeare" had for the door of her room in the Fourth Ward hotel, was found to be missing, and, although detectives attached the greatest significance to the loss of the key, it was never found.

About a year ago, after several vain attempts had been made to have "Frenchy" pardoned, new light was thrown on the murder. A man who said he had had in his employ a Dane whom he suspected of having committed the murder of "Old Shakespeare" was found murdered; his Danish farmhand came home with a peculiar key. He had read of the murder, and when his farmhand disappeared that same night, he suspected that he might have been connected with the crime. He did not, however, make known his suspicions until a year ago, when a newspaper reporter got in communication with him. The new facts in the case were made known to the lawyers who had defended "Frenchy," and an appeal was made to Governor Odell to pardon the convicted murderer.

THE OTHER "JACKS"

AUTHOR'S COMMENTARY

By the late 1800s, the nickname "Jack the Ripper" was known worldwide. It invoked mystery, fear, and human nature; people had an insatiable hunger to learn more.

The media understood by labeling a story with "Jack the......" it always fascinated the general public, which meant more newspapers sold. Today's media readily employs the same tactic.

The following stories of lesser criminal behavior than the Whitechapel and New York Rippers demonstrate that salient point. These men did commit crimes, which in most cases, would be considered a misdemeanor involving a small fine or short stay in jail. However, their attacks on women cannot be condoned and would have caused great anxiety among these cities.

Some will find the following stories humorous. But remember, all attacks on women are unacceptable.

The Macon Telegraph

Monday, February 15, 1892

CUT THE GIRLS BRAIDS

"Jack the Haircutter"

Steals the Thick Tresses of Kate Mayer

"Jack the Haircutter" is at it again. The miscreant appeared in Yorkville at 11 o'clock yesterday morning and cut two heavy braids of hair from the head of a pretty German girl, 16 years old, who was looking in at a shop window. Detective Doyle of the E. 88th St. police station, has been sent out to look for "Jack," but has only a poor description of the fellow.

Kate Mayer is the daughter of a dry goods merchant living at number 1712 1st Ave. She has a remarkably thick growth of black hair, which hung down her back. She wore it in two long braids.

TWO TEMPTING BRAIDS.

She set out to do some shopping yesterday morning, and paused for a few moments to examine some articles in the window of a dry goods store at number 1570 3rd Ave. which is near 88th St.

She had been standing there only a few moments when she felt a tug at her hair. Turning quickly, she saw a man hastening up the Avenue and stuffing a braid of hair in his pocket as he ran. The girl put her hands to her head and could not find her braids. Like a flash, the thought of "Jack the Haircutter" ran through her mind. She was too excited to know what to do and stood bewildered on the sidewalk with her hand still clutching the thick stump of hair which the fellow left. She watched the fellow run until he disappeared down a side street. She made no outcry, but in a low voice said, "Oh! Oh! Gracious me, where is my hair?"

CUT WITH A RAZOR

The two braids had been tied close to the head with a ribbon. They were cut off as clean as steel could cut them. It is believed that the fellow used a razor. The braids are fully 18 inches long and very thick.

The girl hastened to a grocery store at the corner of 88th St., where she purchased some articles and went home. Her parents were the only ones she informed of the loss of her hair.

Mr. Mayer, the girl's father, reported the matter to the police. The only description Kate can give of "Jack the Haircutter" is that he looks like a tramp and is about 30 years old, with a dark complexion. He wears a sort of grizzled mustache. She does not know what street he turned down.

OTHER HAIRCUTTING JACKS

This is the first time in almost a year that "Jack the Haircutter" has made his presence manifest. During last spring and for some months prior, he committed many similar offenses for which the police of the city and Brooklyn made unavailing efforts to apprehend him. The offender known by this sobriquet has appeared in several guises.

A colored man on February 3, 1891, cut off the long golden braids of Hannah Shannon, a 15-year-old girl living at number 2396 2nd Ave. The deed was committed on Second Avenue, in Harlem, at 8 o'clock at night. The fellow got away.

Maggie Dorn, of number 318 E. 35th St., was watching the parade of Barnum's Circus, at Broadway and 13th St., on the evening of March 25, 1891, when she felt a tug at her hair and found that one of her three braids in which she wore it had been clipped off.

Prior to these, numerous cases were reported. "Jack the Haircutter" appeared on the Eastside in October 1889, and their clipped braids of hair from Sophia Menkes and Katie Schuman while they were looking into store windows.

AT WORK IN BROOKLYN

He then transferred his operations to Brooklyn, and in January, 1890, many young girls were bereft of their tresses. Among them were Lulu Hewitt of No. 151 Schermerhorn

Street, Mamie McMurray of No. 224 Leonard St., Eva Whitehead of No. 475 Kosciusko Street and Gertie Breast of No. 368 St. Mark's Place.

Ms. Hewitt described her assailant as a middle-aged man, while Miss Breast said her hair was cut off by a slim young fellow with a blonde mustache.

A short, stout man, wearing a dark suit and coat and derby hat, attempted to cut off Rachel blonde's hair, in Lexington Avenue, at 78th St., this city, on the evening of February 12. She felt a pull at her braids and screaming, turned around, when she saw the fellow, shears in hand. He escaped.

AUTHOR'S COMMENTARY

A segment in the following article is titled, *a lady of color kissed*. I did not change the wording or spellings used. The reporter opted to write the story as he or she heard it. By leaving the language as it appears in the story, it provides a window as to how many reporters viewed African Americans at the time. Neither the publisher nor I condone the slang spelling of the words. However, the story is history, and history can not be changed. We must learn from it.

Lincoln Evening Caller

Sunday, February 10, 1889

JACK THE KISSER

A Bold Man Who Drives a Ghostly Cab

His Mission on the Earth Is to Kiss and Love the Women.

He Occasionally Makes Mistakes—Girls Look for Him But He Does Not Come.

(Written for The Sunday Call)

"Jack the Kisser."

The career of "Jack the Kisser" has not yet been cut short. He still roams at large, notwithstanding efforts of the police, irate fathers, husbands, brothers, and lovers of the ladies who have been kissed by the Kisser to capture him.

Jack seems to bear a charmed existence, so for at least, clever traps have been laid for him, but he is too wary to fall into them. As a consequence of the continued exploits of the osculator, ladies of the West End are in constant care. They are afraid to appear on the streets after dark, and those who are compelled to flirt through the streets like frightened deers. Even the little girls to whom Jack also turns his attention, are afraid of every man who looks at them.

On Sunday night, a little girl not more than ten years of age, rushed into Connor's Drugstore, corner of Garrison and Sheridan Avenue's, all out of breath.

"What's the matter?" Asked Mr. Connor, but it was some time before the frightened child could explain that she had met Jack the Kisser.

"He grabbed me up in his arms, called me a little darling, and then he kissed me so much he almost took my breath away," said the little girl.

"Where did he go to?" Asked the druggist excitedly. "I'd like to get my hands on the rascal."

"Oh, he ran away up the Glasgow place. He told me not to be frightened, I would be a little angel soon," said the little girl. "He carried me a long way in his arms, and I didn't feel much afraid, because he was so nice and kind and talked to me so pretty, but when he put me down and said 'Now, run away, and tell people you saw Jack the Kisser,' I got awfully frightened, 'because I've heard mama say that this Jack is a bad man.''

The druggist sent his clerk home with the little girl, and her father immediately went out on the warpath, but Jack was invisible to the enraged parent.

HE RIDES IN A CAB.

On Saturday night, Jack was out in a cab. He sat on the driver's box, and when he saw a lady in a lonely place, he would hold, alight from his seat and asked her for some number on the street, and before it could be given, he would throw his arms about her and kiss her. As quick as a flash, he would mount the driver seat, whip up his horse and whirl away.

It was on Webster Avenue, near Sheridan, that Jack came near being captured, but, to the surprise of the gentleman who had him for a moment in his grasp, two men sprang from the cab and, before he knew what was up he was sprawled out on the sidewalk and Jack and his confederates, were merrily rolling away.

The gentleman, who for a moment thought himself a hero, relates his experience with the kisser, not generally, but to a few intimate friends:

"I was going home on Saturday night about 9 o'clock. As I reached Sheridan and Webster Avenue's, I heard a woman scream. As I had been hearing stories of Jack the Kisser, I immediately made up my mind that he was in the locality. I ran as fast as I could north on Webster Avenue, when I suddenly came upon a woman and a man struggling on the sidewalk.

"Save me! Save me! Scream the woman.

"I caught the man by the collar and gave him a jerk, and he immediately let go of the woman. I got a good grip on the fellow, and I think I could have got away with him, but two men came rushing at me from a cab that was standing a short distance upon Glasgow place. I didn't know whether they were friends or foes, but before I could make up my mind, they jumped on me. One of them grabbed me by the shoulders, put his knee in my back, and the other fellow hit me a blow in the face, and between the two of them, I was knocked out.

WOULDN'T HURT A MAN WHEN DOWN.

The big man whom I had grappled within the first place said: "Don't hurt him, comrades. He knows not who he was endeavoring to thwart. Go in peace, my friend," he continued, speaking to me, as I lay upon the sidewalk, uncertain just what to do. "My mission is to kiss and to save, and not to bruise or maim. I am Jack the Kisser."

"Then the three, without another word, went to the cab, the man who had declared himself Jack the Kisser mounted the box, and the others entered the vehicles. I heard a crack of a whip, and then I saw the cab move rapidly away. I don't know whether the wheels were muffled, as well as the horse's hooves, but I declare not a sound came back to me, and yet I saw they can move at a rapid gait and disappear in the distance. After they had gone I looked about for the lady who screamed and led me into the unpleasant predicament, but she, like the kisser in the cab, had flown, and I concluded to get home and say as little about the affair as possible."

The next heard of Jack, and his cab was at Elliott Avenue and Dixon Street. A lady who lives but a block from that point was on her way home from the market, where she had been sent by her mother to order things for Sunday. On the southeast corner, there was a vacant lot, and, not thinking of any molestation, she was walking leisurely along when a cab came hurriedly down the street and stopped right in front of her. The driver jumped down from his seat and accosted the lady with the question: "Can you tell me on what St., John I. Martin lives?"

"Oh, yes," replied the lady; "Mr. Martin lives on Thomas Street, between Elliott and Jefferson. I don't know his number, but he has a great big sign out with his name on it. You can't miss the house."

"Thanks," said the man. "Did you notice the new moon? Young ladies generally pay some attention to the nights luminary when he first hangs his silvery crescent in the evening sky."

UNDER THE NEW MOON

"There was something so sweet and sentimental," said the lady, "about the man's way of addressing me that I forgot for a moment that it was a cab driver who stood by my side. I turned my eyes to the west, and there, just gliding below the housetops, I saw the young moon. It did not look as new moons usually do, but more like a full moon almost entirely eclipsed. I was about to remark on the particular appearance and move on when an arm was thrown about my neck from behind, my head was drawn back, as I attempted to raise my hands, they were grasped and held firmly. Some women would have screamed, but I looked into the face bending down in the kindly eyes looking into mine, I was mesmerized.

"I don't know why, but I was in that man's power as much as a wren in the talons of a cat. He could have carried me away, and I don't think I could have made, or care to make, and outcry. He seemed to know that I was an easy victim, for he said gently:

" Let not a thought of fear enter your heart. You are in the embrace of Jack the Kisser. In a moment, I will be gone, and you will be on your way home a happy woman, for I will have kissed you, and my kisses always bring happiness. Make any wish your heart desires by the pale young moon yonder, and before it ripens into the fullness of its splendor, your wish shall be granted.

The moon was young when I kissed my love.

but not so far as she, the moon was young when I kissed

and then my love kissed me.

"No lover could have been more earnest than Jack when he pressed his lips to mine, and when he withdrew them, I was really busy with the ardor of the embrace. But he left me, mounted his box, lifted his head, cracked his whip, and then silently but swiftly the cab – the way down Elliott. The swift flight of the vehicle left no more sound in its wake than the flight of a bird. For a moment, I thought there must be something supernatural about the whole occurrence, and then I began to experience a feeling of awe creeping over me. I hurried home, and I have had a headache ever since. But I am firm in my belief that Jack the Kisser is not a bad man by any means. I hope I shall never meet him again, but if I do, I shall not do anything that is likely to bring the police down upon him."

"Well," remarked the reporter, "you must have enjoyed Jack's style of kissing?"

"No, I can't say that, but I think he cast a spell over me. I don't wish him any harm, and I wouldn't have my father know of the affair for the world."

A LADY OF COLOR KISSED.

Hugh Patterson, who lives on Howard Street between Elliott and Leffingwell, and until a few days ago in the water rates office, tells a good story to which Jack really gets badly left.

"Sunday night," said Mr. Patterson, "I had been up at Kelly stable, on Cass Avenue, discussing the political situation and was on my way home when I met a colored girl who works in a family a few doors from where I live. She is rather a trim looking, neat dressing negro woman, but still, she is pretty dark. When I met her, she was indignantly repeating:

"' Nigger! Nigger! I guess I'm as good as some white people.'

"I asked her what was the matter, and she blurted out: "I's bin kissed by Jack, de kisser. He thought I was a white woman, and when he made de discovery dat I was a cullud lady, he insulted me.'

"Tell me all about it," said Mr. Patterson. "When and where did it happen?"

"Right aroun' de corner. A big man follered me for a long ways, and when I was a long back uv de stables, where it is dark and spookyish, he throwed his arms aroun' me and smacked me squar' on de mout.' He was goin' to kiss me some, I guess, when he discovered I was cullud. An' he said: "'Old Lord! It's a nigger,' an' den run away as hard as he could. I could furbib him fur kissen' me, but fur callin' me 'nigger' never, Mr. Patterson. He's no gen'men, that's w'at, that Jack, the kisser ain't."

"How do you know the man who kissed you was Jack the Kisser?" Asked Mr. Patterson.

"Didn't he say so himself? An' and who's goin' aroun' kissin' respectable people but dat mean, good for nothin' crank?"

Miss Bouldier, the young lady who is mentioned in the Globe–Democrat last Wednesday as having been kissed twice in one night by the kisser, received a letter from Jack the other day it was written with a typewriter and runs as follows:

ST. LOUIS, Feb. 1, 1889, – MY DEAR SISTER: I will call you such now, as you have taken the second degree in our order. I am somewhat pained that the Globe-Democrat should have got on my track. I do not fear the police, but I dread the publicity a newspaper gives to such affairs. The public cannot be convinced of the sincerity of my mission and the purity of my motives. But time will prove that I am a laborer in the field of righteousness. The God that rules the universe is a lovely woman. What is romance without women? Where would poets get their inspiration were not for lovely women? The lily of the field is beautiful; the violent and the rows are fragrant and sweet, but woman, the flower of humanity, sways the specter overall, and I came to save her and her kind.

From whence I came or whit I go, it would be as hard to find me out as it were to trace the summer zephyrs from its inception to its destination.

I have traveled the world over. I have tasted the fair lips of all lands, but never yet have I been captured. I belong to a band that human power cannot reach. I will come to you again someday. When we meet, you will not expect me, but you will be overjoyed when I kiss you again. Don't part with the card I gave you; it is blessed.

When the sun had kissed the earth good night,

and darkness robes land and sea,

the world is mine – for when old Sol don't shine,

the kissing all is left for me.

Affectionately yours,

MISUNDERSTOOD JACK, THE KISSER.

The place in the district which Jack is working are doing all in their power to catch him, but he is too smooth for them. They have questioned ladies who have been kissed by the kisser, their description of the man is so uncertain and vague that they can get no clue.

It is now becoming a popular recreation for parties or girls to go out in search of Jack, but he never appears to those who seek him. He seeks his own times and places to operate, and he generally succeeds whenever he undertakes to kiss a woman.

St. Louis, February 6, 1889.

The Post Standard

Thursday, November 24, 1904

"JACK THE HUGGER" TERRIFIES WOMEN

Pounces Upon Them from Clump of Bushes Beside the Street.

SPECIAL POLICEMEN WATCH THE SPOT

Residents of the Neighborhood Carry Weapons to Protect Themselves—Mothers Meet Their Daughters Returning ==From Down Street in Order to Guard Them.

Terrorized at the invasion of an alleged "Jack the Hugger" in their district, women residents in the vicinity of Highland Avenue are timid about venturing out of doors after dark. They are so wrought up over it that they have found no comfort in the fact that policemen in plainclothes patrol the territory nightly searching for the bold, bad man.

The attention of the police was called to "Jack the Huggers" appearance in the 100 block in Highland Avenue two weeks ago last Saturday night in a written communication to Commissioner of Public Safety Ralph S. Bowen. The Commissioner immediately ordered an officer to be detailed in the locality and in civilians' clothes. Although a faithful watch was maintained, they failed to apprehend the culprit.

Their efforts have been without result, the special surveillance was withdrawn, but the resumption of "Jacks" operations last Monday and Tuesday nights necessitated another detail. Accordingly, another policeman guarded the scene again last night, and tonight in plainclothes, another policeman will be given the watch. All the while, however, anxious parents, who fear that their daughters, on the way home from the department stores and offices, will be molested, have met the girls as they alighted from the Rapid Transit cars. Others who walk home are met at the corner of James and Highland streets and are conducted home.

One indulgent mother said last night that she did not fear encountering a "Jack the Hugger" because she arms herself with a heavy stick which she carries under her cape. Revolvers and other weapons equally as uninviting to intruders guarantee protection.

On Saturday night, November 5, as Miss Josephine Courtney, a servant in the employ of Mrs. M. Louise Clary of number 204 Highland St., was on her way to the home of Forbes Herman's at number 217 Highland Ave. to visit Miss Mary Whelan, a domestic, she was rudely accosted by the alleged "Jack the Hugger." This was at 630 o'clock.

The man hid himself in a clump of bushes in the vacant lot on the north side of the street and adjoining number 109 Highland Ave. on the east. The bushes border on the walk and command an advantageous view of it in either direction. At this point, district takes a drop. Dense trees which line the space between the sidewalk and the gutter shade the spot from the glare of the electric lights at the intersecting streets of Highland and Graves.

Without warning, "Jack the Hugger" jumped from his hiding place and almost upon Miss Courtney, when she gave a terrified scream and frightened the man. It was such a shock to her nerves that Miss Courtney seems to be held fast to the walk.

Mrs. Anna Couvrette of number 126 Jasper St., was a block away at the time, was attracted to the scene by Miss Courtney's yells and went to her assistance. When she reached the young woman, the miscreant was not in sight.

At the time, Miss Courtney screamed Miss Mary A. Sullivan of number 109 Highland Ave. looked out of the window, but could not see the man disappearing through the vacant lot, which is thick with trees, and the course "Jack the Hugger" is said to have taken. It is said that the man was scantily attired. No description of him from which to get a clue could be furnished the police.

Mrs. Couvrette escorted Miss Courtney to the Herman's home, where she nearly collapsed. Her friend, Miss Whelan, was immediately dispatched to Commissioner of Public Safety Bowen's home at number 203 Highland Ave. with a note advising him of the incident. It was the next night that the Commissioner caused a plainclothes policeman to be detailed on the case. The officer remained there for ten days in order to relieve from that duty "Jack the Huggers" operations were resumed, but the scene changed to Oak Street in the shadows of the trees between James Street and Highland Avenue, two blocks away.

On Monday night Miss Josephine Quigley, who is employed as a second girl at the home of attorney Charles W. Andrews at number 216 Highland Ave., was frightened by a man who suddenly confronted her at this point. She rushed by him and ran breathlessly into the house. The man disappeared, he is said to be tall and, on this occasion, wore a long, dark coat.

The locality has been a favorite one for "Jack the Hugger's." Last year, as winter set in, women reported similar attacks. In most cases, the depredations were done on Saturday evenings at about 1030 o'clock, when young women were homeward bound from the various department stores. Several reported that they were roughly handled, some knockdown, and their pocketbooks taken from them. No arrest were made.

A majority of these assaults occurred in Highland Avenue, while others happen in East Willow Street, midway between Highland and Lodi streets. The assailants leapt over the fence of the Rose Hill Cemetery, where a tool house throws its inky black shadows on the sidewalk.

Suspicions have been concentrated on two men who have frequently been seen in the neighborhood, and their actions it is said to warrant a close inquiry.

Oakland Tribune

Monday, February 24, 1913

HUGGED MAID AND EARNED A BIG BEATING.

Athletic Sisters Administer a Summary Punishment to

"Jack the Hugger."

SAN RAFARIL, Feb. 24. –

"Jack the Hugger," a tartar in the person of Miss Gwendolyn Carter at a dark corner on South C. Street this city, late last night and annexed a sound flogging for his trouble. The thrashing was administered by Miss Gwen Carter, and her older sister Katherine, who came upon just as "Jack the Hugger," grappled with the young girl.

The Misses Carter, ages 25 and 23 years, are both ardent devotees and exponents of golf, basketball, and other athletic games. The girls were walking along South C. Street late last night – Gwen slightly in advance of her older sister – when "Jack the Hugger" suddenly leapt from behind a tree and, announcing that he had waited a week for an opportunity to embrace the fair athlete, started to take advantage of what he considered his opportunity. A start is as far as he got, however, for the next instant Katherine had jerked a picket from a handy fence and was plying it no less adroitly than savagely over the head of the much surprise man.

In the meantime, Gwen had been as busy as her sister, although perhaps with less telling, if equally as painful, effect. A hatpin which she chanced to be carrying in her hand was her weapon, and she piled it vigorously about the hands and arms of her assailant. Although knocked to his knees once, the girls declare, "Jack the Hugger" regained his feet and made off in the darkness, but not until the girls had an excellent description of him.

The Des Moines Register

Tuesday, November 14, 1889

"JACK THE CUTTER"

Washington, D. C., is entertaining a gentleman who would be a welcome guest in every city throughout the length and breadth of our land. He is familiarly known as "Jack the Cutter," and has come into considerable prominence through a habit which he has of walking down Pennsylvania Avenue these autumn afternoons, armed with a big pair of shears, with which he cuts off every lady's skirt which does not clear the ground by at least 3 inches. That he has made himself a terror to the ladies, need hardly be said, but by clumsy mankind and by that great army of street cleaners, who were thrown out of employment when trailing dresses became the fashion, "Jack the Cutter" is hailed hero and reformer.

The Washington Post is in receipt of the following communication, which gives Jack's own view of the matter.

He writes:

Editor post: You seem to be exercised a great deal over "Jack the Cutter," who is doing no more than his duty in endeavoring to bring about a reform in dress skirts. So long as women will persist in wearing's skirts that drag on the pavement, so long will they pay the penalty of their foolishness. The wearing of long, trailing skirts is unclean, and it should be abolished. I am doing, with others, all I can to bring about a much-needed reform, and when I have brought about the desired result, I will devote my attention to the idiots who wear collars 3 inches high. Yours for reform, **Jack the Cutter.**

Men should not be too quick to smile approvingly over Jack the Cutters unique reform method, for it is noted he says, once all the long skirts in the capital city are cut, he will turn his attention to "the idiots who wear collars 3 inches high," in which class, it is presumed, the masculine portion of the race will be included.

To many, who doubt, the measures adopted by Jack the Cutter will seem severe, but the cause has long since called for strenuous treatment. How a woman, lovely woman, can sweep along the streets of this country where Raleigh made his discovery, with her eyes directed in front telling what her dress is kicking up behind, has long been a mystery. The only reasonable explanation has been that women, in their spirit of self-sacrifice, determine that as long as men would defile the streets of our cities with expectoration, they would do their share toward the removal of filth. But this is a sacrifice which Jack the Cutter, who is evidently a friend of womankind, is not willing they shall make. Hence, he has begun at the capital city, with his long shears, to cut off the street cleaning appendage of a woman's dress. Among the world's pictures, Jack the Cutter, with his shears, should be represented along with that other celebrated picture of Atropos, who cuts the thread of destiny.

THE OLD WEST

Butch Cassidy and the Sundance Kid

AUTHOR'S COMMENTARY

The annals of the old west are brimming with stories of famous outlaws. Perhaps the two outlaws best known in America are Butch Cassidy and the Sundance Kid. For decades, their criminal exploits have been romantically and, at times, humorously depicted in books, movies, magazines, and folklore.

In 1969, actors Paul Newman and Robert Redford portrayed the outlaws in a feature film titled Butch Cassidy and the Sundance Kid. The movie shadowed their lives as they committed crimes and always stayed just a step ahead of the pursuing posse. In some movie scenes, they are depicted as fun-loving outlaws, with a romantic twist. Many left the movie theater believing the romantic tale of the old west they just watched. In their minds, the two desperadoes were nothing more than misguided, fun-loving scamps.

However, we must not forget they were ruthless criminals, and that is how they should be remembered.

The Daily Morning Journal and Courier

Saturday, April 30, 1898

TERROR OF FOUR STATES

"BUTCH" CASSIDY AND HIS FIVE HUNDRED.

Governors Hold a Meeting to Talk Up a Way of Exterminating the Gang.

In our Western states, if for no other part of the earth, the bid saying that truth is stranger than fiction holds good. Who would believe in these days there could exist among the vastness of the Rocky Mountains a band of 500 outlaws whose defiance of the law should call for a conference between the governors of four states to determine upon a plan of campaign against them? Yet such a conference was held last Monday between the governors of Colorado, Utah, Wyoming, and Idaho, and "Butch" Cassidy and his 500 followers have brought about this unwanted proceeding.

"Butch" Cassidy is a bad man. He is the worst man in four states. The states are Utah, Colorado, Idaho, and Wyoming, and where the four governors met in secret conclave on Monday, it was for the purpose of deciding upon a plan of campaign against the most notorious outlaw the West has ever had to cope with. The achievements of Jesse James and his followers pale into tawdry insignificance before those of "Butch" Cassidy and his 500.

For several years – in fact, ever since the livestock commission drove the Wyoming rustlers out of business, in 1892 – "Butch" has proven a thorn in the flesh of the authorities of the four states in which he carries on his operations. He has laughed the militia to scorn. Sheriffs and deputies, he regards with pity and contempt. He is a power unto himself.

After the ordinary method of hunting, outlaws had been tried unsuccessfully; it was decided that drastic means must be employed. Rewards have been repeatedly offered for "Butch" Cassidy, dead or alive, and after each fresh outbreak, these rewards have invariably been increased. If all the offers which have been made from time to time hold good, the slayer of "Butch," should he ever live to claim his reward, would be entitled to upward of $20,000 in blood money.

But the rewards have proven as futile as have the efforts of the militia and the deputy sheriffs. And that is why Gov. Wells of Utah, Gov. Adams of Colorado, Gov. Richards of Wyoming, and Gov. Steunenberg of Idaho got their heads together to see what could be done. Just what the result of their conference has not been divulged. The governors believe in still hunt methods, and it is thought that a large number of experienced mountaineers and bandit hunters will be placed in the field, each state to furnish its quota and that the bandits will be rounded up in much the same fashion that cattle are. Any attempt to exterminate this desperate band is certain to be attended by bloodshed.

"Butch" and his band are the outgrowth of the rustlers of six years ago. Since then, they have broadened their field and increase their numbers. It is no idle boast to say that the leader of this notorious band has 500 men at his beck and call. Their depredations are upon a scale never before reached in the history of frontier crime. All the conditions are favorable to them. They know every foot of the vast territory in which they operate, taking in, as it does, the wildest and most inaccessible portions of four states. Every man of them is thoroughly familiar with frontier life and its rougher phases.

The forces are subdivided into five bands, each controlled by its own leader, with Cassidy as the supreme power. The outlaws now practically control the sparsely settled regions extending from central Wyoming southwesterly through Northwestern Colorado, and Utah, and almost to the Arizona line. Marauding and murderous bands conduct their raids without restraint. The thefts of livestock run into the millions. Ranchmen are murdered and driven out of business, and the officers of the law are powerless.

There are five camps where the various bands make their headquarters, each of which is well-nigh inaccessible except to the bandits themselves. Two of the most famous are "Robbers Roost" and "Hole-in-the-Wall." The former is in south-central Utah, on the San Rafaele River. The latter is hidden away somewhere in that wild, mountainous district to the northwest of Casper, Wyoming.

The other camps are located in Teton basin, near the eastern border of Idaho and south of the Snake River; Powder Springs in Southwest Wyoming, near Colorado, and about 50 miles east of the Utah line, and Brown's Park, taking in the northwestern corner of Colorado in the northeastern portion of Utah. It is not definitely known in just which state the Brown's Park camp lies, but it is thought to be across the line in Colorado.

The five camps form a chain extending for hundreds of miles. Between these posts, communication is maintained by a regular system of couriers and cipher dispatches, facilitating the cooperation of two or more bands when an enterprise of more than usual magnitude is undertaken.

These bands are composed of men of the most reckless and desperate character, long accustomed to deeds of crime. Whenever a murder is committed in the mountain states, or a convict escapes from a penitentiary, the criminal flees to the nearest of these retreats, where he is safe from pursuit. In this manner, the ranks of the bandits have been recruited up to a strength conservatively estimated at 500. While each band has its chosen leader, "Butch" Cassidy exercises some sort of authority over the federation.

Each of the strongholds is both a rendezvous and a fortress absolutely impregnable. They can only be reached by *traversing deep and narrow gorges, scaling the lofty and rugged peaks, and penetrating the wildest recesses of the Rocky Mountains. In many places, the only trail lies over a narrow shelf of rock, cut by the bandits along the face of a precipice. Holes have been drilled into which in case of close pursuit dynamite can be placed in and the trail blown from the face of the cliff into the chasm below, thus baffling all pursuers.*

There are also many places where one robber can hold 50 officers at bay, and as the bandits are armed to the teeth and will fight to the last man, any effort to exterminate them by ordinary process of law is regarded as a useless sacrifice of life. In their retreats are numerous caves, luxuriously fitted up and containing subsistence sufficient for months. Thus are the bandits enabled to set at defiance all the forces of law and order.

The outlaws roam the adjacent country and smaller settlements without molestation. Many settlers purchase immunity by extending assistance in various ways, and the robbers even attend country dances and other functions, occasionally "shooting up" the town or indulging in other forms of recreation. It is only when closely pursued by officers of the law that they retire to their mountain retreats.

"Butch" Cassidy, however, by reasons of the price upon his head, considers the higher altitude more conducive to his health and seldom ventures into the towns, unless he is making a raid or surrounded by a band of his trusty men, in which case he never fears molestation. As a killer, he has earned a reputation during the last ten years, probably equaled in the West only by that of "Wild Bill" Hickok, peace to his ashes.

Few men who knew him would care to arouse his ire for although a man of wonderful nerve, unlike most men of his class, he is possessed of a fearful temper. Sometimes he gets beyond his control, and then he throws all caution to the winds and becomes utterly reckless.

About four years ago, he was shot at from ambush near Green River by a cowboy known as "Hackey" Hughes, whose only object was to secure the reward offered by the state authorities of Utah. The bullet pierced the lobe of his ear, and the blood streaming down his face acted upon Cassidy as a red flag might to a maddened bull.

With a howl of rage, he turned his horse just as another bullet passed through the rim of his sombrero. A puff of smoke from a clump of bushes showed where the assassin was concealed. For picturesque profanity "Butch" Cassidy hasn't his equal in the states, and on that occasion, he is said to have fairly surpassed himself. Ripping out a string of oaths that would reach from Dan to Beersheba, he jumped from his horse and dodged behind a boulder.

He waited for 20 minutes, and then the cowboy shot the outlaws horse, which had been grazing in the open. That was more than "Butch" could stand. Throwing caution to the winds, he ran toward the clump of bushes, with a pistol in each hand barking at every step.

But Hughes, considering discretion the better part of valor, had jumped on his horse and succeeded in making good his escape. But the vindictive nature of "Butch" Cassidy asserted itself. He had recognized his assailant, and every member of the band received instructions to be on the watch for him. Hughes left the Green River country, and it was not until six months later that he was located, on the North Fork of the Powder River, up in Wyoming.

Cassidy was notified, and with a dozen men, he reached the ranch where Hughes was working. It was during the spring round-up. The two men met face-to-face. Hughes knew what was coming, and pulled his gun. But he wasn't quick enough. Cassidy's pistol cracked first, and the cowboy dropped from his saddle with the bullet through his right eye.

"That's the way I serve any skunk that tries to shoot me in the back," remarked Cassidy. "If any of his friends want to take up the quarrel, I am ready."

But if the dead cowboy had any friends, they failed to respond. "Butch" Cassidy was well known, and it wasn't safe to pick quarrels with him. So he rode away with his escort, cursing the cowboys for a pack of cowardly coyotes.

Cattle stealing is the chief source of income for Cassidy and his followers. One company alone in central Utah has lost 2000 head during the past two years, worth at the present price of $80,000. These are driven through Colorado and into New Mexico. It is in driving the stolen cattle from one state to another and out of the country that their system of cooperation is beneficial.

However, any operation that promises adventure and financial reward is never overlooked. Trains are held up, express companies and banks robbed, and even individuals, when known to have money in their possession, are relieved of their possessions in true Road Agent style.

There are women among these outlaws, too, who ride with them on the wild forays and take pride in their association with these bold and daring freebooters. Even "Calamity Jane," in the old days of her association with "Deadwood Dick," could not surpass these picturesque females in their wild career.

About a year ago, "Butch" Cassidy and "Bill" Ferguson, one of his trusted lieutenants, dashed into the town of Price in broad daylight, held up the paymaster of the coal company, and rode off with $8,000 before the crowd of bystanders realized what had happened. This is but a sample exploit.

Bank robberies are but side issues with them, merely incidental to their grand chief operation of cattle stealing. If a victim resists or an officer pursues, murder is regarded as a professional duty, to be cheerfully performed, but they are not given to wanton slaughter. In several instances, foolhardy officers who have invaded their strongholds have been disarmed, dismounted, and sent home.

An instance of this kind occurred just after the raid on the coal company at Price. Two deputies traced Cassidy and Ferguson to their lair at "Robbers Roost." They were fully 24 hours behind, and their approach was known long before they arrived at the narrow trail leading up into the rendezvous. Cassidy was in a jovial mood, and he conceived that it should be more fun to capture the deputies and make sport of them than to kill them. So he acted accordingly.

The deputies were about halfway up the trail when, just at the bend around a sharp point of rocks, they heard the sharp command, "Hands up!"

Half a dozen guns were staring them in the face, not 20 paces away. The deputies realized that not to obey meant sudden death. Up went their hands, Cassidy stepped up to them, roaring with laughter.

"You are a couple of fine dubs to come and catch peaceable citizens, ain't you?" He cried, "Gimme your guns. Here, Buck," calling to one of his men, "search these tenderfeet, and if they have got any tobacco, you can keep it."

The outcome of it was that the deputies, relieved of everything but their clothing, were bound hand and foot to their horses, conducted to the foot of the pass, and sent *about their business. To add to their discomfiture, a rudely scrawled note was pinned on the breast of each, which read: "We are Deputy Sheriff's sent out to capture 'Butch Cassidy' and his gang. When found, send us home." San Francisco bulletin.*

Salt Lake Telegram

Saturday, October 8, 1910

FORMER TERRORS OF UTAH, "BUTCH CASSIDY AND "KID" CURRY, NOW IN ARGENTINE REPUBLIC

"Butch" Cassidy, was the terror of bankers and little towns of Utah in the good old days, and "Kid" Curry, who held up banks, who was a train robber and a general bad man, with capital letters on both words, have formed a partnership in crime down in Argentine Republic that is of such formidable proportions that it's taxing the ingenuity of that country to meet it. Finding itself baffled in its efforts to round up these nervy lawbreakers that Republic has, through its representatives, asked the United States to detail a corps of its most tireless and shrewd mountaineers on the job, with instructions to stay on the trail until the men are either in prison or in their graves.

A parallel condition has probably never before existed. The case that probably came nearest to being a parallel was the capture of Miss Stone and her missionary companion by Raisoult, the Moorish bandit, a few years ago, and the dispatching of an American gunboat to Turkish waters to capture the bandit, or to compel the return of the missionaries without the payment of a ransom.

This is of such recent historical date that the public is still familiar with the conditions, and the repetition of the story would not be in point at this time.

Experts Go After Bandits.

But the Argentine Republic has appealed to her Uncle Samuel to send some of the best and bravest men into her domain and capture and punish the bold and daring bandits who have been a terror of two great republics.

Within a week after the State Department of this government had been appealed to for aid in a ridding the sister Republic of the gang, five of the best mountaineers in America are on their way to that country. These men went from five different states, and each was given full power to act as his best judgment would dictate, but the instructions in each case were to capture or kill "Kid" Curry and "Butch" Cassidy.

John H. McIntosh, a former detective, tells an interesting story of the career of "Kid" Curry. It is of interest to Utah people because of his reported partnership with "Butch" Cassidy, a native of this state, whose story was told in the telegram a few weeks ago. Mr. McIntosh's story is told in the October number of "World Wide" magazine. He says:

The names of the five men who have undertaken the hazardous task to capture and bringing this daring outlaw back to the United States are withheld for obvious reasons. In time the world will know them, for they will either report their venture a failure or will achieve success – and failure in a case of this kind may mean death.

Bankers Want Curry.

One of the five went as a detective for the National Bankers Association, which would like to see the outlaw brought to trial for three bank "holdups"; a second was sent *direct from Chicago by the Pinkerton National Detective Agency; a third was equipped and commissioned by Maj. Sylvester, head of the International Association of Police Chiefs. Three big western railroads combined to send the fourth, while the fifth criminal hunter started out at the investigation of Capt. W. S. Swain of Spokane, Washington, who is now head of a big detective agency and who himself spent years trying to bring "Kid" Curry to justice.*

The news from Argentina is the first authentic information the American authorities have had for five years concerning Curry. It has been repeatedly stated that this notorious western character had met his death. In the summer of 1906, for instance, a report came from Tucson, Arizona, to the effect that a man positively identified as Curry had been killed while cattle rustling. The cowboy who shot him even put in a claim for the immense reward offered by the railroads, banks, states, and the government. It was later, however, proven that the dead man was not Curry.

Early in January, 1907, a relative of "Kid" Curry, living in the Little Rockies, northern Montana, gave it out that he had received a letter from a man in Brazil who had known Curry in the latter country, and who stated that the "Kid" had been killed in a fight with a Spaniard. But it was not long after that the same relative declared the report of Curry's death to be false, and he accompanied this with a promise that Curry would live to return to the United States and settle old scores with some of his enemies.

Real Name Harvey Logan.

It has since transpired that most of these reports were started by Curry himself. Who used the news of his death as a means to throw pursuers off the track. In fact, it is now pretty well established that the desperado has, for the past four years, been carefully laying his plans and reorganizing his band. Now he is in a position to strike, and strike hard.

"Kid" Curry's real name is Harvey Logan, but the outlaw has been known so long by the former name that it has stuck to him. The American members of his band are George Leroy Parker, alias "Butch" Cassidy, and Harry Longbaugh, alias "the Sundance Kid."

Curry operated in northern Montana for years. His home was in Choteau County, about 20 miles from Chinook, and it was in that section that he started on his career of outlawry. Later he became leader of what was known as the "Wild Bunch," a gang of outlaws who infested the Hole-in-the-Wall country, Wyoming. Parker held forth in "Buzzard's Roost" and inaccessible mountain retreat near the point where the Colorado, Utah, and Wyoming boundary lines run together. Longbaugh was a dreaded cattle rustler and horse thief of eastern Montana. Each of these men, with his followers, preyed upon the railroads; they participated in scores of train robberies and are credited with many murders. Curry was the most desperate and by far the most resourceful of all. No prison has been strong enough to hold him, and it is said that the Union Pacific Railroad alone has spent half a million dollars trying to capture him.

At one time, the rewards for the capture of Curry, dead or alive, aggregated $40,000. Of this amount, the Union Pacific offered $10,000, the Great Northern $10,000, the National Bankers Association $5000, and the states of Montana and Utah each $5000 each. Yet more was offered by a great detective agency as an incentive to its employees.

His Long Criminal Record.

According to Mr. Eugene Van Buskirk, superintendent of the National Bureau of Criminal Identification, with headquarters in Washington, D. C., Curry holds the distinction of having the longest criminal record ever known in the United States.

No chance has ever been too desperate for this daring outlaw. He has seven murders to his credit in the states alone. The largest robbery in which he participated was near Wagner, Montana, in 1901, when, with "Butch" Cassidy and one other, he held up a Great Northern train and obtained $41,500 in banknotes from the express car.

The earliest date of any felonious crime committed by Curry in the possession of the detectives of the west is December 25, 1894, when he killed a man named Pike in Landusky, Montana. In 1897 he participated in a bank robbery at Belle Fourche, South Dakota, was arrested at Dylan, Montana, under the name of Tom Jones, and placed in jail at Deadwood.

In less than two weeks, he had figured out a plan that gave him his liberty. Nothing more was heard of him for nearly two years, when he took a leading part in the holding up of a Union Pacific train at Wilcox, Wyoming.

Headed by Sheriff Hazen, a posse started out after the robbers. Two days later, they came upon the gang at Teapot Creek, near Casper, Wyoming. The posse was closing in on the gang when Curry stepped from ambush and shot Hazen through the breast, killing him instantly. Curry and the men with him got away.

Killed Two for Revenge.

The band separated, and one of the members was run to cover. Refusing to give himself up, he was shot and killed by John Hyler, Sheriff of Grand County, Utah, and Sam

Jenkins, and acting deputy sheriff. Curry at the time was being sought in the southwest, where he was supposed to be hiding. In some way, word reached him that one of his compadres had been killed by the officers. Purely for the purpose of revenge, he went to Moab, Utah, where he sought out the Sheriff and Deputy Sheriff and murdered them. Posses of citizens scoured the surrounding country for miles, but no trace of the outlaw was found.

Curry again stepped into the limelight in August, 1900, when he held up a Union Pacific train at Tipton, Wyoming. A year later, he held up a Great Northern train near Wegner, Montana, and got away with $41,500. All this time, the state and county officers of half a dozen different states were anxiously seeking him.

The next crime charged to the outlaw occurred on July 26, 1901. When he killed James Winters for revenge, as Winters had been assisting the authorities in their efforts to apprehend him.

Shortly after killing Winters, Curry was seen in Helena, accompanied by a woman, with whom he traveled through the southern states for several weeks. In Nashville, Tennessee, the woman was arrested while trying to pass some of the money stolen in the great Northern robbery: but Curry, as usual, got away. He was next heard of in Knoxville, Tennessee, where he shot and dangerously wounded two policemen who were trying to arrest him. Other officers came to their aid, however, and Curry was overpowered and locked up.

Sentenced to 130 Years.

Convicted of assault with intent to kill, he was later convicted on ten counts for altering banknotes. The sentences aggregated 130 years in the Columbus, Ohio, state penitentiary.

While awaiting removal to the Ohio penitentiary, Curry managed to escape from Knox County jail. This escape was one of the most cleverly planned, as well as one of the most daring in the criminal annals of the country.

In some way unknown, the prisoner got hold of a small length of brass wire. With this, Curry made a noose and waited his chance. The next morning, as the jailer was making his rounds, the desperado accosted him.

"Hey, Bill!" He said pleasantly. "There is a big spider crawling on the back of your coat. Step close quick, and I'll brush him off."

Curry was in his cell: the jailer was in the corridor, and, in the circumstances, never suspected a trick. He stepped against the cage holding the outlaw, with his back to the man who he believed was to brush a spider from his coat. Quick as lightning, the outlaw's hand slipped through one of the holes in the grating, but instead of attending to the supposed spider, he deftly slipped the wire noose over the jailer's head.

The turnkey's hand darted to his holster, but Curry was quicker. The wire, drawn tight, cut like a knife across the jailer's windpipe while his tongue protruded from his mouth.

"Quick! Out with that gun and give me the keys or I'll give this wire an extra poll and choke you to death like in a rat trap," said Curry in a fierce whisper.

His Daring Escape.

It was a life-and-death matter with the officer, and he had no option but to hand over the articles demanded. Having obtained them, Curry coolly fastened his end of the wire inside the cell, the noose remaining about the unfortunate jailer's throat. For the prisoner to unlock his cell, meanwhile keeping the revolver aimed at the helpless jailer, was the work of a moment. Next, he securely tied and gagged the man held tight by the wire and unlocked and swung open the big door leading to the jail proper. The Sheriff's office stood open between the front door of the building and the jail: yet Curry sauntered by as unconcernedly as though he were going to church.

"Who was that man?" Asked the Sheriff of one of his deputies.

"I didn't get a good look at him. Why?"

"Well, he looked very like our prisoner, Curry." Replied the Sheriff carelessly.

While this conversation is going on, Curry ran out to the stable at the rear of the jail and forced the astonished man in charge there to saddle and bridle the best horse available, a spirited animal belonging to the sheriff. In the meantime, his escape had been discovered, and the officers rushed out pell-mell just as Curry waved his hat at them before turning the street corner, riding at a gallop.

Quickly organizing a posse, the sheriff gave chase. The trail led into the Blue Ridge Mountains and time, and again it seemed the pursuers would surround and capture the pursued, but in the end, Curry made good his escape. He traveled northward by easy stages, then west to the Jackson Hole basin of Wyoming, and still, later, he turned up at his old haunts in Choteau County, Montana.

It must not be understood that Curry eluded the clutches of the law year after year without aid. He had friends, most of whom helped him because they feared him, but they counted as friends just the same. I had occasion to learn this and will here tell of my first and only experience with this noted outlaw.

His Friends Stand by Curry.

About a year after Curry's spectacular escape from the jail in Tennessee, I was sent to Montana by a big detective agency for which I was working with instructions to visit Curry's hometown in northern Montana and learn, if possible, whether the outlaw was in the state. I had no instructions to try to affect a capture.

My experience as a detective cover less than a year, but I had been successful in a big case and was delighted on hearing that I was to trail the most noted outlaw in all the west.

"You are young," the superintendent told me, "but we have faith in your nerve and judgment. Go to Chinook, Montana, and then in some sort of disguise learn, if possible, of Curry's whereabouts. If you think his capture is possible, advise us at once, and we will detail a dozen tried man on the case."

Ten days after that, a soap "drummer" (commercial traveler), hailing from St. Paul, stepped off the Chinook and with his case of samples put up at the only hotel in the little cattle town. That evening, as the "drummer" was reading a paper in the hotel, to uncouth looking men dropped in.

"Join us in having a drink, pardner?" said one.

The "drummer" was about to decline the invitation, but his visitors were insistent, and he joined them. He was plied by his host with questions, some of which were embarrassing. Later he was glad to part from his newfound friends and retire for the night.

In the morning the "drummer" called on the proprietor of a general merchandise store with his samples, but was taken aback when the merchant gave him a cool reception.

"I don't want none of your goods, stranger," he said. "You may be all right, but your looks are agin' you. There's talk aroun' here that you're workin' up a case agin' "Kid" Curry. Now, I am an honest man an' don't uphold no thief; but "Kid" Curry didn't never bother nobody nor nobody's property in Chinook. I ain't givin' help to those what's lookin' for him."

Ordered Out of Town.

The "drummer" protested that he was what he represented himself to be but to no avail. Then it occurred to the supposed soap salesman that he might get the hotel proprietor, who seem to be well known and popular, to say a few words in his favor.

"Nothin' doin'," said the hotel man, laconically, after the salesman had recounted his experience with the merchant. "My business is in this little town, and Curry's friends are my customers. If you ain't a detective, the gang around town is fooled, and that's all about it. Anyway, stranger, it'll be a whole lot healthier for you somewhere else, no matter what you are. Butch Cassidy sent word this mornin' that him an' his pals give you one hour to get out o' town."

The "drummer" looked at his watch. The eastbound Great Northern express would be in at 11:45. It was then 11. The "drummer" gave up the struggle and took the express.

Thus baffled and humiliated at being outwitted, he returned to the headquarters of the detective agency and voluntarily resigned. The "drummer" was none other than the writer of this article. I had had enough of detective work and gave it up in sheer disgust.

My experience, however, had demonstrated how well Curry's friends protected him in certain parts of the west and that any plan that would affect his capture must be out of the ordinary.

For two or three years following, Curry jumped from place to place about the west, stealing horses and robbing trains. In the spring of 1906, two boys got a clue that Curry was in Arizona; they traced him to St. John's and were murdered just outside the town. Although there were no witnesses to the shooting, authorities say there is no doubt that Curry killed the boys when they tried to close in on him.

Killed The Sheriff.

After the murder of the boys, the sheriff of Apache County endeavored to apprehend the outlaw. The sheriff found his hiding place in the woods, but when the officer stepped up to place him under arrest, Curry drew his gun and shot him dead.

After that, the search for the desperado became more determined than ever; it was also better organized. In Colorado, Utah, Arizona, Wyoming, and Montana, huge rewards were offered by the local authorities, and many fearless sheriffs swore they would "get" Curry or forfeit their own lives in the attempt.

Whether the hunt became too warm for the outlaw or whether he hoped for bigger booty in foreign lands, it is not known, but certain it is that "Kid" Curry suddenly dropped from view. Then came the news that he was living in South America, but all records from there were hazy until the American Consul notified the State Department that the former terror of the western states was operating on a big scale farther south.

It is reported that the Argentine robberies have been of the most daring character in that those who have tried to stop them have been put out of the way with bullets.

Riding to the scene of a robbery on horseback, the outlaws leave one of the members in charge of the horses while they hold up the employees of banks with revolvers and rifle the safes and vaults.

How Curry Started His Career.

Reading of the lawless doings of an outlaw of the Curry type one wonders what could start a man out on such a career of wanton crime.

In Curry's case, it seems that it was a conviction and small fine for a petty theft that launched him on the downward path. After that, he considered all officers of the law as his natural enemies, and all property as his for the taking.

An old Justice of the Peace – Tim Hobbs by name – tried Curry for the theft of a yearling calf near Fort Benton, Montana. The justice thought the evidence conclusive and fined the prisoner $50. Curry continued to protest his innocence so strenuously that the justice fined him an additional five dollars for contempt of court. Thereupon Curry jumped to his feet, knocked the constable down, pushed the heavy table over on top of the justice, and, mounting his horse, rode away.

Up to that time, he had been employed as a cowboy on a ranch in northern Montana and was considered unusually quiet and well behaved. After the episode near Fort Benton, however, Curry became known as a cattle rustler and gunfighter. He was scarcely 20 years of age when he started on the career of an outlaw.

Curry is now 45 years of age. He was born in Missouri but moved to Montana when a boy. He is a medium-sized man, with black hair and a dark mustache. He is a dead shot, and in spite of his many encounters, he has only one scar from a gunshot wound, one on the right wrist.

The old-timers Montana, recall Curry as a quiet, industrious boy 25 years ago, will marvel at the sequence of events which has made him one of the most notorious bandits in the Argentine Republic.

The Journal and Tribune

Sunday, February 6, 1910

HAD A WILD TIME IN BOLIVIA

Butch Cassidy and Sun Dance Kid Shot to Death.

Killed Ten Men There After Being Forced to Flee From the Argentine.

Many readers will recall the stir. The arrival of Harvey Logan, his ring days in this vicinity caused by capture after shooting to Knoxville policeman, his subsequent arrest, trial before a federal court, and his later sensational escape from the Knox County jail. In Harvey's band or the Hole-in-the-Wall gang, which held up many a train in the West, were "Butch" Cassidy and the "Sundance Kid," and their recent deaths as told in the following story reprinted from the New York American, doubtless wipes out all members of this gang, and the others being either dead or in prison serving long sentences for their depredations. The New York American story follows: –

The mystery of the disappearance of "Butch" Cassidy and the "Sundance Kid," two members of the old "Hole-in-the-Wall" gang which terrorized Montana and Wyoming for so many years, has at last been explained.

Cassidy and the Kid disappeared from Wyoming and Montana several years ago, each man carrying an immense reward on his head. It was rumored that they had escaped from the country by way of the Mexican border, but this was doubted as no trace of the outlaws was ever found on the other side of the line.

The men met their death in a little adobe house ten leagues outside the town called Uyuni, in Bolivia, after leaving a trail through South America, which was marked by the death of at least ten men, the daylight looting of three banks and numberless other ventures of the sort. They were shot to death by a troop of Bolivian Calvary – at least Cassidy was shot to death, but is supposed that before he died, he killed the "Sundance Kid," who was responsible for Cassidy's predicament.

Two years after "Butch" Cassidy and Lauterbaugh, better known as the "Sundance Kid," left Wyoming two "Yankees" turned up in Argentine country. They were well supplied with ready money and invested in a ranch some distance inland in the agricultural district. They called themselves Maxwell and Brown. Maxwell was Cassidy, and his partner was, of course, none other than the Sundance Kid.

Detectives Find Them.

Every police department in South America had pictures of the two men, and it was the Pinkertons who trace them to the Argentine. In some way, the two men heard that the Pinkertons were after them and hastily sold their ranch. It is believed that had the men been let alone, they would have turned into farmers and left other people's money alone, but when they were driven to fight, no part of their Wyoming record can compare with what followed.

They struck first at Mendoza, in the Argentine. Walking into the bank in broad daylight, they held up the cashier and helped themselves to all the money in sight, riding away unharmed.

The next heard of them was at a Chilean town, where they entered the British Bank of South America, and while Lauterbaugh held up the two clerks, Cassidy picked up 25,000 pesos in paper money.

Then they gave a fancy exhibition of shooting, writing their initials on the walls with shots from their revolvers, each man using two guns.

At Antafgasta, the "Sundance Kid" had a small love affair. It happened that the local lieutenant of police was also in love with the same lady, and he waited outside one night, sending word that he would kill Lauterbaugh on-site. The Kid buckled on his guns and walked out at the front door with Cassidy at his elbow.

Lauterbaugh warned the policeman that he would shoot to kill, but the Chilean made an attempt to draw his gun, and the Kid fired just once. The bullet struck the lieutenant squarely between the eyes, killing him instantly. Cassidy's guns came out in time to drive back the crowd, which gathered as the men walked to the office of the United

States Consul. They told this man that they were peaceable Americans who had been persecuted by the man whom the Kid had killed, and Cassidy turned over all the funds in his possession in order to get the Kid out of jail. It costs the pair every cent they had, but in time the Kid went free.

They next turned up in Bolivia, where they held up a German American paymaster and made their biggest hall, 40,000 bolivianos, equal to $20,000.

Cashed Their Gains

This money they cashed and, in order to go into hiding, went to work on the new railroad line near Oruro, on which several Americans were working.

One day the foreman of the gang, a man named Joseph Peters, entered Cassidy's tent without giving a warning. As he stepped through the flaps, he found himself looking into the muzzle of two guns – Cassidy was ready to shoot at an instant's warning. Peters tumbled out the tent backward, but Cassidy, feeling that some explanation was necessary, took the foreman into his confidence and made a full confession. He also showed a new revolver which he bought when he first came to Argentine, remarking that he had been forced to kill a man with it.

For a year, the two men worked hard as laborers, and the few Americans who were let in on the secret befriended the outlaws, even going to the limit of warning them that their pictures were openly displayed in the near city.

After one year on the embankments, the two men disappeared again, leaving friends behind them. The Sundance Kid, a man of fine presence, good manners, and many accomplishments, had succeeded in making himself a general favorite.

Then came the last raid. The man robbed the stage near Uyuni. The booty was small, and perhaps it was the disappointment which caused Lauterbaugh's spree. At any rate, he filled himself with a fiery brandies of the country and Cassidy dragged him into a small adobe hut in a settlement 30 miles from Uyuni. Word came to the Commandant of the Regiment of Cavalry stationed at Uyuni, that two "Yankees" were hidden in the adobe house, and he sent a troop after them.

Two soldiers were sent to knock on the door. Cassidy opened fired as he did so, killing one soldier instantly. The other started to run at the flash of the revolver, but Cassidy shot him through the back of the head as he ran.

The officer in command of the troop stationed his men behind mud walls, and they fired volley after volley through the hut until it was certain that nothing alive remained inside.

When the door was opened, Cassidy was found literally shot to pieces, but there was only one wound on the body of the Sundance Kid. He had been shot between the eyes. Cassidy had told Peters that he had a "suicide agreement" with Lauterbaugh, neither man wishing to be taken alive. They had settled it that if escape was impossible, each would kill the other. It seems that neither was willing to kill himself. Because of the one wound on the Kids body, it is believed in Bolivia, Cassidy, seeing that escape was impossible, carried out his part of the agreement.

The bodies were never positively identified. There were some Americans in that part of the country might have made the identification possible, but they refused to view the remains, giving as a reason that they did not want the Bolivians to secure the big rewards.

Thus passed, with their boots on, the two remaining members of the Hole-in-the-Wall gang. Their mates are buried in Montana, Wyoming, Colorado, and New Mexico, but Cassidy and the Sundance Kid lie in unmarked graves close to the adobe hut where they died.

AUTHOR'S COMMENTARY

The Mankato Executions
38 Sioux Hung

In 1862, the United States faced its darkest days as the Civil War raged. It was unknown if the nation would survive. President Lincoln was worried and highly discouraged by the lack of success of the Union Army and ordered his commanding generals to attack the Confederates. Lincoln desperately needed the Union Army to win a significant battle to inspire the nation.

Lincoln's prime concern was defeating the Confederate States to keep the country united. Unfortunately, Lincoln's attention was drawn away from the war with the Confederates to Minnesota. War parties from the Sioux National were conducting raids on white settlements and killing many. The president knew he had to act quickly and decisively. However, he could not afford to wage war with Native Americans in the northern states or within the Indian territories; the soldiers and supplies necessary to fight a protracted Indian War would severely hamper his Civil War efforts. Plus, Lincoln rightfully worried that bloody conflict with American Indians would not be useful or play well in many regions of the Union or Confederacy. By slaughtering thousands of North American Indians, he worried other tribes would take up arms against the Union and side with the Confederacy, as the Cherokees had.

The Cherokee Nation considered their options and chose to join forces with the Confederate States. Their chief at the time was Stand Watie, who held the rank of Brigadier General in the Confederate Army. He commanded the 1st Indian Brigade, also known as the 1st Cherokee Mounted Rifles. They were fierce and accomplished horse-mounted ambush fighters and caused great consternation to the Union Army.

The Cherokee's reason for siding with the Confederates was straightforward; they sought to maintain their population of black slaves, which numbered between 2,500-5,000.

Additionally, as with many Indian conflicts, the Sioux employed violence after the US Government failed to keep promises it had made. The government did not provide the funds or supplies it guaranteed. As settlers encroached on Indian land and killed much of their natural food sources (deer, bison, elk, bear), the Northern Dakota tribes fought back.

Dakota hunting party engaged and killed five settlers. It was the start of the war.

The War Begins

For six weeks in 1862, the war raged in southwestern Minnesota.

The war was fought primarily by Mdewakanton and Wahpekute men. Of the estimated 6,500 Dakota people living on Minnesota reservation land in 1862, historians think no more than 1,000 fought, including some who were strong-armed into the battles.

Before the war broke out, a group of Mdewakantons had formed a soldiers' lodge. Traditionally, the soldiers' lodge regulated hunting efforts within a village. Increasingly, though, this lodge attracted young men who resisted U.S.

assimilation policies. Dakota farmers were not allowed to join.

TIMELINE TO WAR

Timeline courtesy of the Minnesota Historical Society.

August 17: Four young Dakota men murder five white settlers near Acton Township, Meeker County. Fleeing to their village, they beg for protection. Leaders of the soldiers' lodge appeal to Little Crow (Taoyateduta) to lead them in war on the whites. Reluctantly, he agrees.

August 18: Mdewakanton warriors open fire on white traders and government employees at the Lower Agency and defeat a relief force sent from Fort Ridgely. Dakota warriors attack isolated farms and settlements in Renville and Brown counties.

There were an estimated 1,200 settlers in Renville County in 1862. On the 18th and 19th, more than 160 residents are killed; more than 100 more are taken captive. With few exceptions, the bodies of those who died are in unmarked graves, where they fell.

Milford Township also suffers many losses. Located just west of New Ulm in Brown County, Milford Township was populated by mostly German immigrants. More than 50 residents are killed, making it one of the hardest-hit communities during the war.

In all, more than 200 settlers are killed in these raids, and more than 200 women, children, and mixed-race civilians are taken hostage.

August 19: The Upper Agency is evacuated, and its white inhabitants are led to safety by Aŋpetutokeça (John Other Day). News of events at the Lower Agency reaches St. Paul; Gov. Alexander Ramsey commissions Henry H. Sibley, a former trader, congressman, and governor, to lead a force of volunteer state militia against the Dakota. As thousands of refugees began arriving in eastern Minnesota towns, bearing tales of atrocities real and imagined, panic sweeps the state.

New Ulm comes under siege by a relatively small group of Dakota warriors. This skirmish lasts several hours and leaves five settlers dead. The following day the people of New Ulm elect Judge Charles Flandreau, a prominent citizen from St. Peter, as their military commander. Over the next few days, more than 1,000 refugees balloon New Ulm's population to 2,000 people, while only 300 are equipped to fight.

August 20-22: The Dakota made two attacks on Fort Ridgely and are turned back. The Lake Shetek settlement is attacked, and the women and children taken hostage are carried into Dakota Territory. An attack at West Lake (Norway Lake or present-day Monson Lake) occurs, killing 13 people.

August 23: The second battle of New Ulm. This time, more than 600 Dakota soldiers fight under the guidance of Chiefs Waŋbdí Tháŋka, Wabaśa, and Mankato. This is the largest battle over a US town since 1776. After holding off the attack, Charles Flandreau leads the evacuation of New Ulm on August 25, leaving much of the city in ashes. Little Crow's camp retreats to the upper reservation.

August 25: Missionaries fleeing from the vicinity of the Upper Agency reach Henderson safely.

August 26: Upper Dakota men form a soldiers' lodge to oppose the war, crystallizing the Dakota Peace Party.

August 28: The force led by Sibley reaches Fort Ridgely, where some 350 refugees who have been under siege for ten days are gathered.

September 2: A burial party sent out by Sibley is attacked at Birch Coulee. The Peace Party opens negotiations with Sibley.

September 3-4: A Dakota force led by Little Crow fights a skirmish at Acton and attacks barricaded settlements at Forest City and Hutchinson. Fort Abercrombie on the Red

River is attacked and surrounded. Sibley learns that the Dakota holds more than 250 hostages; he begins negotiating for their release.

September 18: Sibley's forces leave Fort Ridgely and advance up the Minnesota River Valley.

September 23: Sibley defeats a Dakota force led by Little Crow at Wood Lake near the Yellow Medicine River. A relief force sent from Fort Snelling by way of St. Cloud reaches Fort Abercrombie.

September 24: Little Crow and his followers flee westward.

September 26: The Dakota Peace Party surrenders hostages at Camp Release.

On September 28, 1862, two days after the surrender at Camp Release, a commission of military officers established by Henry Sibley began judging the Dakota men accused of participating in the war. Several weeks later, the trials were moved to the Lower Agency, where they were held in one of the only buildings left standing, trader François LaBathe's summer kitchen.

As weeks passed, cases were handled with increasing speed. On November 5, the commission completed its work. 392 prisoners were tried, 303 were sentenced to death, and 16 were given prison terms.

President Lincoln and government lawyers then reviewed the trial transcripts of all 303 men. As Lincoln would later explain to the U.S. Senate:

"Anxious to not act with so much clemency as to encourage another outbreak on one hand, nor with so much severity as to be real cruelty on the other, I ordered a careful examination of the records of the trials to be made, in view of first ordering the execution of such as had been proved guilty of violating females."

When only two Dakota men were found guilty of violating females, Lincoln expanded the criteria to include those who had participated in "massacres" of civilians rather than just "battles." He believed he needed to set an example for the Dakota and other tribes. He then made his final decision and forwarded a list of 39 names to Sibley. Lincoln worried that if he failed to execute enough men, that may embolden other tribes. But, if he executed too many, it would cause outrage in the Union and weaken his position. In the end, he settled on executing 38 Dakota men and teens. Tragically, two innocent men were hung in error. One a young Dakota boy and the second an adopted white teen.

On December 26, 1862, 38 Dakota Men Died by a Hangmen's Rope

At 10:00 am on December 26, 38 Dakota prisoners were led to a scaffold specially constructed for their execution. One had been given a reprieve at the last minute. An estimated 4,000 spectators crammed the streets of Mankato and surrounding land. Col. Stephen Miller, charged with keeping the peace in the days leading up to the hangings, had declared martial law and had banned the sale and consumption of alcohol within a ten-mile radius of the town.

As the men took their assigned places on the scaffold, they sang a Dakota song as white muslin coverings were pulled over their faces. Drumbeats signaled the start of the execution. The men grasped each other's hands. With a single blow from an ax, the rope that held the platform was cut. Capt. William Duley, who had lost several members of his family in the attack on the Lake Shetek settlement, cut the rope.

After dangling from the scaffold for a half-hour, the men's bodies were cut down and hauled to a shallow mass grave on a sandbar between Mankato's main street and the Minnesota River. Before morning, most of the bodies had been dug up and taken by physicians for use as medical cadavers.

Following the mass execution on December 26, it was discovered that two men had been mistakenly hanged. Wicaŋhpi Wastedaŋpi (We-chank-wash-ta-don-pee), who went by the common name of Caske (meaning the firstborn son), reportedly stepped forward when the name "Caske" was called and was then separated for execution from the other prisoners. The other, Wasicuŋ, was a young white man who had been adopted by the Dakota at an early age. Wasicuŋ had been acquitted.

The below letter expresses the passion of betrayal. Chief Wabasha was told by General Sibley if the warriors surrendered, they would be treated fairly. Again, the US Government failed to keep its word.

Letter from Hdainyanka to Chief Wabasha written shortly before his execution:

"You have deceived me. You told me that if we followed the advice of General Sibley, and gave ourselves up to the whites, all would be well; no innocent man would be injured. I have not killed, wounded, or injured a white man, or any white persons. I have not participated in the plunder of their property, and yet to-day I am set apart for execution, and must die in a few days, while men who are guilty will remain in prison. My wife is your daughter, my children are your grandchildren. I leave them all in your care and under your protection. Do not let them suffer; and when my children are grown up, let them know that their father died because he followed the advice of his chief, and without having the blood of a white man to answer for to the Great Spirit."

Courtesy: Isaac V. D. Heard, History of the Sioux War and Massacres of 1862 and 1863, NY: Harper & Bros., 1863

AUTHOR'S COMMENTARY

By today's societal norms, the executions at Mankato would shock the nation and most of the world. It is beyond imagination that a contemporary president would personally select 38 American citizens for execution for engaging in a war on US soil. Yet, it was the accepted norm during President Lincoln's administration, as demonstrated by the following newspaper articles. The Sioux and other Native Americans were viewed by most as vermin requiring extermination, and the executions were simply an unpleasant necessity of a civilized nation.

From the Summit County Beacon, the hangings were less than a filler article with a single sentence announcing the executions.

Nearly 20 years later, *The Saint Paul Globe* dedicated a paragraph announcing one of the wooden beams from the gallows was now a "cherished" relic in the State University Museum.

Roughly 30 years after the executions, The *Fort Scott Daily Tribune* and *Fort Scott Daily Monitor* announced the proud display of a souvenir Sioux scalp.

The Summit County Beacon

Thursday, January 22, 1863

26th. Thirty-six Sioux Indians hung in Minnesota.

The Saint Paul Globe

Monday, May 2, 1881

In the New Ulm Review: One of the beams forming a part of the gallows on which the 38 Sioux Indians were hung at Mankato, December 26, 1862, has recently been removed from an old building, the notches cut in the timber where the ropes were placed are to be observed. This timber has been presented to the State University Museum and will soon be forwarded to Minneapolis, to be placed among the cherished relics of the past.

Fort Scott Daily Tribune and Fort Scott Daily Monitor
Thursday, April 24, 1890

Mr. J. Banning residing at Devon, was in the city today and showed us a scalp from the head of one of the 38 Sioux Indians that were hung at Mankato, Minnesota, in 1862, for participating in the massacre near that place during the Sioux outbreak. Mr. Banning had a brother-in-law who was a Sergeant in the United States Army at the time.

BILLY THE KID

AUTHOR'S COMMENTARY

History indicates the Kid was born into a New York Irish family. His legal name was Henry McCarty, and he later adopted the name William H. Bonney. As his criminal life grew, he became known as "Billy the Kid."

Without question, he was one of the most renowned killers of the old west. Records indicate he killed eight men, perhaps as many as nine. In all likelihood, he killed others that were not credited to him or his gang.

The Kid's murderous career was short by years but vast in crimes. After being on the run for two years, a former friend and now Lincoln County Sheriff Pat Garrett arrested Billy for the murder of Sheriff Brady. In April 1881, Billy was found guilty of murder and was sentenced to hang the following month.

On April 28th, just 14 days before his date of execution, he wrestled a gun from his jailer and shot him dead. Moments later, he shot and killed another deputy sheriff. The murder of two law enforcement officers and his escape drew immediate national media attention.

It was reported that on July 14, 1881, Sheriff Pat Garrett learned Billy was hiding out on a remote ranch. He quickly rode to Ft. Sumner, New Mexico, and placed the ranch house under surveillance. After dark, Garrett stealthily entered the house, surprising Billy. Garrett fired, and Billy the Kid was killed. The Kid was 21 years old when his life and criminal career ended.

However, as with Butch Cassidy and the Sundance Kid, many believe the Kid was not killed that night. He escaped to live out his life. They claim Garrett shot and killed another man and falsely claimed the corpse was that of Billy the Kid. When Garrett was murdered years later, rumors erupted that an unproven conspiracy killed him. And so, the legend of Billy the Kid remains alive today.

The Times

Wednesday, July 20, 1881

THE STORY OF AN OUTLAW

MURDEROUS CAREER OF BILLY THE KID

But Twenty-One Years of Age and One of the Most

Noted of Desperadoes—Shot Down at

Last by a Sheriff—His Exciting Life

Las Vegas, N.M., July 19

There is no doubt about it that "Billy the Kid," the notorious bandit, is dead. He was killed on Saturday by Sheriff Pat Garrett, of Lincoln county, at Fort Sumner, 120 miles from here. The Coroner's jury has returned a verdict of justifiable homicide coupled with a statement that Par Garrett deserved the thanks of the whole community for ridding the country of the desperado. The Kid was a beardless youth and is said to have been born in New York, and it is said that his real name was McCarthy. His boast was that he had killed a man for every year of his age, which is probably true.

Sheriff Garrett received the reward of $500 from the Territory, and $200 will be raised for him by the rejoicing people. The verdict of justifiable homicide is rather queer, as the Kid was shot down without warning. He had been in the neighborhood of Sumner for some days, disguised as a Mexican. Sheriff Garrett got upon his track and, on Saturday night, was waiting for him in the cabin of Pete Maxwell, a cattleman. Garrett had not been in the room over twenty minutes when the Kid entered in his stocking feet, knife in hand, and ostensibly for the purpose of buying some meat. He observed Garrett's crouching form near the bed, but before he could ascertain who it was, Garrett fired, the ball passing through the desperado's heart.

The Kid has shot a number of men since his escape from jail, about two months ago. He was tried and sentenced to be hanged and taken to Lincoln, near Fort Stanton, for safe-keeping. He gave warning he would escape. One day he felled his guard with a blow from his shackled fists, snatched a revolver, and sent a bullet through his heart. Then he walked across the street to the house where another guard lived, waited for him to come up the street, and shot him dead. Then he armed himself with a Winchester rifle and a lot of revolvers and as the crowd, attracted by the noise, gatherer scattered people right and left. He ordered one of the men to get him a horse and file. He mounted the former and, with the latter filed off the shackles upon one of his legs, and, not stopping to remove the other, tied the severed manacle with its chain to his belt so that it should not impede is movements. Not a man in the crowd dared draw a bead on him, and, saying that he did not intend to steal the horse and would return it, Billy started out of town on a gallop. Before he had gone far, the horse "bucked" and threw him. He jumped up, and at the muzzle of his pistol compelled one of the men to catch his horse, which he remounted and rode away. Soon after, he went to Fort Sumner, where he had a sweetheart, and disguised himself.

A NOTED BANDIT'S CAREER

His Castle in the Wilderness—Shooting People Off-Hand—His Band

Fort Sumner, N.M., July 10,

A month ago, it was generally believed that the famous bandit known as "Billy the Kid" was dead, and as the belief in the truth of the report grew, there was more and more rejoicing. Now, however, comes the report that Billy is still in the land of the living and that he is living in disguise at Sumner. There is considerable excitement over the news. Billy the Kid, who has been greatly feared in this portion of New Mexico, in Texas and part of Colorado for several years past, is the desperado concerning whom less is known than any other American outlaw who even cuts throats, robbed stagecoaches or stole cattle in the far Western country.

Your correspondent has accidentally made the acquaintance of a young gentleman, the son of a former distinguished member of General Sherman's staff, who had a wonderful experience with the celebrated bandit, whose deeds have been so much heralded of late.

Young Duncan is now a successful trader at Alamosa, New Mexico, in the "Black Range." The news of the renegades death was to the effect that "Billy the Kid," disguised and going under another name, was shot and killed by passengers of a stage-coach within five miles of Alamosa, New Mexico, on the afternoon of May 16, at thirty minutes past one o'clock—just twenty-five hours and thirty minutes later than he would have died by the rope had he remained in jail of a little New Mexico town, where he was confined under sentence of death, which sentence was to have been executed on the 15th of May, at twelve o'clock noon. On the 2d of May, he escaped from jail by knocking his jailer senseless with the manacles on his hands and got away, after killing the Deputy Sheriff and one other citizen. During the two weeks' freedom which followed, this young terror of the plains succeeded in taking seven more lives than he already had to answer for, bringing his grand total of known butcheries up to some thirty-three of thirty-four in number. The news of his death proves false, and there is no doubt that the desperado is now in this vicinity, in spite of the price set upon his head.

A MYSTERIOUS BANDIT

But little is know of the true history of the little more than youth called "Billy the Kid," and there is not an individual living within a radius of several hundred miles of this region (where all the desperate exploits of the murderer have taken place) who even knows the Kid's true name. This is something he would never tell, and his reasons for withholding it will be found further along in this history.

The young man who tells me the story of the Kid's life is one of the best-known young fellows in this whole wide country. Never is danger threatened the settlement, but he is the first man to be on the alert to protect his interests, and it has not been many days since he headed an expedition to go in pursuit of a party of Indians who were suspected of murdering a young miner. Some time ago, young Mr. Duncan was a member of McBroom's surveying party, surveying for one of the new railroads through New Mexico and Texas. He had, at this particular time, been several months in the country and was pretty well used to its ways. He could talk, eat and sleep with "Greasers" and hold fluent converse with nearly all the different tribes of Indians.

"It was about the middle of April, in 1880," said he, "that I was with McBroom's party, and, after several weeks' hard work, we found ourselves somewhere close to that dangerous locality, the Llano Estacado, or Staked Plain, occupying an immense territory in the counties of Lincoln and Dona Ana, in the extreme southeastern corner of New Mexico, and where it is, as you know, very hard work to find anything in the shape of water or greenness. In fact, there is no verdure in the whole immense area. One hot evening, when what water we carried was exhausted, we were unsuccessful in finding a creek or spring. The night was rapidly approaching when we finally went into camp, and several of us were dispatched in different directions to look for precious fluid. I was given three burros (small Mexican donkeys) and started in a northerly direction, with instructions if I did not strike water before darkness came to return to camp.

LOST ON THE PLAINS

"I found no water and at dusk started in a direction which I supposed would take me to the camp. It did not, however, and I wandered about all that night, hearing no noises except now and then the screeches of night birds peculiar to this region. I cannot describe to you my feelings when, *at the close of the second day of my bewilderment, I sank down exhausted and made a pillow of one of my faithful little animals which, like myself, were nearly famished through hunger and thirst. It came to me all at once that I was lost on the Llana Estacada! For three days, I was alone on that desolate plain, and the fourth day had set in before I became delirious. On the afternoon of the fourth day, when I was about ready lie down and die, the burros struck what is known as a 'blind trail' and followed it up. I was startled a short time after to have one of the burros break away from me and dash forward. The two others followed, and a few moments later, I saw the poor beast rolling and plunging in a greenish, stagnant pool of foul water, out of which grew a heavy rank vegetation. I thanked God, go I knew there must be clear water somewhere near from which the pond is fed. At length, I found it---a tiny, silvery rivulet, very shallow, but every sparkle of which in the clear sunlight was more precious to me than so many diamonds. I threw myself prostrate by its side and drank. Getting up, I walked to the top of what is called mesa, or high plain, that was just before me, and was surprised when my eyes fell on the valley beneath to see a cluster of what appeared to be cottonwood trees. Immediately on the other side of them rose another high plain.*

The trees were in the valley and in the midst of them stood one of the queerest looking building I have ever seen. It was around, cone-shaped affair, that might have been the castle of some Mexican grandee, the rancho a cattle herder of a fort. Situated as it was between the two abrupt high plains, it could not be seen until one was completely upon it. The building appeared to be built of adobe, and I could notice all around its sides holes, which I took to be loopholes. I was getting deathly sick, made so by drinking so much water, and determined to approach the strange building. Going down the hill, I looked for the door, found it, cried 'halloo,' and would probably have fallen to the ground had I not been brought to my senses by seeing the cold, cruel bores of eleven Winchester rifles staring me in the face. The rifles were pointed at me from cracks in the door and the loopholes surrounding it. I suppose I cried, 'Don't shoot; I'm a friend,' or something of that sort, for they didn't shoot, and the next moment the door was opened and a young man with an eye brighter than an eagles' stepped out. I knew him. I had seen him in Sumner, and I had seen him shoot down a man in his tracks and saunter leisurely down the street. I was in the presence of the bandit known as Billy the Kid. When I had seen him in Sumner, he had also noticed me, and as I was a stranger, he had inquired as to who I was and had received the information. He now recognized me, and when he saw my condition greeted me kindly. I said,' How are you, Kid?' and he answered, 'Well, you're a pretty sick kid.' He then looked carefully around and, seeing that I was entirely alone, invited me in. I caught a glimpse of a very handsome young woman. He ordered her to do something, and soon she brought me about a pint of raw cornmeal and water. She told me to drink it. I did, and it saved my life. I laid myself down on a pile of skins, and, I guess, being quite a healthy young fellow, very tired and with a tolerably easy conscience, I performed the feat of sleeping for about thirty hours, without eating or drinking. When I saw all of my arms and ammunition lying beside me on a stool, and then I knew I was safe among people who would not harm me."

THE KID'S STRONGHOLD

The young man then described to your correspondent this peculiar and secret hiding place of one of the most lawless and desperate bands of renegades the country has ever know. When it is stated that only in one place for probably fifty miles around this section of country can water fit to drink be found and that this water bubbles up from a spring situated in the middle of the floor of the outlaws' stronghold, one of the advantages of the site will be obvious. It was from this gushing spring in the adobe ranch of the desperadoes that the little stream trickled on to feed the slimy pool, accidentally discovered by the young surveyor.

The fearful exposure to which young Duncan had been subjected caused a fever to set in, and he could not think of leaving his bed for some time. During the days of his convalescence, he had several long talks with the Kid and other members of his band. They all treated him with great kindness, and many were the allusions made as to the jolly life they led, intended, no doubt, to influence the young man to join them. The thoughts that occupied the mind of the young Washingtonian where references were made to a possible onslaught on the stronghold by Texan Rangers, who were then in the Territory, were not very pleasant, for being found in the renegades' company he would have shared a like fate with them.

THE BANDIT'S APPEARANCE

Billy the Kid was a remarkable looking person, and the following is something of a description of him at the time of which I write: He was about twenty years of age, small of stature, smooth-faces, spare built, with several peculiarities that would distinguish him from equally wicked spirits as himself. One of his chief marks was that of extreme cruelty. His lips were thin and his upper lip very short; two sharp, fierce-looking teeth, much longer than any others in his head, grew out from under that upper lip in an extremely cruel and vicious manner. He was exceedingly vain, not only of his position as leader of a band of between two and three hundred desperadoes but of his personal appearance and his skill with the rifle. In the latter specialty, he perhaps had a right to be proud, for it is known that in all the

Western country there was not such a quick and perfect shot as "Billy the Kid."

He took delight in showing the young man who had so unwittingly fallen into his hands the nicety with which everything in his "Castle," as the called his retreat amidst the loneliness of the New Mexico Plain, was arranged. And verily, from the description of it which I received, it must have been a wonderfully built place of defense. The main room was about thirty feet in diameter and about ten feet high. There were complete cooking arrangements in one of the "ante-rooms," and a great number of berths fixed one about another on one side of the apartment. In two other partitioned spaces, there were enough stores packed away to last a hundred men thirty days. The great spring in the middle of the hard floor was of the most cooling and refreshing nature. There were specimens of nearly all kinds of pillage to be found in abundance in the place.

ON AN EXPEDITION

At the time the young man who gave me these particulars went to the "Kid's" headquarters, there were only eleven or twelve men "at home." The rest of the gang were out stealing cattle and at his other strongholds in different parts of the country. Young Duncan noticed that a close watch was always kept at the loopholes during the day and that the men never were separated from their arms. On inquiry, it was made known to him, that which has long been apparent to everybody in New Mexico and parts of Colorado and Texas, viz., that there are about three classes of society in those regions. Which may be thus divided: Followers of bands of organized horse and cattle thieves, murderers and bandits, such as "Billy the Kid" led on to victory; the "Texan Rangers," or movable vigilance committees, who have the law of Texas on their side, but are, in fact, about as great rascals as those who steal openly. These "Rangers" the desperados hate with deadly hate, but they also fear them. When bandit cowboy and "Rangers" are about the only organized sort of police the State of Texas employs, and they frequently make excursions over into New Mexico to "whoop up the Greasers." The third class in New Mexico society is the honest, quiet, hard-working citizen, and his is the prey of both "Rangers" and desperadoes.

READY TO TAKE A TOWN

In an immense corral adjacent to the "Kid's" castle, there was placed on the fourth day of Mr. Duncan's sojourn in the adobe rancho some two hundred cattle, the fruits of one expedition of the gentleman who had been absent. There was much feasting and great hilarity on the night of their return home. The next morning when the stranger woke up and looked out where the cattle had been, lo! They were gone—spirited away, after having been rebranded, to some still safer place! On that day, the famous young cut-throat got himself up regardless of the cost and went away. Before his departure, one of his men brought a magnificent black gelding up to the door of the hidden rancho, and Billy, while the horse was neighing and pawing, sprang into the saddle. This is how he looked as he sat giving his last orders to McCabe, his first lieutenant in villainy: He wore a blue dragoon's jacket of finest broadcloth, heavily loaded down with gold embroidery; buckskin pants, dyed a jet black, with small, tinkling silver bells sewed on down the sides. These pants were cut tight and fitted closely his shapely leg. Underneath this garment was his drawers of fine scarlet broadcloth, extending clear down to the ankle and over his feet, encasing them like stockings. But his hat was the most gorgeous and the crowning feature of is get-up, as it is with the Mexicans. It was what is knows as a "chihuahua," made of costly beaver, with a flat crown and a brim ten inches wide. And this whole structure of a hat was covered with gold and jewels until it sparkled and shone in a dazzling and blinding manner when one looked upon it. There was a gold cord around the crown as large as a man's thumb, and a great, bright rosette at the left side set it off in all its glory. This hat cost nearly $300. The shoes worn by this young prince of the plain were low quartered, with patent silver spurs fixed in the heels, which took the place of the common, clumsy arrangements that ordinary equestrians use.

Rigged out in this gaudy, saucy way the boy demon (for he can hardly be described as anything short of a mixture of the devil and humanity) would dash into a town—take it; this is, the citizens would give way to him, let him race like a meteor through the streets, drink at their bars without paying when he pleased, and one man in Sumner, a leading spirit and the owner of the largest store in the place, so much feared the Kid and his gang that he would allow them to use their pleasure in regard to paying him for articles to which their fancies might lightly turn and which they would confiscate.

THE KID'S HISTORY

It was about ten days before the young king of the renegades returned to his hidden castle. Coming back from his secret mission to no one knows where he became very much attached to Duncan, admired his bravery and, in a remarkable degree, made him his confidante. Fourteen days after the young man fell into the den of the Kid, that individual announced to his new acquaintance that he had been discovered and the whereabouts of McBroom's party (somewhere on the Vegas river) and would in-person guide his guest to his friend. Then he called one of his men, had a splendid horse saddle for Duncan, caused his own steed to again magnificently caparisoned, and the two set out on *a cool morning for a ride that must have been full of very unpleasant sort of mystery to one of the party at least.*

The Kid seemed to be in a melancholy sort of mood and became communicative, giving to his young and honest companion the fullest history of his life that he ever gave to anyone. This desperado has been given many names by those correspondents who have written concerning him, and not one of these names, he himself stated, was correct. He was known as Billy Conley, Billy Coyle, Donovan, and by several other cognomens, but none of them were right. He was of Irish birth, he told my informant, and was one of a large family who at the time of his birth, lived near Springfield, Ill. His father was very poor and, to better his fortunes, went to Sherman, Texas, when Billy was about nine years old. Here and in different towns of Texas, the boy became a celebrity on account of the wonderful way in which he could handle a rifle.

Old marksmen stood in awe of him whenever he appeared, a grinning, saucy boy, at shooting matches, country fairs, or ox-roasts, to compete with them for the prizes offered.

THIS FIRST MURDER

In Sherman or some small town near to that city, when he was 16 years of age, Billy killed his first man. He was very pathetic when he related the circumstances of this tragedy. In a barroom, one night, a swaggering youth, whose father was wealthy, threw out a slur to the Irish boy, which reflected seriously upon his birth and particularly upon the kind of work in which his (Billy's) father was engaged. The boy dared him to fight, and in the melee that ensued killed his antagonist. Immediately he reflected that his victim's family, being rich, they would hunt him to the death, and he would stand no chance of getting justice should he remain and be tried.

So he fled and went direct to Lincoln county, New Mexico, where several cattle-herders were in want of boys. Later on, he was defrauded by one of these men, who refused to keep his agreement of dividing at a certain time the profits of his business (cattle stealing) with the cow-boys who aided him. The boys revolved, and a desperate and bloody contest ensued. This was during the years of 1878 and 1879 and has continued up to the present time. In the Lincoln County cattle war he came to the front at once, although one of the youngest boys engaged in the business; and that position he ever after maintained, not hesitating to kill at a moment's notice any man, even of his own band, who aspired to gain any sort of influence over the men or who questioned his authority. He also told Mr. Duncan that the reason he always refused to give his real name and the genuine place of his residence in Texas was that he had an old mother and three sisters, the latter being happily married to law-abiding and honorable citizens. At that time, he was anticipating death. Heavy rewards were everywhere offered to anybody who would take him, dead or alive, or who could give authentic information as to is hiding-places. He lived in imminent danger of any moment being shot down like a dog, and he was honest enough to own that he deserved it.

The ride was a long and circuitous one, and the "Kid," no doubt, guided his companion in such a manner that it would be a hard task for Duncan ever again to find the spot where the secret rancho was hidden. Billy acted honorably towards his captive. On the night of the day on which they left, the Llano Estacado Duncan was returned safe and sound to his friends. Billy bade him good-bye and vanished.

In the first town, the surveying party stopped my informant saw a notice posted up offering $500 reward for "Billy the Kid," dead or alive, and less amounts for any of his band, or for information whereby his retreats might be discovered.

The man who had slept in Billy's rancho would rather have cut off his right hand than betray him, even could he have done so.

HOW "THE KID" MURDERED

For years this young desperado has been engaged in the task of systematically killing off all persons in this (Valencia) and Lincoln counties who he considered his enemies. These people were all engaged in the cattle-stealing business. The chief end of his life of late has been expressing it, to kill off a man named Gillis, a rich cattle herder, and who was the first man, Billy said, who "went back" on him. Often he would ride up to where Gillis' men were, shot down one or two of them, and then send word to Gillis by those whom he allowed to live that he (Billy) was on his tack and intended to hunt him to his death.

At the time the desperado had this remarkable conversation with young Duncan, he was suspicious of his first lieutenant, a Texan named McCabe. He said that McCabe had committed a great number of crimes against the settlers, which were attributed to himself and which he deprecated. It was not many weeks after this that Duncan heard that McCabe had been shot down by his superior. Persons at this place who witnessed a tragedy in which the "Kid" was the chief act of described it to me as one of the most remarkable feats of quick and accurate shooting they have ever seen.

An enemy of one of Billy's fast friends was in Sumner one day when some of the "gang" were on a jamboree. This enemy of the renegade's friend was a "Ranger," and by prying around and hiding behind doors and store boxes, he thought he had escaped identification. When the renegade whom he was bent on slaughtering entered the store, the "Ranger" drew a bead on him, and in three seconds Billy's stanchest friend would have been food for worms had not the Kid sprang about six feet, seized his Winchester and with rapidity of lightning let fly the leaden messenger that sought refuge in the heart of the "Ranger." He fell over against a barrel and expired without a groan, while the entire party, including the renegade who had so narrowly escaped death, marched up to the bar and took a drink. After his last escape from prison, Billy was almost maniacal and was more of a daredevil that ever before. His band is now pretty well scattered.

The York Daily

Wednesday, July 20, 1881

BILLY THE KID KILLED

Shot down by the Sheriff from

Whose Custody he had Previously Escaped

Las Vegas, N.M., July 18—The notorious outlaw, "Billy the Kid," was killed last Saturday morning at Fort Sumner, 120 miles distant from here, on the Pecos River. Billy had been stopping with the Mexicans in that vicinity disguised as one of them ever since his escape from the Lincoln County jail. Pat Garrett, Sheriff of Lincoln County, has been on his track for some time, and on the day above mentioned arrived at Fort Sumner, having been put on the track by some Mexicans. He had to threaten their lives in order to get them to divulge the Kid's whereabouts.

About midnight, Sheriff Garrett entered the room of one Pete Maxwell, a large stock owner residing at the Fort, and supposed to have knowledge of the fugitive's exact whereabouts. Garrett had been in the room over twenty *minutes when the Kid entered in his stocking feet, knife in hand, and ostensibly for the purpose of buying some meat.*

He immediately observed Garrett crouching at the head of the bed, and asking Maxwell what that was, drew his revolver. Maxwell made no answer but proceeded to crawl toward the foot of the bed. Had he answered, giving Garrett's name, Billy would have killed him at once, as he is a dead shot. Billy moved slightly, getting into the moonlight then shining in at the window. Garrett, recognizing him, fired, the ball passing through his heart. He fell backward, his knife in one hand and revolver in the other. Garrett, thinking him not dead, fired again but missed. Had his first shot failed, he would have been riddled with bullets, as the Kid is coolly desperate and very accurate in aim when in close quarters. His death is hailed with great joy throughout this section of the country, as he had sworn that he would kill several prominent citizens, and had already slain fifteen or eighteen men. His real name is McCarthy, and he is a New Yorker by birth.

JESSE JAMES

AUTHOR'S COMMENTARY

Jesse James proved to be perhaps the most ruthless murdering outlaw of the 1800s. The total number of men he killed is unknown; however, it is safe to estimate it hovered near 100.

During the Civil War, Jesse, as a young teenager, joined his older brother, Frank, as a member of "Quantrill's Raiders," a Confederacy-allied band of murdering marauders who slaughtered hundreds of innocent men and boys during their raids.

In August 1863, their murderous raid on Lawrence, Kansas, accounted for the cold-blooded murder of nearly 200 civilian men and boys. This brutal attack so infuriated the Confederate Government it withdrew its support for Quantrill and his field commission under the Partisan Ranger Act. It was in this raid a teenage Jesse bragged he killed 36.

The following year, Quantrill lost control of the raiders, and they dispersed into smaller individual gangs. Ultimately, Quantrill and many of the others met a violent death. Some lived on, and Jesse and Frank James transferred their killing skills to a life of crime.

The Chicago Tribune

Tuesday, April 4, 1882

JESSE JAMES KILLED.

A Companion Assassinates Him in a Shanty at St. Joseph, Mo.

Profound Excitement Throughout the Region Which Gloried in His Deeds.

The Mother—The War—Massacres of Lawrence, Kas., and Centralia, Mo.

Jesse Killed Thirty-Six Men at Lawrence— List of Bank Robberies.

Russellville, Ky., Gallatin, Mo., Mexico, Corydon, Ia., Columbia, Ky., Kansas City.

St. Genevieve—The Stage and Train Robberies—Death of Capt. Lull, of Chicago.

West Virginia—The Great Minnesota Expedition—Glendale and "Blue Out."

JESSE JAMES' DEATH

THE OUTLAW SHOT DEAD IN HIS OWN HOUSE BY A MEMBER OF HIS OWN GANG.

Special Dispatch to the Chicago Tribune.

St. Joseph, Mo.,--April 3.—This morning, the city was startled by the report that Jesse James had been at last brought to grass by a murderous revolver in the hands of a young man claiming to be a detective, who gives several names. He and others say it is Charles Ford, of Ray County, while still others say it is Charles Roberts. The man who did the shooting is a mere boy, both as to years and general appearance. He is heavily and compactly built, smooth, round face, light complexion, and rather pre-possessing.

THE FACTS OF THE CASE,

so far as can, under the exciting circumstances, be learned, are about as follows: Last November a man and wife and two children, a boy of four and a girl of five, came to the city and took a small one-story frame house on a bluff in the south part of the city, where they set up housekeeping. They lived greatly to themselves and seemed to mix with no one. Yet no one thought strangely of this. They claim to have come from Baltimore, and the wife said to your reporter that they came here with a view to go to farming near here this spring. Some three or four weeks ago, or perhaps longer.

TWO YOUNG MEN,

claiming to be brothers, came here, got acquainted, or were previously so, with the family, and went there to live. One of them, the wife says, was her nephew. They and James were almost constantly together. This morning at 8 o'clock, James got up, came out of his bedroom into the front room, and was in the act of dressing, having only his pants and a few other articles of clothing on. Robert, who was at the time in the kitchen conversing with Mrs. James, went into the sitting room and soon

A SHRILL REPORT,

was heard, followed by a groan. Jesse fell to the floor with a 42–ball in the back of his head, and the blood flowing freely from the wound. He scarcely breathed from the time he fell. The man, with a revolver in each hand, walked deliberately out of the room, and he and his brother walked to the Chief of Police and gave himself up, and said

HE HAD KILLED JESSE JAMES,

and wanted to be taken in charge until the man's identity was proven when he should demand the reward. Soon the rumor spread, and great crowds flocked about the little out-of-the-way house, and great and intense excitement prevailed. The two men were taken in charge and marched up to the jail and turned in, after having been guarded in the Marshall's office for an hour or two. As the two men went through the streets, an immense throng followed, and the police and two men carried revolvers in each hand.

AT THE CORONER'S INQUEST

the wife said there was no use concealing the fact further, as the dead man was certainly Jesse James, a desperado who had filled all hearts with fear and terror. Upon the person of the dead man was found a fine gold watch, one that was taken from Gov. Crittenden some years ago, and a valuable ring with the words "Jesse James," was taken from his finger. His looks answered the description of the outlaw. Upon searching the house this afternoon

A CARTLOAD OF REVOLVES, DIRKS, BOMBS, AMMUNITION, ETC.,

were found, and taken to the Marshall's office. The man who did the killing says he has been watching and waiting for weeks to get the drop on James, but never could find him unarmed, and that, from a long acquaintance with him, it was the first time he had ever known him to leave his room totally unarmed, and at the mercy of his enemies.

THE ASSASIN

stepped between James and his armory and fired, having two revolvers ready for use, and the brother was waiting at hand ready to take a hand, if needed, but the aim was sure, and no help was needed, and the notorious Jesse James has been taken off, not going with his boots on, either, as he has so often declared he would. The dead man was laid out in the courthouse, and thousands of persons have called to see the most noted outlaw that ever robbed and killed on this continent.

THE WIFE

took the death in a very cool manner, and, while her grief was quiet, it was profound, and showed plainly that she was a woman of nerve and master of herself. She said she was not surprised. She had expected as much, and it was no more than she thought would come sooner or later. In fact, she said, for years, she had expected this every day and hour.

GOV. CRITTENDEN

was telegraphed, but has not answered up to this hour. There is no doubt, but the man is Jesse James, as the wife telegraphed Mrs. Samuels, the mother of Jesse, and others at Kansas City that Jesse was dead and for her to come up. At last, the long reign of terror is over.

DICK LIDDEL BROUGHT ON A SPECIAL TRAIN.

Dick Liddel, an old comrade and fellow outlaw with Jesse James, was brought here tonight on a special train, and recognized his old friend Jesse. He says there is no question. He would know him anywhere. Dick was brought from the Kansas City jail to settle the dispute, and his word seems to ease all minds, and our people are satisfied the outlaw's race is run.

THE EXCITEMENT.

To the Western Associated Press.

ST. JOSEPH, Mo., April 3, – a great sensation was created in the city this morning by the announcement that Jesse James, the notorious bandit, and train robber, had been shot and killed here in St. Joseph. The news spread with *great rapidity, but most people received it with doubts until investigation establish the fact beyond question. Then the excitement became more and more intense, and crowds of people rushed to that corner of the city where the shooting took place, anxious to view the body of the dead outlaw and to learn the particulars.*

IN A SMALL FRAME SHANTY

in the southwest part of the city, on the hill, not far from the World's Hotel, Jesse James has lived with his wife since sometime in November last. Robert and Charles Ford, two of his gang, have made their headquarters at his house, and Charles, it is said, has lived with him in that shanty ever since November. Robert arrived about ten days ago, and the three had been making preparations for a raiding expedition in which they were to start tonight. James and the two Fords being in the front room together, about nine this morning, the former took off his belt and laid his pistols on the bed, preparing to wash himself, when Robert Ford sprang up behind him and sent a bullet through his brain. The ball entered the back of his head at the base of the right brain, coming out over the eye. The Ford brothers at once made known what they had done, and gave themselves up. They are now under guard at the courthouse.

THE BODY OF JESSE JAMES

was conveyed to an undertaker's, where it was prepared for burial, and where a photograph was taken. James' wife telegraphed to his mother the news of his death. A number of men have identified the body, and there is no question about it being Jesse James. A Herald reporter viewed the body at the undertaker's when it was being photographed. Jesse was a fine-looking man, apparently 40 years old, with the broad forehead, and his physiognomy was that of an intelligent as well as a resolute and daring man. Jesse was in the habit of

WEARING TWO BELTS,

with a brace of very fine revolvers and 25 extra cartridges. In a small stable nearby were discovered several fine horses, the property of James. The Ford brothers claim that they are detectives; they have been on Jesse's track for a long time. It is believed they were with James in the "Blue Cut" robbery, and that they were influenced in killing him by the hope of getting the big reward which has been offered for James, dead or alive, by the Governor and by the express and railroad companies.

CHARLES FORD HAD BEEN AN ACCOMPLICE OF JESSE JAMES

since the third of last November, and entirely possessed his confidence. Robert, his brother, joined Jesse near Mrs. Samuel's house last Friday a week ago and accompany Jesse and Charles to the city Sunday, March 23. Jesse, his wife, and two children removed from Kansas City, where they had lived several months until they feared their whereabouts would be suspected, in a wagon to the city, arriving here November 8, 1881, accompanied by Charles Ford, and rented a house on the corner of Lafayette and 21st St., where they stayed two months when they secured the house No. 1318 Lafayette St., formerly the property of Councilman Aylesbury, paying $14 a month for it, and giving the name of Thomas Howard.

THE HOUSE

is a one-story cottage, painted white with green shutters, and romantically situated on the brow of a lofty eminence, cast of the city, commanding a fine view of the principal portion of the city, the river, and the railroad, and adapted *as by nature for the perilous and desperate calling of James. Just east of the house is a deep, gulch like a ravine, and beyond a broad expanse of open country, backed by a belt of timber. The house, except from the west side, can be seen for several miles. There is a large yard attached to the cottage, and a stable where James had been keeping two horses, which were found there this morning. Charles and Robert Ford have been occupying one of the rooms in the rear of the dwelling, and have secretly had an understanding to kill Jesse ever since last fall. A short time ago, before Robert had joined James, the latter proposed to*

ROB THE BANK AT PLATTE CITY.

He said the Burgess murder trial would commence there today, and his plan was if they could get another companion to take a view of the situation of the Platte City Bank, and while arguments were being heard in the murder case, which would engage the attention of the citizens, boldly execute one of his favorite raids. Charles Ford approved of the plan and suggested his brother Robert as a companion worthy of sharing the enterprise with them. Jesse had met the boy at the latter's house, near Richmond, three years ago, and consented to see him. The two men accordingly went to where Robert was and arranged to have him accompany them to Platte City. As stated, all three came to St. Joe a week ago Sunday. They remained at the house all that week. Jesse thought it best Robert should not exhibit himself on the premise, lest the presence of three able-bodied men who are doing nothing should excite suspicion.

THEY HAD FIXED UPON TONIGHT

to go to Platte City. Ever since the boys had been with Jesse, they had watched for an opportunity to shoot him, but he was always so heavily armed that it was impossible to draw a weapon without him seeing it. They declare they had no idea of taking him alive, considering the undertaking suicidal. The opportunity they had long wished for came this morning. Breakfast was over. Charles Ford and Jesse James had been in the stable currying their horses preparatory to their night ride. Returning to the room where Robert was, Jesse said: "It's an awfully hot day." He pulled off his coat and vests and tossed them on the bed. Then he said

"I GUESS I'LL TAKE OFF MY PISTOLS,

for fear somebody will see them if I walk in the yard." He unbuckled the belt in which he carried two .45 caliber revolvers, one a Smith & Wesson, and the other a Colt, and laid them on the bed with his coat and vests. He then picked up a dusting brush with the intention of dusting some pictures which hung on the wall. To do this, he got on a chair. His back was now turned to the brothers, who silently stepped between James and his revolvers, and at a motion from Charlie, both drew their guns. Robert was the quicker of the two. In one moment, he had a long weapon to level with his eyes, with the muzzle no more than 4 feet from the back of the outlaws head. Even in that motion, quick as thought, there was something that did not escape the acute years of the hunted man. He made a motion as if to turn his head to ascertain the cause of that suspicious sound, but too late. A nervous pressure on the trigger, a quick flash, a sharp report, and the well-directed ball crashed through the outlaw's skull. There was no outcry, just a swaying of the body, and it fell heavily back onto the carpet. The shot had been fatal, and all the bullets in the chamber of Charles revolver, still directed at Jesse's head, could not more effectively have decided the fate of the greatest bandit and freebooter that ever figured in the pages of the country's history. The ball had entered the base of the skull and made its way out through the forehead over the left eye.

It had been fired out of a Colt 45, improved pattern, silver-mounted and pearl-handled, presented by the dead man to his slayer only a few days ago.

MRS. JAMES

was in the kitchen when the shooting was done, divided from the room in which the bloodied tragedy occurred by the dining room. She heard the shot, and, dropping her household duties, ran into the front room. She saw her husband lying on his back and his slayers, each holding his revolver in hand, making for the fence in the rear of the house. Robert had reached the enclosure and was in the act of scaling it when she stepped to the door and called to him: "Robert, you have done this. Come back." Robert answered, "I swear to God I did not." They then returned to where she stood. Mrs. James ran to the side of her husband and lifted up his head. Life was not extinct, and, when asked if he was hurt, it seemed to her that he wanted to say something, but could not. She tried to wash away the blood that was coursing over his face from the hole in his forehead, but it seemed to her "that the blood would come faster than she could wash away," and in her hands, Jesse James died.

Charles Ford explained to Mrs. James that "A PISTOL HAD ACCIDENTALLY GONE OFF."

"Yes," said Mrs. James, "I guess it went off on purpose."

HIS EXECUTIONERS.
THE MEN WHO DID THE WORK.

Special Dispatch to The Chicago Tribune

St. JOSEPH, Mo., April 3. – Robert Ford, the young man who shot Jesse James, is 21 years of age. He was born and reared in Ray County, 2 miles from Richmond. He worked on a farm until 15 months ago when he went to Richmond and clerked in his brother's store. He says he has known Jesse and Frank James, the Miller boys, Hite, and others of the celebrated outlaws for four or five years. After the "Blue Cut" train robbery on the Alton Road last fall he said he resolved to hunt the boys down, and went to Kansas City, when he and his brother, who was his companion in the affair, joined the Kansas City detective, and, knowing not only these men, but this country, he self-appointed himself to the task. The two boys are cool, quick, and certainly brave. During the hearing before the justice, they were permitted to retain their two Colt revolvers. This has been a most emotional affair, and

OUR PEOPLE ARE FAIRLY WILD,

some believing the story, while some doubted. A day may develop something. This affair has completely buried the excitement of the hottest and bitterest election contest that ever was to come off in this city. The election occurs tomorrow.

UPON ARRIVAL HERE

at one o'clock this afternoon, your correspondent found the beautiful little city ablaze with excitement over the assassination of the king of the border outlaws. Amusement gave way to incredulity when the identity of the murdered man was asserted, and even at this writing, when the proof seems as clear as sunlight, are a host of doubters, who shake their heads stubbornly and refused to believe that Jesse James has committed the last act in that long catalog of crime which has given him a place among the most daring and famous bandits. All the afternoon, a multitude of excited people have been assembled about the shop of Sidenenfaden, the undertaker, struggling for precedence in the long line of persons admitted to view the body of the fallen chief. The latter lies on a rude stretcher in the middle of a small, dark room, through which entrance and exit is effected by the same door so that the procession of the curious moved slowly and inharmoniously.

THE BODY

is that of a man of magnificent physique, who, in the pride of health and strength, must have been a commanding figure, 6 feet tall, and weighing 195 pounds, with every muscle developed and hardened by active life. It is a body that would fill with light the surgeon seeking material for demonstrating anatomy. The features, but little disturbed in death, are not unpleasing, and bear the imprint of self-reliance, firmness, and dauntless courage. To look upon that face is to believe that the wonderful deeds of daring ascribed to Jesse James have not been exaggerated. The hair is dark brown, the eyes half open, glazed, a cold steel gray, upon the upper lip a close-cropped mustache, stained by nasal hemorrhage, and the lower part of the face covered by a close brown beard about 4 inches long. Over the left eye is the blackened wound caused by the bullet of Robert Ford, the beardless boy, whose cunning and treachery, animated by greed of gold, brought to an ignoble and the desperado who has so long snapped his fingers contemptuously at the law and its myriad of agents.

A SUPERFICIAL EXAMINATION OF THE BODY

would alone afford strong proof that the dead body is that of Jesse James. He has been literally shot to pieces in his daring exploits, in his old wounds, would have killed anyone cast in a less rugged mold. Two bullets pierced the abdomen, and are still in the body. There is a bullet *hole in the right wrist, and another in the right ankle. Two more disfigure the left thigh and knee. The hands are soft and white and unstained by manual labor, and the middle finger of the left hand has been shot away at the first joint. Hundreds of people have passed before the body, and while there was a unanimous expression of relief that the country was rid of so formidable a desperado, there were not a few who did not hesitate to condemn the manner of his taking off. Nevertheless, the young Ford brothers are undeniably the heroes of the hour. As they sat in the County Clerk's office this afternoon, awaiting the call before the coroner's inquest, then progressing in an adjoining room, they were the coolest and most unconcerned persons present, and the very last that a stranger would pick out as*

THE SLAYERS OF JESSE JAMES.

It was Robert E. Ford, the younger brother, who fired the fatal shot, but his brother Charles was at his side with cocked revolver in hand to second his attempt. Charles is said by old Missourians to bear a wonderful resemblance to the once-famous Basil Duke. He was 24 years old, with black hair banged over the forehead, heavy black eyebrows, a faint and foppish mustache, high cheekbones, sunken cheeks, and square jaws, denoting great firmness.

Robert, the killer, is but 20 years of age, 5 feet 10 ½ inches tall, and weighs 135 pounds. His hair is brown and close-cropped, and his round ruddy face is smooth-shaven. He has hazel eyes as sharp as a hawk's, which constantly move about with restless and penetrating gaze. There was not the faintest trace of excitement in the young man's manner as he detailed the story of his act. "There is nothing to conceal," he said, "and I am proud of what I have done. I was born in Richmond, Ray County, Missouri, and raised on a farm until 17 when I clerked for two years in a grocery store. Then I went back on the farm.

"So they say that the dead man isn't Jesse James, do they? Then they are mistaken. I first met Jesse James three years ago, and I have made no mistake. He used to come over to the house when I was on my oldest brother's farm. Last November he moved here to St. Joe and went

UNDER THE NAME OF THOMAS HOWARD.

He rented a house on 31st up on the hill back of the World's Hotel, a quiet part of the town, and not thickly settled. My brother Charley and I had known nearly all of the gang, but had never worked with them otherwise. I was in collusion with the detectives, and was one of the party that went to Kentucky and arrested Clarence Hite, last February. Hite got 25 years in the penitentiary. Jesse never suspected that we were false to him, and, as his gang was all broken up, he wanted new material and regarded us favorably. Two weeks ago, he came to Clay County to see his mother, Mrs. Samuels, who lives 40 miles east of Kansas City. Charley and I told him then we wanted to join him and be outlaws, and he said all right. Charley came here with him a week ago Sunday, and I followed last Sunday night. We both stayed at his house, a one-story building with seven rooms. Gov. Crittenden had offered $10,000 reward for Jesse, dead or alive. We knew that the only way was to kill him. He was always cool and self-possessed, but always on watch. During the day, he would stay around the house, and in the evening, he would go downtown to the news depot and get the papers. He said there were men here who ought to know him, but they never did.

HE TOOK THE CHICAGO "TRIBUNE,"

Cincinnati Commercial, and Kansas City Times regularly, and always knew what was going on all over the world. About a week ago, he read a piece in one of the papers that Jesse James' career was over, and Charley said he was *awful mad about it. He said he would show them before long that Jesse James was not done yet. He had not done any job since the "Blue Cut" train robbery last September, and I don't believe he had over $700 or $800 in money. He was thinking of robbing some bank nearby and then running in under close cover. It was for this he wanted our help. "'Well,"' continued the youth, Conway relighting his cigar, "we knew he had to kill him. But there was no chance to get the drop on him until this morning. His wife, and boy of seven, and a girl of three were in the kitchen. Jesse was in the front sitting room, where he slept."*

I NEVER KNEW HIM TO BE SO CARELESS.

He commenced brushing the dust off some picture frames, but stopped and took off his weapons, and laid them on the bed. There was a Colt's revolver and a Smith & Wesson, each 45 caliber. He also had in the room a Winchester repeating rifle, 14 shots, and a breach loading shotgun. As he turned away from the bed, we stepped between him and his weapons and pulled on him. I was about 8 feet from him when he heard my pistol cocked. He turned his head like lightning. I fired, the ball hitting over the left eye and coming out behind the right ear. Charley had his finger on the trigger, but saw he was done for and did not shoot. Not one of us spoke a word. He fell dead at Charlie's feet. We then got our hats, went to the telegraph office, and telegraphed what we had done to Gov. Crittenden, Capt. Harry Craig, of Kansas City, and Sheriff Timberlake, of Clay County. The latter replied: 'I will come at once. Stay there until I come.'"

FORD TOLD THIS STORY

in the most matter-of-fact and un-impassioned way, without a particle of the dramatic in the delivery. He said that he wanted the reward, and all that he had done was with the consent of the officers who employed him. He was very willing to repeat his recital to everybody who asked him, and, producing a big bag full of murderous looking bullets, identical with that which pierced Jesse's fertile brain, gave them away to the bystanders as souvenirs until his brother checked his prodigality by remarking that he might need some of them before he got through. At 6 o'clock,

AFTER THE WIDOW HAD FINISHED HER TESTIMONY

before the coroner, the Fords were arrested on Squire Mitchell's warrant charging them with murder. They took this with great unconcern, as a matter of mere form, waived examination, surrender their deadly looking weapons and cartridge belts, and were remanded into custody. Their discharge, however, seems to be regarded as a foregone conclusion. The excitement continues intense, and the tragedy is discussed by crowds on every street corner.

FRANK JAMES,

The shrewder but less daring of the outlaw brothers, has been lost sight of since last September. There are many who think that Mrs. Samuels will yet avenge the murder of her favorite son if Frank fails to do so.

THE NEWS

AT JEFFERSON CITY—THE GOVERNOR KNEW OF THE PLOT.

Special Dispatch to the Chicago Tribune

ST. LOUIS, Mo., April 3, – the manner in which Gov. Crittenden received the news of the killing of Jesse James is described by a Globe-Democrat correspondent as follows: Gov. Crittenden on stepping off the train from Sedalia, shortly after 1 o'clock this afternoon, was handed a telegram from St. Louis, Missouri. It was from a man who, the governor says, has been with Jesse James for the past ten days. It read: "Have got the man. Meet me at Kansas City tonight."

This was supplemented by another, two hours later from Police Commissioner Craig, of Kansas City, dated at St. Joseph, saying Jesse was dead. The dispatch continued no particulars of the killing. The governor immediately telegraphed to S. R. Timberlake, at St. Joseph, to take the body to Kansas City, and that he would meet him there tomorrow morning. He is instructed to have it well guarded.

IN AN INTERVIEW

with Gov. Crittenden late this afternoon, he said: "I have no particulars yet, and do not know that I shall receive any before I reach Kansas City. I leave on the train at 1 o'clock today. I am satisfied that they have killed the right man, and that Missouri will never be bothered by Jesse James again. People have no idea how much trouble I have had getting my men to work together and keep at it. Some of them would work it while getting tired and want to quit, but I would encourage them, and they would try it a little longer.

TRUE RESULT IS

I have succeeded in suppressing train-robbing, and have broken up the gang of bandits. I tell you my mysterious man 'Bob.' As I call him, did the work."

"That I am not at liberty to tell. The papers in the dispatches and interviews made 'Bob' out to be Wood Hite, and had him killed. He is not Wood Hite. Wood Hite is dead, and 'Bob' is another individual. My great point in the whole business has been secrecy. My success has been entirely brought about by keeping quiet and not revealing my information before I had effected my purpose." Gov. Crittenden was seen at 7 PM. He said: "I have no particulars of the killing yet. I don't doubt the truthfulness of the report, for I feel that

I CAN RELY UPON MY MEN.

I shall go to Kansas City on the first train. I received a dispatch from O. M. Spencer, County Attorney of Buchanan County, dated at St. Joseph, late this afternoon, saying, "Jesse James was killed here today." I also received this from Gen. Carson, General Superintendent of the Hannibal and St. Joe Railway: "'Hannibal, Missouri, April 3. – If the reports from St. Joseph are true, I sincerely congratulate you. John B. Carson.'

"Do you expect any particulars tonight?"

"I do not think there will be anything further from the men who have the body in charge. Their time will be taken up, removing it to Kansas City, and I do not expect to learn anything more until I reach that city. Of course, I may receive telegrams and hear reports, but I shall not consider them reliable unless they come from

THE MEN WHO ARE WORKING UNDER MY AUTHORITY."

"Where is Frank James? Is he in the vicinity of St. Joe?"

"No. Frank James was in Kentucky a few days ago, and is not in Missouri unless he has come here very recently. I gave up some time ago the idea of catching the train robbers in the country, and stop looking for them at crossroads. I came to the conclusion, from information in my possession, *that Jesse was in the habit of spending a good deal of time in the towns."*

AT INDEPENDENCE, MO.

INDEPENDENCE, Mo., April 3. – It has just been learned that Dick Liddel, the bandit, was in Kansas City last night. It appears that late last evening as his wife, Mattie Collins, and in company with W. C. Woodward, a St. Louis journalist, formerly of Memphis, were walking on the street Liddel rode up, accusing her of having informed Woodward of things she should not have done. A fuss then ensued between the two latter, in which a shot was fired by one of the two. Liddel rode off, fearing arrest by the officers. Woodward, an hour later, boasted that Jesse James will be killed the next day. His prophecy was verified. Independence is wild with excitement over the death of Jesse James. Fear of his vengeance has restricted the people taking extreme action against all the accused train robbers. Men are huddled together in groups on the street, and rumors of a lynching party to be organized tonight are very prevalent.

AT KANSAS CITY.

KANSAS CITY, Mo., April 3. – The news of the killing of Jesse James created an immense sensation in the city, although the report was generally treated as incredulity, and, even at this late hour, many unbelievers can be found. This afternoon as soon as the news was received here, Police Commissioner Craig left for St. Joe with a heavily armed posse of men to guard the body of Jesse James and as protection for the man who killed him.

AT QUINCY, ILL.

QUINCY, ILL., April 3. – The news received here today from St. Joseph, Missouri, that Jesse James was shot and killed caused great excitement.

EXTRAORDINARY CAREER.

NOT EQUALED IN PREVIOUS CAREERS OF CRIME.

KANSAS, CITY, Mo., April 3. – Here, the James boys were reared and here has ever been their harbor of refuge when chased from pillar to post and state to state by detectives. Here many of their old guerrilla comrades live, and here, too, they have friends and relatives residing.

The James boys were raised in Clay County, within 12 miles of Liberty, the Youngers in Jackson County, within 4 miles of Independence. There is something suggestive in the names of their homes, for Liberty and Independence with them have been carried beyond the limits of criminal license.

Frank James was born in Kentucky in 1841, Jesse, in Clay County, Missouri, in 1845. The father was the Rev. Robert James, a prominent and eloquent Baptist minister, a pleasant and courteous gentleman, possessed of more education than was common within the ministers of his church in the frontier days of 1843 in the state, when the James family moved from Kentucky to Clay County. He was one of the first trustees of the William Jewell College, located at Liberty, and, though a resident of that vicinity only from 1843 to 1849, he has left a kindly remembrance of himself among the old settlers. In the latter named year, he went to California, and there died in 1851. To this day, the old settlers about the James home say, and it has become a tradition, that the Rev. Robert James was driven from home by his wife.

THE JAMES BOYS' MOTHER

is still alive and vigorous, and resides on a well-cultivated farm 4 miles east of Kearney, a station on the Hannibal and St. Joseph Railroad, 17 miles northeast of the city. She was a Miss Zerelda Cale, of Scott County, Kentucky, and, though she has attained the advanced age of 58, she wears the traces still of what in her young womanhood must have made her the famed beauty in all the country roundabout. Her neighbors say that Aunt Zerel, as she was commonly called, has transmitted to "the boys, all the deviltry they possess. If so, what an exuberant abundance she must have had in her day. No wonder her meek Baptist husband went on a mission to California.

She is 58 years old, well preserved, vigorous in body as well as in spirit. Her hair is gray – quite white – her eyes are steely blue, her face is a long oval, set off by a firm, determine expression about the mouth, marked by a few lines of age, and flushed with a ruddy glow of health. In figure, she is a commanding woman, weighing fully 170 pounds, and is 6 feet high – way above the medium run of womankind. She is shrewd, has dauntless courage, and displays a devotion for "the boys" that can be likened to nothing else but a tigress love for her cubs. After six years of widowhood, she married Dr. Ruben Samuels, a respectable citizen.

THE YOUTH OF THE JAMES BOYS.

It was here in about Kearney that Frank and Jesse James led uneventful lives until the breaking out of the 1861 to 1865 war. They were not over-fond of attending school in their youth, preferring squirrel hunting, and in horsemanship, they became famous. As the other boys in the neighborhood were, so were they. There was nothing vicious about them, though high-spirited, and they are remembered today as a voice of pleasing manners and general favorites. When their comrades got to rollicking, the boys never took part, for then, and now they never drink. The latent devil in them was brought out during the war. Both sides in Missouri were *guilty of the greatest atrocities, and each party vied with the other in devising devilish and horrible ways of retaliation. It finally became not war, but murder, unsanctioned by anything but the lust of blood. In this school of crime, the James boys learned the lesson that has made them, at this date, the most daring, desperate, and bloodthirsty criminals known to the West.*

Frank James joined Quantrill's guerrillas when he was 20 years old. He soon became noted for his daring and murderous ferocity. Jesse, only 14 years old, sought service at the same time, but was rejected as too young. Returning home, he became serviceable as a spy for the guerrillas infesting Clay and adjoining counties. His stepfather, Dr. Samuels, was a pronounced secessionist, and old Mrs. Samuels gave unbridled license to her tongue in advertising her sympathy for the South. The family thus making themselves conspicuous or marked for vengeance by the union militia of the state, who were stationed at Kearney and other towns in that locality.

Sometime in the early summer of 1862, the Federals, in pursuance of the vow of vengeance against the Samuels, visited the farm. Dr. Samuels was encountered and abruptly told it was there designed to hang him. A rope was produced, and, conducting him a few rods from the house, he was actually strung up, without being given time even to expostulate. His wife, fearing danger, having seen the squad of soldiers meet her husband and go off with him, followed, and reach the scene of the hanging just after the Federals had turned from the work as a completed job, and cut him down. He was resuscitated with great difficulty. Jesse James was threatened with hanging, but his youth saved him; he escaped with many cuts and blows at the hands of the soldiers. His mother and sister were imprisoned in St. Joseph. This so enraged Jesse that he again sought Quantrill's band and implored to be admitted. He was accepted, his brother Frank interceding for him. Thus the lad of 15 began a life of murder and crime, a career of daring and desperate deeds that has no parallel in history. Frank had already attained eminence in Quantrill's gang of murderers and cutthroats, and Jesse, emulating his example, soon eclipsed him, and became the leader in all expeditions or nerve, daring bravery, and a reckless disregard for his own or other lives were required.

WHOLESALE MURDER OF WOUNDED SOLDIERS

in Quantrill's command, the James boys found congenial spirits and Cole and Jim Younger, Jarette, Clell Miller, George Sheppard, and others who have been partners in the robberies since the war. Both were in Quantrill's band of 200 when Lawrence, Kansas, was sacked, burned, and nearly every male inhabitant ruthlessly murdered. Jesse James boasted at the time to have shot down 36.

Probably no horror of equal enormity or atrocity was ever perpetrated than the massacre at Centralia, Missouri, a waystation on the Wabash Railroad in Boone County. Here, on September 27, 1864, Bill Anderson, assisted by Jesse and Frank James, killed 32 invalid soldiers in cold blood. They first raided the village and sacked the stores. Then, waiting for the eastbound train, they stopped it and robbed the passengers of their money. Among the passengers were 32 sick soldiers en route from St. Joseph to St. Louis for better hospital accommodations. These poor wretches were marched out and aligned by Frank and Jesse James, and Bill Anderson, with his own hands, shot and killed every one of them, a pistol being handed him by either Frank or Jesse as fast as he emptied the one in hand.

Scarce had the diabolical massacre been finished before the company of Iowa Volunteers appeared in the distance, *and they, too, became victims of the unerring aim of these bandits. Thus within two hours, 80 slain were piled about the village. Such scenes as these hardened the James boys and made their latter-day crimes merely trivial in comparison.*

When the war ended, this country became too hot to hold the guerrillas. Jesse James accompanied George Shepherd to Texas.

THE FIRST BANK ROBBERIES.

For three years, the James boys sank from the public gaze. In the spring of 1868, Jesse James, accompanied by Cole Younger, Al Shepherd, George Shepherd, and Jim White, dashed into Russellville, Kentucky, and robbed the bank $14,000. Part of the party entered the bank, while the others remained outside and began a fusillade up and down the street to intimidate the inhabitants. After securing the money, the robbers rode off, and, though vigorously pursued, escaped. George Shepherd, however, was captured two weeks after the robbery, fully identified, and served a three years term in the penitentiary.

The first robbery in Missouri took place in Gallatin, where not only did they rob the bank, but deliberately shot and killed Capt. Sheetz, the cashier, after they had collected all the money in the bank. Frank and Jesse James and Cole Younger were the only ones concerned in the robbery. Frank guarded the avenues of approach, while Cole Younger and Jesse entered the bank and forced the tribute.

For two years the James boys hung around the Rio Grande frontier, and Mexico. In 1870 they returned. Corydon, Iowa, a prosperous village near the Missouri line, was invaded, and the bank relieved of $40,000. At the time of this robbery, a political meeting was in progress near the town, and when the boys had effectually gutted the bank, they rode to the public gathering. There Cole Younger interrupted the speaker, and announced the fact of the bank robbery. The crowd was fairly stupefied, and, derisively laughing at the consternation produced, the bandits put spurs on their horses and rode off. Pursuit was given, but in vain.

Two years now intervened before the gang was heard of again. Kentucky was a second time the sufferer. Columbia was a scene of the robbery, and the two James boys, Cole, Jim, and John Younger, were the five who did it. Here, again, murder signalized the visit of these highwaymen, the bank cashier being shot down in cold blood, and another party in the bank being seriously wounded, though effecting his escape by a rear door. Only $200 was obtained by this raid.

A DARING ROBBERY IN KANSAS CITY.

In the fall of this year, Kansas City was for the first time visited by the outlaws in an official capacity. The county agricultural fair was in progress, and it was on Thursday, the big day, that three men not only might have been, but were seen to ride up to the gate of the grounds. They were mounted and wore long linen dusters and the usual wide-brimmed slouched hat commonly affected by Missourians. On reaching the gate, one dismounted, handing his bridle reins to his comrades. He approached the ticket office, and, looking through the window, said to the cashier: *"What if I was to say I was Jesse James and told you to hand out that tin box of money – what would you say?"*

"I say I see you in hell first," was a contemptuous reply.

"Well, that's just who I am – Jesse James: and you had better hand it out pretty damn quick, or – –" and the rest of the sentence was finished by leveling a huge Navy revolver at the cashier.

The box was handed out, with its contents of $10,000. Returning with the cash, Jesse remounted, and the three desperados began firing the pistols and hurriedly rode off. The alarm became general almost immediately. Pursuit was organized, but the boys got away with the money.

Only three nights after this occurrence, two men rode up to the front of the Times building and, hailing a passerby, politely requested him to go upstairs and tell Major John N. Edwards, the editor, that two gentlemen would like to see him at the bottom of the stairway. In a few moments, Major Edwards came down, and one of the horsemen accosted him by saying: "Major, we are the James boys, and we wish to present you with this gold watch and chain because of the fair treatment you have always given us."

At this, the taller of the two, and the spokesman, Jesse, pulled out a handsome and costly gold watch, and holding it by the chain, pass it over to the editor of the times, now editor of the Sedalia Democrat. So soon as the watch was accepted with an astonished "thank you," the boys said, "Goodbye, old fellow," in a jovial sort of way, and rode off. This occurrence was made known to the police within five minutes after took place, but the boys were not caught.

This daring exploit was followed in six weeks by the robbery of the bank at St. Genevieve. Nobody was killed here, but $4000 was poured into the capacious mouth of the bandit's saddlebags. They were followed northwest to the Missouri, where all trace of them was lost.

THE FIRST RAILROAD ROBBERIES.

The next heard of them was in June 1873. The James boys were recognized around home in Clay County, and shortly after their appearance, a train on the Chicago, Rock Island and Pacific Railroad was wrecked, and the express messenger was robbed of $6000. Eight men were engaged in this affair, and it is credited to the James boys, Cole, Bob, and Jim Younger, and three of the bandits whose names are not known. Following this event, several stage robberies took place about the Hot Springs, Arkansas, in which the old gang are said to have been implicated.

They put a climax to their audacious career in this section of country by the robbery of an Iron Mountain Railroad train at Gads Hill. They took possession of the station, switched the train on a sidetrack, and, at their leisure, Clell Miller, Jesse, and Frank James, and Jim and Cole Younger stripped the passengers of their surplus wealth, and robbed the express car of $11,500.

The robbery following so fast upon numerous others, aroused the authorities, and especially the railroad and express companies to do something to protect their large interests. Pinkertons Detective Agency was empowered to hunt down and bring these daring outlaws to justice. From the appearance of Pinkertons detectives on the scene in 1874 until the undertaking was hopelessly abandoned two years after, the most thrilling events of the story occurred. The detectives put forth their best efforts to compass the capture of the brigands, but their most adroit schemes were frustrated, and the detectives who undertook their capture came to an untimely end at the hands of the enemy.

THE FATE OF SEVERAL DETECTIVES.

John W. Wicher first undertook the perilous task of finding and capturing the James boys and their associates. He found them, but it was he and not they who was captured. Disguised as a laboring man, he visited the Samuels farm and applied for work. The boys were at home, and with them Clell Miller. For some reason, whether advised of imprudent inquiries made by Wicher in Liberty or not, the boys suspected him. Against every asseveration he was just what he represented himself to be, Wicher was made a captive. Bound and tied on a horse, he was marched by the three and across the Missouri, and his body was found near Independence, Jackson County, with three gunshot wounds in the head.

CAPT. LULL, OR CHICAGO.

This failure did not deter others of the detectives from continuing the work. Wicher had undertaken to ferret out the James boys. Capt. Lull, of the Chicago police, and James Wright took upon themselves the task of uncovering the Younger brothers. Disguised as cattle buyers, they invaded the Younger country in Cass County, en route taking into their confidence the employee Ed McDaniels, a Deputy Sheriff at Osceola. In the course of their travels, they stopped overnight at a relative's of the Youngers, where John and Jim were at the time, but they kept out of sight. The three strangers being together awakened the boy's suspicions. The next morning they followed the three strangers, and overtook them on the road. An unguarded exclamation, "My God, here is Jim and John Younger," gave the trio away. The Youngers ordered them to hold up their hands. McDaniels and Lull obeyed, but Wright put spurs to his horse and fled, Jim Younger pursuing him. John, in the meantime, poured the contents of a double shotgun into McDaniels and killed him.

Lull at this pulled out his pistol, and, firing at John Younger, struck him in the neck, from which wound he died. Jim Younger, attracted by the firing, gave up the pursuit of Wright, and returning took part in the fight, and firing at Lull, he fell from his horse, and it was supposed by the robber, dead. John Younger being sore hit, his brother took him in charge and returned to the house they had just left on their murderous mission. Capt. Lull was found that night by some negroes, was taken to a neighboring town, and after lingering for six weeks, died.

ROBBING A TRAIN ON THE KANSAS PACIFIC.

For some time, the gang disappeared from sight. In December, 1874, however, they robbed a train on the Kansas Pacific railroad, near Muncie. The band comprised Jesse James, Clell Miller, Thompson, Bud McDaniels, and Jim Hinds. The five first placed obstructions on the track an hour before dark. When the train stopped, two men jumped on the engine with revolvers in their hands, and ordered the engineer to move slowly ahead, the express car having in the meantime been detached from the train. Moving had about half a mile, Jesse James, Clell Miller, and Bud McDaniels broke into the express car. At the mouth of a pistol, the express messenger handed over $24,000 in money and a large consignment of jewelry and route to New York from a Lawrence house. The gang then fired several shots in order to frighten the train hands, and then mounting horses concealed in the woods escape.

Three days afterward Bud McDaniels, whose father kept a livery stable on Grand Avenue, in this city, was arrested on Main Street while drunk, and, upon being searched at headquarters, $1100 and some of the sample jewelry taken from the Kansas Pacific train was discovered on his person. It was the first suspicion the police had that McDaniels was one of the train robbing gang, but the proof was absolute, and he was taken to Kansas for trial. He finally broke jail at Lawrence in May of the year following, was shot by a farmer named Bauerman while escaping. Bauerman went into a field to mow, and took a rifle with him, it having been reported that the train robber was in the neighborhood. He saw McDaniels one-quarter of a mile distant, and as he was mounting a horse, he had stolen Bauerman fired, and the noted bushwhacker was mortally wounded.

With the exception of the killing of John Younger by Capt. Lull, the death of McDaniels, was a first violent ending of any member of the famous robber band. Clell Miller and Hinds were arrested for the Muncie robbery, Miller in Carroll County, and Hinds at independence, the county seat of Jackson County, 10 miles from Kansas City. Miller, after his arrest, captured the sheriff in charge, and, holding him in front of his body, made him send his deputies away, and, with a revolver muzzle in his ear, the officer complied, and the bold highwayman escaped; but his end was not many years distant. Hinds escaped in about the same manner from the officers of Independence and has never been heard from.

DESPERATE EFFORT TO CAPTURE THE BOYS.

Out of the Muncie, robbery grew the tragedy enacted at the home of Mrs. Samuels, in Clay County, in January 1875, which added one more to the many fancied causes why the James boys should continue their career as brigands. The proffered rewards of Kansas Pacific and Express Officials for the rest of the perpetrators of the Muncie outrage again brought Pinkerton's men into the field. One cold evening in January, a special train having on board a posse of eight heavily armed men stopped near Kearney, Missouri. Wagons being in waiting, they were quietly driven to the neighborhood of the Samuels home. In a few minutes, they had surrounded the house, supposed to contain Jesse and Frank James. In order to light up the inside of the house, a prepared cast-iron shell, about 3 inches diameter, filled with oil and supplied with a fuse, was hurled through a window into the kitchen. Mrs. Samuels quickly pushed it into an open fireplace with her foot, where it exploded, killing her 14-year-old son Arthur, blowing her right arm off near the elbow.

What followed has never been made public, but it is known that the boys were in the house at the time of the attack, and that a terrible fight took place. A fence on the east side of the house was perforated with bullet holes made by bullets coming from the house. The next morning when the special train reached Quincy, a badly wounded man was transferred on a stretcher to a Chicago, Burlington, and Quincy car for Chicago, but who he was, or who his companions, is housed in the archives of Pinkerton's agency. This much is known, however. The boys were not killed or captured, but five days afterward, a neighbor of theirs, named Daniel Askew, was called to his door and riddled with bullets. The murderers, awaking a man close at hand, said: "We have killed Dan Askew, and if anyone asked who did it tell them Pinkerton's Detectives." Askew was killed because suspicious circumstances pointed to him as one who carried information to the detectives that the outlaws were at their mother's house that night their half-brother was killed. For fear of a like death to officials of Clay County took an indifferent interest in the search for the murderers of the innocent farmer.

ROBBING A BANK IN WEST VIRGINIA.

So hot and determined was the pursuit of the gang after the train robbery at Muncie, which resulted in Bud McDaniels death, that the robbers separated, the James boys going to the panhandle of Texas, where their brother-in-law, Allen Palmer, owned a fine ranch. Frank, however, soon went to Kentucky, where he was joined by Cole Younger, Thompson McDaniels, and a man known as Keen, alias Webb, alias Hinds. The Huntington, West Virginia, robbery was then planned and carried into execution. The robbery occurred in September, 1875. It has always been thought that Frank James and McDaniels entered the bank, leaving their companions as a guard outside. The cashier was compelled

TRUE CRIME CHRONICLES | 209

to deliver up what money he had, about $6000. With this booty, the four-men road rapidly out of town. In less than two hours, a posse of over 100 men started in pursuit. In the mountains, nearly 100 miles from Huntington, a fight took place between the officers and fleeing robbers. Thompson McDaniels was killed, and Keen alias Hinds, captured, but, as usual, Cole Younger and Frank James escaped. Keene was sentenced to 14 years in the penitentiary, and is now serving his time. He has never told his name or home, and steadfastly refuses to open his mouth regarding his companions at Huntington.

ANOTHER PACIFIC RAILROAD ROBBERY.

Frank James join Jesse in Texas, and the band was increased by the addition of several outlaws from the Indian Territory. In July, 1876, the plans were completed, and the Eastbound passenger train on the Missouri Pacific Railroad was robbed at a point about 20 miles east of Sedalia, called Otterville. The party consisted of Jesse and Frank James, Cole, Jim, and Bob Younger, Clell Miller, Bill Chadwell, Charlie Pitts, and Hobbs Kerry, a green country miner, who eventually was captured, and at Boonville made a full and free confession of the plot. The train was stopped in a deep, rocky cut after midnight by obstructions placed on the track. Seven of the gang jumped on board. Jesse James and Cole Younger entered the express car and forced the messenger to open its safe, for which they took nearly $15,000 in currency. None of the passengers were disturbed. After a hasty division of the spoils, five of the party went directly south, while the James boys, Clell Miller, and Chadwell return to Clay County. They rode about 50 miles before daylight, and the second night reached a safe hiding place in the county.

Kerry was arrested at Joplin, Missouri, in August of the same year while playing faro, and is now in the penitentiary at Jefferson City, serving out a seven-year sentence. In his confession, he named all the above parties as participants in the robbery at Otterville, hoping by this to escape himself, but having no attorney, his case was hopeless, and an easy conviction followed.

Several threatening letters were received by Kerry while in jail at Booneville from Jesse and Frank James, and one from the man Pitts. He was told that the most terrible death would be his if he gave them away to the officers, and at the head of both letters was a cross of blood as a fearful reminder of what was in store for him. After his conviction a last letter was sent to Kerry, informing him that the entire gang has sworn a solemn oath to kill him as soon as the time was out in the penitentiary, and that until the last one of the party was dead this deed of blood would be held as a sacred trust. In less than three months from that date, three of the party were dead and three in the penitentiary for life, leaving Jesse and Frank James alone to carry out the provisions of the oath.

ROBBERY OF A MINNESOTA BANK.

The immediate pursuit of the Otterville robbers being given up, a plan was arranged for a trip up into Minnesota, where it was proposed to rob the Northfield Bank. Bill Chadwell, who was recruited to the ranks of the Missouri band from the Indian Nation, was an outlawed horse thief from Minnesota, and was undoubtedly the originator of the fatal journey, which ended in the almost total extermination of the entire party. There were plenty of banks in Missouri and Iowa as easy to access as the one at Northfield, and Chadwell must have used some powerful incentive to draw the James boys and Youngers on that fated trip, so far from home, into a country of the topography of which they knew nothing. Chadwell and one of the Youngers were sent in advance of the other several days to reconnoiter, *the main body of the expedition leaving Clay County, Missouri, sometime during August, 1876. Cole, Jim, and Bob Younger, Jesse, and Frank James, Clell Miller, Charlie Pitts, and Chadwell comprise the party, the same who operated so successfully at Otterville. And a little station near Northfield the eight desperados held a consultation on September 6, and on the afternoon of the Sabbath, they entered the last name town at a furious pace, shooting their revolvers right and left in order to intimidate the people on the streets. With their horses on a dead run, the party halted directly in front of the bank. While Frank and Jesse James and Bob Younger entered, the other five remained outside to guard against attack. J. L. Hayward, cashier, and two clerks were in the institution at the time. For refusing to open the timeclock, Jesse James sent a ball into Hayward's brain. Meantime the citizens on the street realized what was going on, and opened fire on the robbers. Chadwell was shot from his horse by a man from the courthouse window, just opposite the bank, and in a few seconds Clell Miller, who had escaped dozens of times in Missouri, was also killed.*

By this time, the firing became general, and Jesse James was in the tightest place of his life. Jim Younger had a bullet in his mouth and Frank James one through his left leg, but the entire six succeeded in mounting their horses and escaping from town. Then began a flight and pursuit, which for persistence and endurance is almost without parallel. The robbers were in a strange and unknown country, followed by 50 armed men. When it was seen that the chase was to be to the death, a proposition was made to separate. Before this time, Jesse James wanted Bob Younger killed, as a blood from his wound made a plain trail, but Cole Younger would not allow it, and said he would kill the first man who dared lay a finger on his wounded brother. Jesse and Frank James rode off in a northerly direction, while the three Youngers and Charlie Pitts remained in a body. As on all previous occasions, luck followed the James boys, for, while they escaped after being pursued nearly 500 miles, the Youngers were shot down and captured, and Pitts was killed. The three former were terribly wounded before they would surrender, and are now serving life sentences in Minnesota penitentiary at Stillwater.

Jesse and Frank James, after being chased for weeks, succeeded in reaching Texas, and at Waco, Frank had a surgical operation performed upon his leg in consequence of the bullet he received at Northfield. The wound was so many days without care that it made Frank a cripple for life, and a detective told your correspondent that Frank James would be captured either in bed or on horseback, as he could never walk again for any distance.

THE ROBBERY ON THE CHICAGO & ALTON.

In the fall of 1879, the boys returned to their old haunts in Clay County, and very soon had about them a new gang ready to follow wherever a rich hall was in sight. Among the recruits were Ed Miller, brother of Clell, killed at Northfield; Jim Cummings, a noted Clay County horse thief; Tucker Baasham, Ed Ryan, and Dick Little. The last three were young farmer's sons, who, led on by the persuasive power of Jesse James, went blindly into the work, and two of them are now in the hands of the law. Frank James, in consequence of the wounds received in Minnesota, did not leave Texas with Jesse, but remained on the ranch of his brother-in-law, Allen Palmer, and was not one of the gang who again made Missouri soil obnoxious to persons from abroad.

After looking about for a few days, Glendale, a little station in Jackson County, 17 miles of Kansas City, on the Chicago and Alton Railroad, was selected as the scene of their next exploit. On the evening of October 8, the attack was made by Jesse James, Ed Miller, Jim Cummings, Ed Ryan, Tucker Baasham, and Dick Little. Like all preceding train robberies, it was a success. After battering down the door of the express car, Jesse James and Ed Miller entered revolvers in their hands and compelled Grimes, the messenger, to unlock the safe and hand over the contents, variously estimated at from $25,000-$30,000. With this amount, the gang left that section, and in less than 24 hours were centered about Jackson and Clay Counties. James Ligget, at the time Marshall of Jackson County, at once organized a strong party to capture the robbers, if possible, and George Shepherd, a former friend of Jesse James, and one of the Russellville, Kentucky bank robbers, was taken into the confidence of the officials.

THE FIGHT WITH GEORGE SHEPHERD.

Shepherd was a lieutenant under the noted guerrilla Quantrill, and was known as a brave and desperate man. He had an old grudge against Jesse James, who he claimed murdered his nephew and robbed him of $5000 shortly after the trip into Kentucky, which resulted in Shepherds capture and imprisonment for three years. A plan was arranged whereby Shepherd was to go and join Jesse James, who was thought would try and reach Texas, and when the right time arrived, he was to betray him into the hands of the officers. Shepherd accepted the trust and did join Jesse James, and remained with him several days. Ed Miller and Jim Cummings are also of the party, but the leaders seem to mistrust Shepherd from the start, and watched him so closely that no chance was given to communicate with Marshall Ligget.

In Southwestern, Missouri, the gang made arrangements to rob the bank at Galena, in the lead district. Shepherd was sent into the town to reconnoiter, but, to be on the safe side, Ed Miller was sent into watch Shepherd and see if he was all right. Shepherd easily fell into the trap, for when he reached the town, he at once sent a telegram to Ligget giving the date of the bank robbery, and also warned the bank officials.

All this Miller ascertained by closely watching Shepherd. After satisfying himself of the treachery of the man, he rode back to camp and related what had taken place to Jesse James. It was at once decided to kill Shepherd when he returned, and about 10 o'clock the following morning, when he came back, the attempt was made. What occurred at that time has never been known except from the lips of Shepherd, who said that as soon as he came in sight of the camp, he saw something was wrong, and immediately determined to kill Jesse James then and there. As the boys saw him returning, they mounted their horses, and when he was close enough as they thought, they opened fire upon him. He returned it, and says he shot Jesse James in the back of the neck, and that the latter fell from his horse dead. Shepherd then turned his horse's head and fled, and was shot through the left leg by Jim Cummings, who followed him 3 miles.

Subsequent events proved that the lucky highwayman, Jesse James, had only been badly wounded. Protected by his friends, he was taken to a place of safety, and his wounds attended to by a doctor from Joplin, who was heavily paid for his services. Before he saw his patient, however, he was blindfolded and driven an hour or more through the heavy timber in the neighborhood of Galena, to the spot where the wounded outlaw had been carried by his friends.

It was weeks before Jesse recovered sufficiently to travel, but in January, he was removed to Texas, where it is thought he remained until he came back and planned the Winston robbery on the Chicago, Rock Island and Pacific Road. Shepherd is now living in Kansas City.

THE WIFE OF THE BANDIT.

Jesse was married to his cousin, Miss Zerelda Mimms, in 1874. At the time, she was a public school teacher in the city. On the occasion of one of Jesse's rare visits to his mother's, she was summoned there, and the two were united.

THIS YEAR.

About daylight on the morning of January 6, 1882, an unsuccessful attempt was made to capture Jesse James, Ed Miller, and Jim Cummings by a posse of 20 armed men, who left the city at 1 o'clock by a special train over the Wabash Railway for a point in Ray County, near Richmond, where the desperados were known to have been. Among the chosen men were Detective O'Hare, Sgt. Distch, and 15 pick members of the police force, armed with carbines. Crossing the Missouri River, a run of about two hours carried the posse by the home of Mrs. Samuels, the mother of Jesse and Frank James, in Clay County, to the Lexington Junction, where the train was switched to the St. Joe branch. About 4 o'clock, the train stopped, and the posse of men dismounted and at once followed a guide through a heavy piece of timber to the locality where the gang was supposed to be. It was quickly surrounded, and shortly after a general descent made, but none of the men were found, they having in some way received notification of the intended rate. It is known that the men were at the point as late as 4 o'clock Wednesday afternoon, and that their horses were stabled in the barn back of the house at that hour. The men came to Ray County from the Indian territory.

LAST WEEK.

The arrest of John Mott, and the confessions of Dick Liddel (Little) and John Land were matters of last week's telegraphic news, the confession of John Land appearing in Saturday's issue of the Tribune.

AUTHOR'S COMMENTARY

Shortly after Jesse James was killed, Frank James surrendered to authorities and was incarcerated in the Independence, Missouri jail. Three weeks later, he was sent to the Gallatin jail to await trial. A year later, Frank James was miraculously acquitted on all charges and never spent a day in prison for his multitude of crimes.

After the trial, he moved to Oklahoma to live with his mother for a time. During the next three decades, it appears Frank lived an honest life. He worked several menial jobs at county fairs, theaters, etc. He died in 1915 at 72 years of age.

In 1899, Jesse James Jr., the son of Jesse James, was indicted for train robbery. He was adjudged, not guilty. The *Buffalo Weekly Express* wrote on March 2, 1899, "Jesse James Jr., was not convicted of train robbery. But without intending injustice to the young man, it may still be said that blood tells. His father before him was not much given to being convicted."

AUTHOR'S COMMENTARY

TIBURCIO VASQUEZ

the

California Desperado

In old west folklore, there are few bandits known for an active criminal life in early California. However, Tiburcio Vasques filled that position. He was born in 1835, in Monterey, California, when it was still part of Mexico. His criminal career spanned the 1850s through the 1870s.

In most cases, he engaged in burglary, cattle and horse stealing, and the occasional robbery of stagecoaches. Although he was accused of several murders, he always denied the killings.

For being an old west outlaw, he was considerably different. He was known as a lady's man. He had lady "friends" throughout California who described him as well-dressed, friendly, charming, and handsome. Unfortunately, Tiburcio had a fondness for sleeping with the wives and girlfriends of his fellow bandits and friends. At no time in history is that wise.

He alleged his criminal conduct was justified because America stole California from Mexico. Did he truly believe this, or was it an excuse? Only Tiburcio could have answered that question.

His name and crimes became notorious throughout California, causing the Governor to offer a wanted dead or alive reward. The state legislature authorized the funds to pay Sheriff Harry Morse and his posse to hunt down Vasques and put an end to his criminal enterprise.

Story continues below

Chicago Tribune

Saturday, March 20, 1875

AT LAST

*Execution of the Most Noted
Desperado of Modern Times.*

Tiburcio Vasquez Expiates His Crimes on the Gallows.

―――――――

The Last Hours of the Celebrated California Brigand.

―――――――

He Views Approaching Death with Perfect Composure.

―――――――

Singular Character of His Three Last Requests on Earth.

―――――――

Quick Ending of a Life Full of Murder and Robbery.

―――――――

No Attempt at Rescue by Brother Bandits and Sympathizers.

―――――――

Complete Account of the Most Remarkable Career.

―――――――

Vasquez's Bloody Exploits and Narrow Escapes.

―――――――

Thrilling Circumstances of His Final Capture.

―――――――

THE EXECUTION.

SCENES AND INCIDENTS.

Special Dispatch to The Chicago Tribune.

San Francisco, March 19.—Tiburcio Vasquez is no more. At 1:30 o'clock this afternoon, he was swung into eternity. Around the jail, everything was quiet and orderly. Sheriff Adams assistant, Mr. Winchell, had taken all necessary precautions. At night sentinels were posted on the roof of the courthouse and jail, and within doors a strong guard, while in the jail yard, three bloodhounds were turned loose to bay and alarm should anyone attempt to scale the walls.

Vasquez retired to rest about 9, but slept only an hour, and that very restlessly. He then rose and walked the corridor, smoking, and occasionally conversing. At about 2 o'clock, he again threw himself on the bed, but did not undress. A second time he rose, and retired for the third time at 4 o'clock. This morning Sheriff Adams paid him a visit, and presented him with a pair of black pants. Vasquez said they were a little tight, but, as he was not going to move around in them much, he supposed they would answer the purpose of execution very well. Then he attired himself in a dark mixture coat and vest, and exercised himself until

THE ARRIVAL OF THE PRIEST,

about 8:30 o'clock. For a short time, the priest conversed with him alone on the solemnity of his position, and then the relatives of Vasquez were admitted, Francisco, Mrs. Mee, and his nieces bring among the number. Breakfast was served at 9:15 o'clock, and consisted of fried eggs, bread, butter, beefsteak, coffee, preserves, wine, and cake. Vasquez ate very sparingly. During the night, he asked for Brandy two or three times, and smoked a great deal.

VASQUEZ MADE A REQUEST

last night to have three favors granted him – first, to be shown his coffin; second, to have the funeral arrangements explained; third, to be allowed to smoke a cigar and drink a glass of wine on the scaffold. He also desired to make an address to the assemblage, but, on the remonstrance of the priest, he agreed to forgo it. This morning, whilst waiting around the corridor, he talked, about different matters of no particular importance – inquired where he was to be buried, and who had paid for the coffin. He was told that his relations and Sheriff Adams and Deputy Winchell had contributed all needful for the purpose.

A COMFORTING ASSURANCE.

The following letter was then read to the condemned: San Jose, March 19 – 10:40 A.M. – to the Rev. Father Luis Basio, Santa Clara: I hereby certify that there is every hope possible that the body of Tiburcio Vasquez, who is to die this afternoon, shall be entitled to Christian burial. He has already been comforted with the sacraments of the holy Catholic Church and is very resigned and willing to accept death. Lawrence Lerda, Catholic Priest.

THE VISITORS INVITED

to assemble in the jail yard included the following, who constituted the only guard necessary; C. Van Buren, E. E. Burke, of Mountain View; Constable C. E. Wade and C. W. Love, Alviso; A. G. Hinman, J. E. Haight, Santa Clara; Deputy Sheriff Albaugh, Saratoga; Capt. Douglass, of San Francisco; Chief of Police Karcher, of Sacramento; Sheriff B. F. Ross, of San Benito; R. Orton, of Santa Cruz; Sheriff Larue, of Sacramento; ex-Sheriff Hume, of Sacramento, and Sheriff Latip, of Santa Rosa; John Edgar, J. H. Stafford, of San Mateo; United States Marshal E. J. Marcellus, Col. H, Finegas, Undersheriff Clouseen, of San Francisco;

Chief of Police Tisdale of San Jose; and, in addition, half a dozen police of San Jose. Tickets of admission, including the above, were issued to about 300, most of whom were present.

BIDDING FAREWELL.

At 12:15 Vasquez expressed the desire to bid farewell to the officers and members of the press present, expressing a wish not to be questioned in any way. He stood in the quarter, accompanied by the priest, and as each one passed, he uttered an expressive "goodbye." At the close of the interview, he sank into a chair apparently exhausted, and was left alone with the priest. Soon after, he was furnished with his last meal, consisting of roast beef, a goblet of claret, pudding, and pound cake. He only ate the cake and drank the wine.

READING THE DEATH-WARRANT

Vasquez listened to the death warrant with admirable fortitude, kneeling part of the time, then seating himself on a chair, crucifix and hand, Father Tedra in front. When Deputy Sheriff Winchell concluded, Vasquez handed him a piece of paper on which was written: "I am destined to die, and I hope that God will have mercy on my soul."

The Sheriff – "That is your answer, is it?"

Vasquez (very firmly) – "Yes, sir."

Deputy Curtis was summoned and led the way to the scaffold, Vasquez following, the priest on his right, Sheriff Adams and Deputy Winchell following, and various Sheriffs, Deputies, and reporters bringing up the rear.

ON THE SCAFFOLD.

Upon reaching the scaffold, the priest began the recital of the litany and prayers for the dead. Deputies Winchell and Sellman strapped the legs and arms of the culprit, and the white shroud was drawn over Vasquez's body, the rope placed around his neck, and, with the prayers of the priest echoing in his ears, the doomed man dropped beneath the platform, falling 7 feet. Up to the last moment, he acted with the most regular composure, and as the black cap was being drawn over his head, he said: "Be as quick as you can with it." Drs. Home, Brown, Turner, and Cory kept record of the pulsations. Life ebbed away in seven minutes and 30 seconds, and a few minutes thereafter, Vasquez's body was lowered for internment.

A WAKE

will be celebrated this evening at the residence of Encarnaccon Garcia, a cousin of the bandit, at Santa Clara. The remains will be interned in the Catholic Cemetery at Santa Clara. Vasquez bequeathed the silver matchbox he usually carried to Assistant Jailer E. J. Shaw, from whom he received numerous favors. To his brother, Francisco, he presented the hat he wore during his confinement. His sisters and other relatives received his other effects.

A REMARKABLE CAREER.

BIOGRAPHICAL

In this connection, a general account of the late lamented Mr. Tiburcio Vasquez, the accomplished ruffian, adroit horse thief, and notorious scamp, may prove of interest to the readers of the Tribune. He was born in the town of Monterey, California, in the year 1838. Both his parents are dead, but he leaves several brothers living; one residing in Monterey, and another in the vicinity of Hernandez Valley, in San bonito County. Tiburcio, in his youth, was naturally smart and intelligent; he received a fair English education, which was cultivated and improved in after years.

At manhood, he possessed a command of the English language much above the average of the California Greaser, while his handwriting was as fine and as delicate as that of the ladies. This is an accomplishment in which every California Mexican excels. The strong suit of that class of which Vasquez is an expert in laziness, and your correspondent, while at college, overheard Prof. remark, when complimented upon the beautiful chirography of his Mexican students, "Oh, yes; they are a good deal more ornamental than useful."

In the year 1854, Tiburcio attended a fandango and became enamored pro tem. of a pretty señorita. She, however, showed little partiality towards another Californian, and Vasquez, not desiring that his "affection" should remain unrequited, primed himself with aguardiente and overtook to

SMASH THE CALIFORNIAN

and everyone else in the saloon. The Constable of the town undertook to quell the disturbance, when Vasques drew a knife and stabbed him to the heart. He wiped his body weapon on his coat sleeves, and fled to the mountains, where he remained concealed until the affair was settled, when he frequented his usual haunts without fear of molestation. As the witnesses were all countrymen of the murderer, the case was misrepresented in the courts, and the matter was looked upon merely as an evidence of the precocity of the average young Californian of the day.

This exploit raised him high in the estimation of his sympathetic countrymen, and he a short time afterward associated himself with a band of horse thieves and cutthroats, who were then the terror of Monterey County.

After the gang had been thinned out by the Vigilantes, he transferred his operations to the section of country North and East of Monterey County, and for two years "interested" himself in the affairs of the large stock owners.

In 1857 he went to Los Angeles County; but, owing to some prejudice against him growing out of a horse transaction, he was sent to the state prison for five years. Yet tired of prison life and having tried it for a year and one half, and escaped with other prisoners on 25 June, 1859, and kept quiet for a few weeks at his mountain retreat near Old Diable, where he was the honored guest of a California rancher. Having recuperated his energies, he visited Amador County, and was again made the victim of the prejudice existing against his communistic method of purchasing horses, and was again sent to the state prison, where he remained until 13 August, 1863, when his term expired.

He had not been out two months before he "borrowed" some money from a fish peddler whom he met in a lonely part of the road of the San Joaquin. In 1864, he honored with his presence the New Almaden, the Guadalupe, and the Euriquita quicksilver mines. At the Euriquita, in the latter part of the year, and Italian butcher was found in his shop one morning with a bullet hole in his head and several knife cuts in his throat and breast. About $400, was known to have been in his possession, was missing. At the Coroner's inquest, Vasquez, who was the only Californian in the place who could speak English, was sworn as interpreter, and he interpreted so well that the jury returned a verdict that the "deceased came to his death from a pistol bullet fired by some person or persons unknown."

A few days afterward, Sheriff Adams received information, which led him to believe that the murder was committed by Faustino Lorenzano and Tiburcio Vasquez, but before he could make any arrest, the precious couple had decamped.

The bandit then changed his quarters to Sonoma and Contra Costa Counties. In 1865, after making one or two predatory excursions near the base of Mount Diable, he fell in with a young and beautiful señorita, the daughter of the Ranchero, who was harboring him at the time. Vasquez was graceful and very dashing in his manner; his hands are small and well-shaped, and his feet, which were of the true Spanish type, – high arched and tapering – were shown to advantage in a neatly fitting pair of fine calfskin boots. The señorita became fascinated with him, and Vasquez, who was a thorough Don Juan, was not tardy in perceiving and taking advantage of it. About this time

A COMMITTEE OF INVESTIGATION

were anxious to interview him, and he was forced to secrete himself in the Manzanita bushes near the house, where his meals were brought to him daily by the devoted girl. The liaison was discovered by the father, and Vasquez eloped with the daughter, and took the road for Livermore, but he was overtaken a few hours afterward by the indignant parent. An interesting discussion ensued, in the course of which Vasquez was shot in the arm, and the girl was stunned by a bullet grazing her temple; she fell senseless to the ground, while the bandit put spurs to his horse and escaped.

The next chapter in the history of the outlaw is dated 1867, when he organized a small band of horse-dealers. He was captured while negotiating for the purchase of a drove of cattle in the nighttime, and was sent to the state prison for four years, where he remained until 1870, when he was discharged by an act of the Legislature. Shortly after his release, he joined a band, headed by Thomas Rodundo, alias Procopio, or Red Handed Dick, a ruffian of the cutthroat sneaking kind. This gang committed numerous outrages and robberies in the counties of Santa Clara,

Monterey, Fresno, and Alameda. Stages were Rob; ranches were plundered, horses and cattle stampeded, and

A GENERAL REIGN OF TERROR INAUGURATED.

Sheriff's Harry Morse, of Alameda, and Adams and Harris, Santa Clara, had been in pursuit of the band for a long time without success, until in the spring of 1871, when Morse, in a pursuit after Procopio, Vasquez, and Juan Soto, came upon the latter in a canyon near the Panoche Grande. Soto made a determined resistance, and fired at the officer, but Morse finally got a beat on him with his Henry rifle, and shot him through the brain. Vasquez and Procopio escaped and went to Mexico, but returned almost immediately by steamer to San Francisco. Procopio was shortly afterward looking down the muzzle of a six-shooter in the hands of Sheriff Morris, in a restaurant on Montgomery St. in San Francisco. He was sent to state prison, where he now remains. Vasquez, who, with a careful regard for that individual known in common parlance as No. 1, had betaken himself to the mountains, selected Cantrua Canyon, near the new Idria quicksilver mines, as a homestead, and established an agency for stock transactions. The place is wild and almost inaccessible, and the entrance is so narrow that one man well armed can keep a Sheriff's posse at bay. Here he organized a new band, with Narcisso Rodriguez and Francisco Barzellas as his aides. His first exploit was

THE ABDUCTION OF THE DAUGHTER OF PEDRO GARCIA,

of San Juan. When the honeymoon was over, he loaned her to Barzellas as reward for his faithful service. The band soon afterward betook themselves to the legitimate business for which they had been organized. The Visalia stage was stopped by the brigands near Soap Lake, and all the passengers were robbed, after which they were tied *and laid on their backs in a field to contemplate for several hours the beautiful blue of the California sky. They next robbed three Teamsters on the road to Hollister, and passed by Wasson of Monterey County without molesting him. He was at that time a candidate for Sheriff. The same day, on the San Juan Mountain, Vasquez, who had separated from his companions, stopped and robbed Thomas McMahon of $750. When the news of these daring outrages reached the authorities, measures were at once taken to capture the bandits. Vasquez was stopped on the road by a Constable of Santa Clara County, who drew a six-shooter and Henry rifle on him; Vasquez went down into his hip pocket for his pistol, and while doing so received a bullet from the Henry rifle in the side. Without moving a muscle, he fired and inflicted a dangerous wound upon the Constable. That day Vasquez rode 60 miles, and reached his headquarters, near the New Idria mines, nearly dead from loss of blood. A few days afterward Barzellas was shot and killed by a Sheriff's posse in Santa Cruz County, and Rodriguez, another of the band, was captured a few days afterward and sentenced to 10 years imprisonment in the state prison, he died there about two years ago from drinking alcohol to excess. The officers of the prison might possibly be able to tell where he got the alcohol.*

For several months after the last mention exploit, Vasquez kept himself very quiet in the fastness of Cantua Canyon, and among his friends near the New Idria Mines. The Mexicans, constitute almost the entire population of the mine and the adjacent mountains, work, with but few exceptions, are partial to Vasquez. On one occasion, an officer of the law and two companions went to the mine to capture him. They knew he was in the vicinity, and they questioned the Superintendent, but he denied all knowledge of the outlaw's whereabouts. When, after an unsuccessful search, the party started to return, they saw a man looking out of a cabin window. It was Vasquez, but they failed to recognize him. After traveling until nightfall, they camped near the Panoche Valley. In the morning

THEIR HORSES WERE STOLEN AND ADDED TO VASQUEZ' STUD.

In the spring of 1872, Vasquez made his headquarters for some time with José Castro, on the San Benito, midway between Hollister and Picucho mines. One day the inhabitants of Hollister were startled with report that the San Benito stage and several people on the road had been stopped and robbed by Vasquez and his gang. The citizens were aroused, and José Castro was captured and swung from the limb of a tree. About one month afterward, Vasquez, who had several female acquaintances in Hollister, paid a visit to the town in the nighttime, and early in the morning quietly departed. The Constable of the town got wind of the proximity of the brigand, and, organizing a posse of four men, he started one day for the house, the front part of which was a saloon. Vasquez, who was on the lookout, saw them coming, and, mounting his horse, which was already saddled and standing in front of the house, rode leisurely away and was not followed.

In January, 1873, Vasquez organized a new gang of desperados for another campaign. The robbery at Firebaugh's Ferry was committed by this gang. The band consisted of August Debert, Anton Leiva, Romulo Gonzalez, and José Garcia. At this juncture, Cleovaro Chavez and Teodoro Moreno joined Vasquez, and the former of whom is still at large, as Vasquez Lieutenant. The next robbery was committed at the 21-mile house, between San Jose and Gilroy. The hotel was entered in the daytime, and four men were robbed and afterward bound and thrown on the floor. Sheriff Adams started out, in company with Under-Sheriff Sellman, in pursuit of the robbers, but, after scouring the country from the Pacheco Pass to the New Idria, they were obliged to return empty-handed. Vasquez, Chavez, Leiva, and Moreno were at this time arranging for the expedition to Snyder's store at Tres Pinos, and they saw Adams pass their hiding place several times. While hiding in the hills at the house of Leiva,

THE ROBBERY OF SNYDER'S STORE

was planned. It was intended to rob the New Idria stage, but on the way to Snyder's the stage passed a portion of the gang earlier than was anticipated, and for fear of an alarm being given the allowed it to pass unmolested.

On 26 August, 1873, the bandits arrived on the Tres Pinos, on the junction of the San Benito Rd. It was nearly dusk, and Leiva Chavez, and Gonzalez went ahead. They entered Snyder's store and engaged in conversation with John Utzerais, the clerk. While they were talking, Vasquez and Moreno rode up. The signal was given, and the persons in the store were requested to lie down and submit to a searching process, while Vasquez and Moreno guarded the door. Before the robbers in the store had completed their work by tying the inmates, a Portuguese sheepherder came along and was ordered to halt. Not obeying the summons, he was shot dead by Moreno. A Teamster named George Redford, who came up with his team, was likewise commanded to halt. He started to run, but a shot from Chavez, who had left the store, prostrated him. He attempted to rise, when Moreno finished him by putting a bullet through his brain. Mr. Davidson, who kept the hotel next door, was standing near the threshold while this was going on. He made an attempt to go into his house, when Vasquez shot at him. The bullet passed through the door and entered his heart, killing him instantly. Snyder was compelled to disgorge all the money he had. After having secured all the booty they could carry, they decamped in the direction of the Picacho mines and the Hernandez Valley. At the latter place, the spoils were divided in the house of Lorenzo Vasquez, who claims to be a brother of the bandit. Sheriff Adams and Wasson organized the posse and started in pursuit, but Wasson gave up the chase after crossing the hills into Tulare County. Adams kept on, and arrested Romulo Gonzalez near Bakersfield, but was obliged to let him go, as there was no jail nearer than Visalia, and, by taking the backtrack, his chances of catching Vasquez would be slim. He spent several weeks in the saddle, and at last, in Rock Creek Canyon, San Bernardino County,

CAME UPON THE ROBBERS.

Sheriff Rowland, of Los Angeles, was with the party, and if a charge, suggested and urged by Adams, had been made, Vasquez would have been captured. As it happened, however, a parlay was had, and, when Adams charged alone to the patch of underbrush where the robbers were concealed, he found that abandoned, the horses stolen at Tres Pinos, and Vasquez escaped. On the same night, Leiva's wife was abducted from Jim Heffner's, near Elizabeth Lake, by Vasquez, and the next day Leiva surrendered himself, almost brokenhearted at his wife's perfidy. He stated that the day before the abduction, he caught Vasquez and his wife in a very paroxysmal situation, and he desired to bring revenge upon his unprincipled chief. After a week of further searching, Adams returned, but soon after, learning that Vasquez had returned to his old haunts in San Benito County, organized another party and spent two weeks in a further search. Soon after this came

THE ROBBERY OF JONES' STORE,

on the San Joaquin, followed by the bold attack on Kingston. Then came the depredations in Tulare and Kern counties, and the robbery of four men at Coyote-Holes Station. After

Anton Leiva had delivered himself to the officers, he gave information concerning the whereabouts of Vasquez' gang, that resulted a week after in the arrest of Teodoro Moreno, near the Hon. E. C. Tulley's Ranch, 45 miles southeast of Hollister. Marshall Orsen Lyon was the arresting officer. Moreno was tried at Salinas city, found guilty of murder in the second degree, and sentenced to the state prison for life.

The Governor of California, and the county's most afflicted by the depredations of Vasquez, offered large rewards for his capture alive or dead, and various posses were organized and went in pursuit of him. Sheriff Henry Morse, of Alameda, disguised himself as a vaquero and traveled on horseback several hundred miles up and down the country, but failed to find his man.

On the night of 13 May, 1874, D. K. Smith arrived in Los Angeles with information which justified Sheriff Rowland in sending out a party to capture Vasquez. At 10 o'clock on the night of the 14th, Undersheriff Albert S. Johnston, Major H. M. Mitchell, Emil Harris, Frank Hartley, Sam Bryant, D. K. Smith, W. E. Rogers, and G. A. Beers, posted themselves in the vicinity of Greek George's cabin, a little outside of the town, and a place where they could get a good view of the country without being seen themselves. About noon a party of Mexicans came along on horseback, and it was observed that among the horses was a white one, which Mitchell recognized as the animal ridden by Vasquez in his previous encounter with the greaser chief. One of the Mexicans started off, and Major Mitchell and two others pursued and caught him. He gave his name as Reales. In the meantime, a wooden wagon coming down the canyon was seized, and the occupants, two Mexicans, compelled to further the plans of the party in a most valuable manner. The men, after securing the horses, sprang into the wagon box, and there lay down so as to be concealed from sight from the occupants of the house. Thus riding to their station, they leveled the revolvers upon two men on the seat in front, and,

UNDER THREATS OF INSTANT DEATH

should they make the least sign towards giving and alarm, they drove in the direction of Greek George's house. While the ostensible wagon load of wood was nearing this point of destination, and when within a few yards of the house, the Sheriff's party rode from their place of concealment and in an instance around the house. So sudden and well guarded had been their advance that they arrived there without raising the least suspicion of their approach.

The house was built of adobe, or mud bricks, with the frame kitchen in the rear. Around this, they quietly gathered and cut off every avenue of escape. As Rogers approached, the door was slightly ajar, and a dusky senorita within attempted to bar it, but before she could do so, it was forced open. Vasquez, who was sitting in the kitchen eating his dinner, took instant alarm, and with a single bound, went through a small window not more than 18 inches square, and landed on his feet in the garden. Here he was met by Hartley, from whom he received the contents of a double-barreled shotgun, and fell to the ground. With catlike agility, he sprang to his feet, and attempted to escape by the westside of the house, but was confronted by Beers, who lodged the shot in his shoulder from a Henry rifle. Turning again, and making another desperate to escape, he was confronted by Hartley, who had thrown away his gun and covered him with his revolver. He then saw that escape was impossible, and throwing up his hands, said in English,

"DON'T SHOOT,"

and quietly surrendered himself. The two men in the house, seeing the fate of their leader, surrendered themselves.

When Vasquez gave himself up, he turned to Hartley and said, "What is your name?"

When asked about his motive, he said, "I want to know the name of a brave man. I am not a coward myself, and I like to know another brave man like myself." This shows that Vasquez was a modest man. Besides the two men taken in the house, the Sheriff's party captured two horses, three Henry rifles, one Spencer rifle, five revolvers, 400 rounds of ammunition, a dirk knife belonging to Vasquez, and other arms. The gold watch, which was taken from C. E. Miles, a short time before, was recovered.

The capture created the wildest excitement throughout the state, particularly in Los Angeles, and there was some talk of organizing a Vigilance Committee and swinging the bandit between earth and heaven. When first lodged in jail, Vasquez expressed some anxiety as to his safety, and had to be assured several times that no further harm would come to him. It was found on examination that he had received two buckshot wounds through the fleshy part of the left arm, between the elbow and the shoulder, one in the right leg, one in the left nipple coming out under the arm, and one shot on the left side of the neck.

On 27 May, 1874, he arrived in San Francisco on the steamer Senator, and was placed in an iron tank in the City Prison. The news of his arrival soon became known throughout the city, and thousands of citizens besieged the office of the Chief of Police petitioning to be permitted to

FEAST THEIR EYES UPON THE CONVALESCENT BRIGAND.

The chief informed Vasquez that a great many people desired to gaze upon him. Then the noble cutthroat said, "Let them come in; charge them half a dollar ahead, and we'll divvy."

The Chief, who has a holy horror of the word "divvy," informed his illustrious guest that it was impossible.

"All right," sighed Vasquez, "Let them come in." And they came in with a vengeance, coming for several hours. Your correspondent mingled with the crowd, and stood for a few moments before the wicket of the cell. The prisoner was lying upon his back on a straw mattress placed on the asphaltum floor. He had his face towards the wicket, and wore a curious expression upon his face, half gratified vanity, and half fear. He wore black cloth pants and coat, and white shirt, without a vest. His physiognomy showed a great deal of self-possession and determination.

About 3 o'clock in the afternoon Mayor Curtis informed the Chief of Police that if he did not stop making a waxwork show of the greaser, he would do it himself. The Chief accepted the hint, and the matinee was concluded. The next morning he was taken to Salinas and lodged in jail. He was shortly afterward taken to San Jose to avoid his being taken out of the hands of the officers by the enraged citizens.

He was tried in San Jose last January for the murder of Mr. Davidson at Tres Pinos, the principal witness against him being the duped husband and former companion, Anton Leiva, whose testimony was so direct and positive that the jury returned a verdict of

GUILTY OF MURDER IN THE FIRST DEGREE.

Vasquez asserted all throughout that he was guiltless of taking human life, but the jury refused to believe him, and confined him to the tender mercies of the court. On the 23rd day of January, Judge Belden pronounced the death penalty, to take effect on the 19th day of March. His counsel moved for new trial on technical grounds, but the court decided there were no valid reasons why a new trial should *be granted. The matter was then taken before the Supreme Court, which sustained the ruling of the court below.*

AN INTERVIEW WITH VASQUEZ.

The subjoined extracts are taken from an interview between J. M. Bassett, editor of Los Angeles Herald, and Vasquez, the day after the latter's capture. After a few questions as to the main points in the life of the prisoner narrated above, the following conversation ensued:

B. – Where did you go after leaving Mendocino County?

V. – I went to my mother in Monterey County, and I asked her for her blessing, and I told her I was going out into the world to suffer and take my chances.

B. – What do you mean by "suffer and take chances"?

V. – That I should live off the world, and, perhaps, suffer at its hands.

B. – Is it true that you are driven to outlawry through injuries inflicted by white men?

V. – To a certain extent, yes. When I lived in Monterey County, I kept a dance house and sold liquor. The Americans used to come in and beat and abuse me, and mistreat my woman.

B. – Is the story true that your wife was debauched by a white man, and were some of your relatives killed by Americans?

V. – I was never married in my life. I have had women when I wanted them, but I never had a wife.

B. – Do you think a woman had anything to do with your capture, or in placing the officers on your track?

V. (laughing) – no; I never trusted one with information that could harm me.

ALWAYS AVOIDED BLOODSHED.

B. – You say you have never killed anyone?

V.-No; I always avoided bloodshed, and always urged by people not to kill or hurt those they robbed.

B. – And what part of the state have you committed your robberies, or most of them?

V. – In Santa Clara, Monterey, Fresno, and Los Angeles counties. I have committed many robberies in these counties, but don't wish to name them or give details. I robbed Firebaugh's Ferry last November, and it was my party who robbed the bank in Fresno and created the terrible commotion there some months ago.

THE TRES PINOS MURDER.

B. – Now give me your version of the Tres Pinos murder.

V. – I will tell you the truth, and, in order that you may hereafter know that what I say is true, I will give you the names of my party. If these men are captured, they will substantiate what I say: at Tres Pinos, my party consisted of five men, all told. Anton Leiva acted as my lieutenant, and when I sent a party, he went as chief. I remained at some distance away from Tres Pinos, and sent Leiva with two men into the place with instructions to drink and smoke, but to draw no weapons nor do any violence until I arrived. Chavez remained with me. We soon followed the advance guard, and when we reached Tres Pinos, we found the murders already committed. I scolded the men for disobeying my orders, and said to the lady whose husband was tied that, if she did not give me the money I would kill him. She gave me the money. I did not kill him.

B. – *How much money did she give you?*

V. – *Oh, very little. The whole amount didn't exceed $200. The goods were taken from the store after my arrival.*

B. – *Who committed the murders?*

V. –*Leiva shot the man in the stable and the one at the store door. Romulo killed the man inside the house. (Here Vasquez gave, under seal of secrecy, the names of the four men who were with him, and also stated that two friends of Chavez whom he did not know were of the party.)*

B. – *Tell me about the affair with Leiva's wife.*

V. – *A criminal intimacy had existed between myself and Leiva's wife long before we left the Rancho in Monterey County, but Leiva never suspected us. At Rock Creek, he caught us in flagrante dilictu. Then he turned against me and sought to have me captured. Leiva had been with me a long time prior to the Tres Pinos murder.*

B. – *What were your general plans of operation?*

V. – *Some time ago, Chavez, Leiva, and myself, and latterly Chavez and I, arranged the plans. I usually had no confederates. When I wanted a party of men, I had no difficulty in finding the requisite number. The work done, the party disbanded, and each went his way. I trusted no one. This plan of operation was the best, for the reason that the men, were not wanted by me, or engage in their ordinary occupations, and were scattered over the country. No one suspicioned them.*

THOUGHTS OF REVOLUTIONIZING SOUTHERN CALIFORNIA.

B. – I have heard that you said you could overrun this portion of the state, if you had money. How would you have acted?

V. – With the arms and provisions that I could have purchased with $50,000 or $60,000, I could raise a force with which I could revolutionize Southern California.

THINKS HE IS NOT SO BAD A MAN AS REPRESENTED.

B. – Do you wish to say anything concerning their present condition and future prospects?

V. – Only this: I am not as bad a man as I am represented. I have robbed men, and I have tied them up, but I never killed a man nor shed human blood, and have always advised those with me not to kill or wound those we robbed. I have been persecuted and driven from point to point from year to year. The white man heaped wrongs upon me in Monterey, and the officers hounded me until I was driven from an honest calling in Mendocino County. Of the future, I shall, at this time, say nothing. Of Sheriff Rowland and the gentleman that captured me, I will say they are all brave men. They took desperate chances, and it was one chance in a million that they succeeded. They could have killed me, but didn't, and they have treated me in the kindest manner.

After the capture, Vasquez, his Lieutenant, Chavez, kept himself pretty quiet. Up to the present writing, he has committed only two or three robberies, but he seems to possess the happy facility of his chief and keeping out of the reach of the officers. His last performance was a letter in the Spanish language addressed to the people of Hollister. It has been translated by a cow- country linguist, but, "' twill serve."

LIFE AND DEATH.

January 1875. – Capt. Cleovara Chavez to the inhabitants of Hollister: know you that, in regard to the acts committed by the Captain of my company, I say that I, knowing myself guilty of those acts, fled to Mexico; but, having been informed, while there, that Vasquez was under sentence of death, I have returned as far as this place, with the aim of disclosing the falseness of the evidence sworn to against him; and, in case Vasquez should be hanged, to quietly mete out a recompense, because I do not believe that I am in need of resources, or lacks sufficient valor, to take him or meet death in the attempt. I wish first to see the result. For this reason, I let you know that if Vasquez is hanged by his enemies, who, through fear, have turned against him, then you will see that I know how to avenge the death of the Captain. I do not exact of you to set him free, but I do not want him to be hanged, because he was not bloodied. This I can prove under oath. In times gone by, T. McMahon will remember that Vasquez saved his life subsequent to the murders at Tres Pinos. I was he who formed the head of the affray. He (Vasquez) certainly was our Captain, but I neglected the orders that were imposed upon us. If this is not sufficient, or if by this means Vasquez did not get his sentence appeased, then you will have to suffer as in the time of Joaquin Murieta. The just with the unjust alike will be punished, according to law. Then you will never more hear of me in this county or the state – neither of me nor my company. If he has mitigation given him, let it be published in the papers. With nothing more,

CLEOVARA CHAVEZ AND HIS COMPANY.

THE ASSASSINATION OF PRESIDENT ABRAHAM LINCOLN

AUTHOR'S COMMENTARY

THE ASSASSINATION OF ABRAHAM LINCOLN the 16th PRESIDENT OF THE UNITED STATES APRIL 14, 1865

It is not surprising Lincoln's assassination filled America's newspapers for months. It was a tragic event coming just six days after Confederate General Robert E. Lee surrendered to Union General Ulysses S. Grant, thereby ending the great Civil War. The nation was only days into healing when this horrible event occurred. From Lincoln's shooting at Ford's Theater to the hanging of the conspirators, thousands of stories filled the nation's newspapers. When selecting the stories to include, I sought a combination that told the beginning, middle, and end. By doing so, the overall tragic story is complete.

    The first article is a real-time running timeline immediately following the shooting. The running dialogue is equivalent to today's 24/7 news outlets providing updates as soon as they are available. Note the various dates and times of the dispatches. They are listed as the newspaper received them. This update covered over five full pages of the newspaper, providing a near minute by minute update on Lincoln's failing condition. I opted to limit this extremely long article to three pages. It gives context, detail, and serves as an excellent example of the overall story. The other accompanying accounts provide excellent coverage of the pursuit and death of the assassin, John Wilkes Booth.

And the arrest and execution of the conspirators to complete this tragic story.

The Nashville Daily Union

Saturday, April 15, 1865

THE REBEL FIENDS AT WORK

President Lincoln Shot

Secretary Seward Stabbed

The President and Mr. Seward both Dead

Grief of Mrs. Lincoln

Seward's Son and Attendants Attacked

Young Seward's Skull Fractured

Wilkes Booth the President's Assassin

Seward's Assassin Escaped

No Celebration in Nashville.

WASHINGTON, APRIL 15TH, 12:30 A.M.—*The President was shot in the Theatre tonight; he is perhaps mortally wounded.*

2nd DISPATCH.—*The President is not expected to live through the night. He was shot at the Theatre. Secretary Seward was also assassinated. No arteries were cut.*

WASHINGTON, April 15,--*President Lincoln and wife with their friends this evening visited Ford's Theatre for the purpose of witnessing the performance of American Cousin.*

It was announced in the papers that Gen. Grant would also be present, but he left by the late train of cars for New Jersey. The theater was densely crowded, and everybody seemed delighted with the scene before them. During the third act and while there was a temporary pause for one of the actors to enter, the sharp report of a pistol was heard which merely attracted attention but suggested nothing serious, until a man rushed to the front of the president's box waving a long dagger in his right hand, and exclaiming Sic Semper Tyrannis, and immediately leapt from the box which was in the second tier to the stage beneath, and ran across to the opposite side of the stage, making his escape amid the bewilderment of the audience, from the rear of the theater, and mounting a horse and fled.

The screams of Mrs. Lincoln first disclosed the fact to the audience that the president had been shot, when all present rose to their feet, rushing to the stage, many exclaiming hang him. The excitement was of the wildest possible description, and of course, there was an abrupt intermission of theatrical performances. There was a rush toward the president's box, when cries were heard, stand back, give him air, has anyone stimulants. After there was a hasty examination, it was found that the president had been shot through the head above and back of the temporal bone, and that some of his brain was oozing out. He was removed to a private house opposite the theater, and the Surgeon General of the Army and the other surgeons were called to attend his condition.

On an examination of the private box, blood was discovered on the back of the cushioned rocking chair, on which the president had been sitting; also, on the partition; and on the floor, a common single-barreled pocket pistol was found on the carpet.

A military guard was placed in front of the private residence to which the president had been conveyed. An immense crowd was in front of it, all deeply anxious to learn the condition of the president. It had been previously announced that the wound was mortal, but all hoped otherwise. The shock of the community was terrible.

At midnight the cabinet ministers Sumner, Farnsworth, Judge Bates, Gov. Oglesby, Gen. Meigs, Col. Hayes, and a few personal friends, was Surgeon General Barnes and his immediate assistance were around his bedside. The president was in a state of syncope, totally insensible, and breathing woefully. The blood oozed from the wound at the back of his head. The surgeon used every possible effort medical skill, but all hope was gone. The parting of his family with the dying President is too sad for description.

The president and Mrs. Lincoln did not start for the theater until 8:15 o'clock. Speaker Colfax was at the White House at the time, and the president stated to him that he was going although Mrs. Lincoln had not been well, because the papers had announced that Gen. Grant was to be present, and as Gen. Grant had gone north he did not wish the audience to be disappointed. He went with apparent reluctance and urged speaker Colfax to go with him, but that gentleman had made other arrangements and with Mr. Ashmead of Massachusetts, bid him good night.

War Department for 10 AM April 15 – Maj. Gen. Dix – the president, continues insensible and is shrinking. Sec. Seward remains without change. Fred K. Seward's skull was fractured in two places besides a severe cut on the head. The attendant is still alive but hopeless. Major Seward's wounds not dangerous. It is now ascertained with reasonable certainty that two assassins were engaged in the horrible affair; Wilkes Booth being the one that shot the president, and the other, the companion of his, whose name *is not known but whose description is so clear that he can hardly escape.*

It appears from letters found in Booth's trunk that the murder was planned before 4 March, but fell through then because the accomplice backed out until Richmond could be heard from. Booth and his accomplice were at the livery stable at 6 o'clock last evening, and left there with their horses about 10 o'clock or shortly before that hour. It would seem that they had for several days spent seeking their chances, but for some unknown reason, it was not carried into effect until last night. One of them has evidently made his way to Baltimore; the other has not yet been traced.

Signed E. M. Stanton.

Washington, April 15. – *When the excitement at the theater was at its wildest height, reports were circulated that Sec. Seward had also been killed. On reaching this gentleman's residence, a crowd and military guard were around the door, and on entering, it was ascertained that the reports are based in truth. Everybody there was so excited that scarcely an intelligent word could be gathered, but the facts are substantially as follows: about 10 o'clock, a man rang the bell, and the call was answered by a colored man.*

He said he had come from Dr. Veerdier, Secretary Steward's family physician, with a prescription, at the same time holding in his hand a small piece of folded paper, and saying an answer to a refusal, that he must see the secretary as he was entrusted with particular directions concerning the medicine. He still insisted on going up, although repeatedly informed that no one could enter the chamber, he pushed the servant aside and walked hastily towards the secretary's room. He was there met by Mr. Fred Seward, of whom he demanded to see the secretary, making the same representation which he did to the servant. What further passed in the way of colloquy is not known, but the man struck him on the head with a billy, severely injuring his skull, and felling him almost senseless.

The assassin then rushed to the chamber, and attacked Mr. Seward, the paymaster of the United States Army, Mr. Hensel, a messenger of the State Department, and two male nurses disabling them. He then rushed upon the secretary who was lying in bed in the same room, and inflicted three stabs in his neck, but severing it is thought and hoped no arteries, though he bled profusely.

The assassin then rushed downstairs, mounted his horse at the door, and rode off before an alarm could be given and in the same manner as the assassin of the president.

War Department, *Washington, April 15 – Maj. Gen. Dix; Abraham Lincoln died this morning at 7:22 o'clock.*

E. M. Stanton Secretary of War.

New York, April 15, *at 9 AM intense sorrow is depicted on all countenances at the horrible events that occurred in Washington last night, and the grief of all good men is apparent everywhere at the death of the president.*

No flags are hoisted in the city this morning until the state of the president was known, when they were all placed at half-mast.

People appear perfectly horrified, and yet most rages undoubtedly felt towards all known secessionists and rebel sympathizers.

The Brooklyn Daily Eagle

Thursday, April 27, 1865

ARREST OF THE ASSASSINS

FURTHER PARTICULARS

THE 16th NEW YORK CAVALRY MAKE THE ARREST

A COLORED MAN GUIDES THE SOLDIERS

LAST WORDS OF BOOTH

WASHINGTON, APRIL 27th

The Star has the following particulars of the capture of Booth:

To Lieut. Col. L.C. Baker, special detective of the War Department, and his admirably trained detective force, and to the 16th New York Cavalry, active participators in the seizure of the criminals, the country owes a debt of gratitude for this timely service. It seems that a detachment of the 16th New York Cavalry, numbering about 25 men, was dispatched from the city on Monday, under the direction of Col. L. C. Baker, special detective of the War Department, in command of Lieut. Dougherty, accompanied by some of Col. Baker's officers, captured and killed Booth, and captured Harold, one of his accomplice alive.

The Cavalry, after leaving here, landed at Belle Plain in the neighborhood immediately started out in pursuit of Booth and Harold, having previously ascertained from a colored man that they had crossed the river into Virginia at Swan Paint in a small canoe hired by Booth from a man for $300.

Proceeding on towards Bowling Green, some 3 miles from Port Royal, Lieut. Dougherty, who was in command of the Cavalry, discovered that Booth and Harold were secreted *in a large barn owned by a man named Garred and were well-armed.*

The cavalry then surrounded the barn and summoned Booth is and his accomplice to surrender. Harold was inclined at first to accede to the request, but Booth accused him of cowardice. Then both peremptorily refused to surrender and made preparations to defend themselves.

In order to take the conspirators alive, the barn was fired, and the flames getting too hot for Harold he approached the door of the barn and signaled his willingness to be taken, prisoner. The door was then opened sufficient to allow Harold to put his arms through that he might be handcuffed.

As an officer was about placing the irons upon Harold's wrists, Booth fired upon the party from the barn, which was returned by Sgt. Boston Corbett, of the 16th New York, the ball striking Booth in the neck, from the effects of which he died in about four hours.

Booth, before breathing his last, was asked if he had anything to say when he replied: "Tell my mother that I died for my country."

Harold and the body of Booth were brought into Belle Plain at 8 o'clock last night, and reached the Navy Yard here at 1 o'clock this morning, on board of the steamer John S. Ides, Capt. Henry Wilson.

The statement heretofore published that Booth had injured one of his legs by the falling of his horse, has proved to be correct.

After he was shot, it was discovered that one of his legs was badly injured, and that he was compelled to wear an old shoe, and use crutches, which he had with him in the barn.

Booth was shot about 4 o'clock in the morning, and died about 7 o'clock. Booth had upon his person some bills of exchange, but only $17 in treasury notes.

It appears that Booth and Harold left Washington together on the night of the murder President Lincoln and passed through Leonardtown, Maryland, concealing themselves in the vicinity until an opportunity was afforded them to cross the river at Swan Point, which they did, as stated.

The man who hired Booth and his accomplice, the boat in which he crossed the river was captured, we understand, but afterward made his escape.

Harold has been lodged in a secure place.

Bowling Green, near which place, Booth was killed, is a post village of the capitol of Caroline County, Virginia, on the road from Richmond to Fredericksburg, 45 miles north of the former place, and is situated in a fertile and healthy region. It contains two churches, three stores, two males, and about 300 inhabitants.

Port Royal is a post village in Caroline County, Virginia, on the right bank of the Rappahannock River, 22 miles below Fredericksburg. It has a population of 600 and has a good steamboat landing near the place.

The Philadelphia Enquirer

Friday, July 7, 1865

JUSTICE!

The Findings of the Military Commission!

SENTENCES OF THE ASSASSINS!

Payne, Atzerott, Harold and Mrs. Surratt to be Hung!

THEY ARE TO BE EXECUTED TODAY!

Mudd, Arnold and O'Laughlin Imprisoned for Life!

SPANGLER MERCIFULLY DEALT WITH!

He Gets Six Years Confinement in the Penitentiary

THE SENTENCES APPROVED BY THE PRESIDENT

The Announcement of the News to the Condemned!

PAYNE MAINTAINS STOLIDITY!

Both Mrs. Surratt and Atzerott Become Agitated.

THE CONDUCT OF HAROLD

His Interview with His Sisters

PREPARATIONS FOR THE EXECUTION

Efforts to Obtain a Commutation of Mrs. Surratt's Sentence!

THE PRESIDENT DECLINES TO INTERFERE

CONDEMNATION OF THE ASSASSINS.

WASHINGTON, July 6.--In accordance with the findings and sentences of the military commission, which the President approved yesterday, David E. Harold, Lewis Payne, Mrs. Surratt, and George A. Atzerott are to be hung tomorrow, by the proper military authorities.

Dr. Mudd, Arnold and O'Laughlin are to be imprisoned for life, and Spangler for six years, all at hard labor, in the Albany penitentiary.

THE OFFICIAL ORDER.

WASHINGTON, July 6.-- The following important order has just been issued: –

War Department, Adjutant-General's Office, Washington, July 5, 1865. – Two Major General W.S. Hancock, United States Volunteers, Commanding the Middle Military Division, Washington, D. C.

Whereas, by the Military Commission appointed in paragraph four, special orders number 211, dated War Department, Adjutant General's Office, Washington, May 6, 1865, and of which Major General David Hunter, United States Volunteers, was President, the following persons were tried, and, after mature consideration of evidence adduced in their cases, were found and sentenced as hereinafter stated, as follows –

Harold's Sentence

First. David E. Harold. – Finding of this specification, guilty, except combining, and confederating and conspiring with Edward Spangler, as to which part thereof, not guilty; of the charge guilty except the words of the charge, that he combined, confederated and conspired with Edward Spangler, as to which part of the charge not guilty.

Sentence – and the Commission does, therefore, sentence him, the said David E. Harold, to be hanged by the neck until he be dead, at such time and place as the President of the United States shall direct, two-thirds of the commission concurring therein.

Atzerott's Sentence.

Second. George A. Atzerott. – Finding of specification, guilty, except combining,

confederating and conspiring with Edward Spangler; of this not guilty. Of the charge, guilty, except combining, confederating and conspiring with Edward Spangler; of this, not guilty.

Sentence. – And the Commission does therefore sentence him, the said George A. Atzerott, to be hung by the neck until he be dead, at such time and place as a President of the United States shall direct, two-thirds of the commission concurring therein.

Payne's Sentence.

Third. Lewis Payne. – Finding of the specification, guilty, except combining, confederating and conspiring with Edward Spangler; of this, not guilty. Of the charge, guilty, except combining confederating and conspiring with Edward Spangler; of this, not guilty.

Sentence. – And the Commission does therefore sentence him, the said Lewis Payne, to be hung by the neck until he be dead, at such time and place as a President of the United States shall direct, two-thirds of the commission concurring therein.

Mrs. Surratt's Sentence.

Fourth. Mary E. Surratt. – Finding of this specification guilty, except as to receiving, sustaining, harboring, and concealing Samuel Arnold and Michael O'Laughlin, and except as to combining, confederating and conspiring with Edward Spangler; of this not guilty. Of the charge guilty, except as to combining, confederating and conspiring with Edward Spangler; of this not guilty

Sentence. – And the Commission does, therefore, sentence or, the said Mary E. Surratt, to be hung by the neck until she be dead, at such time and place as the President of the United States shall direct, two-thirds of the members of the commission concurring therein.

President Johnson's Approval.

And whereas, the President of the United States has approved the foregoing sentences in the following order, to wit: –

EXECUTIVE MANSION, July 5, 1865 – the foregoing sentences in the cases of David E. Harold, G. A. Atzerott, Lewis Payne and Mary E. Surratt, are hereby approved; and it is ordered that the sentence in the cases of David E. Harold, G. A. Atzerott, Lewis Payne and Mary E. Surratt be carried into execution by the proper military authority, under the direction of the Secretary of War, on the 7th day of July, 1865, between the hours of 10:00 AM and 2:00 PM of that day.

Signed Andrew Johnson, President

Therefore you are hereby commanded to cause the foregoing sentences in the cases of David E. Harold, G. A. Atzerott, Lewis Payne, and Mary E. Surratt to be duly executed, in accordance with the President's order. By command of the President of the United States.

E. D. Townsend,

Assistant Adjutant General

In the remaining cases of O'Laughlin, Spangler, Arnold, and Mudd, the findings and sentences are as follows: –

O'Laughlin's sentence.

Fifth. Michael O'Laughlin. – Finding of the specification guilty, except the words thereof, as follows: – and in the further prosecution of the conspiracy aforesaid, on the nights of the 13th and 14th of April, 1865, at Washington City, and within the military department and the military lines aforesaid, the said Michael O'Laughlin did there and then lying in wait for Ulysses S. Grant, then Lieutenant General and Commander of the Armies of the United States, with intent then and there to kill and murder the said Ulysses S. Grant, of said words not guilty, and except combining, confederating and conspiring with Edward Spangler, of this not guilty of the charge, guilty, except combining, confederating and conspiring with Edward Spangler; of this not guilty.

Sentence. – The Commission sentence of O'Laughlin to be imprisoned at hard labor for life.

Spangler's Sentence.

Six. Finding. – Edward Spangler, of the specification, not guilty, except as to the words, "the said Edward Spangler, on said 14th day of April, A. D. 1865, at about the same hour of that day, aforesaid, within said military department and the military lines after said, did aid and abet him (meaning John Wilkes Booth) and making his escape after the said Abraham Lincoln had been murdered and manner aforesaid," and of these words, guilty.

On the charge not guilty, but guilty of having feloniously and traitorously aided and abetted John Wilkes Booth and making his escape after having killed and murdered Abraham Lincoln, President of United States, he, the said Edward Spangler, at the time of aiding and abetting aforesaid, well knowing that the said Abraham Lincoln, President aforesaid, had been murdered by the said John Wilkes Booth as aforesaid. The Commission sentenced Spangler to hard labor for six years.

Arnold's Sentence.

Seventh. Samuel Arnold. – Of the specifications guilty, except combining, confederating, and conspiring with Edward Spangler, of this not guilty. Of the charge guilty, except combining, confederating, and conspiring with Edward Spangler, of this not guilty, the commission sentenced him to imprisonment at hard labor for life.

Dr. Mudd's Sentence.

Eighth. Samuel A. Mudd. – Of this specification guilty, except combining, confederating and conspiring with Edward Spangler; of this not guilty; and accepting receiving and entertaining and harboring and concealing said Lewis Payne, John H. Surratt, Michael O'Laughlin, George A. Atzerott, Mary E. Surratt and Samuel Arnold, of this not guilty.

Of the charge guilty, except combining, confederating and conspiring with Edward Spangler, of this not guilty. The Commission sentenced Mudd to be imprisoned at hard labor for life.

The president's order in these cases is as follows: –

It is further ordered that the prisoners, Samuel Arnold, Samuel A. Mudd, and Michael O'Laughlin, be confined at hard labor in the penitentiary to Albany, New York, during the period designated in their respective sentences.

Andrew Johnson, President.

OUR SPECIAL DISPATCHES

Washington, July 6. – The announcement and findings of the military commission in the cases of the conspirators, made today about noon, completely absorbed public attention during the remainder of the day. Scarcely anything else was talked of in the streets, hotels, and every place where citizens mostly congregate.

The general sentiment seemed to justify the findings of the Commission, but the short period of time allowed *the prisoners between the announcement of the sentence and their execution did not generally appear to meet the public approval. This, however, is in accordance with the practice of court-martial, sentences in such cases being executed almost immediately after the findings are officially published.*

It was intended the announcement should have been made this morning in the papers throughout the country by the Associated Press, the decision of the present having been made yesterday, but owing to some misunderstanding, it was not announced until today.

Judge Holt with the President.

The President having nearly recovered from his indisposition, yesterday invited Judge Advocate-General Holt to the White House, and after mature deliberation, the President approved the findings and sentences in each case as rendered by the commission.

The Sentences Read to the Prisoners.

About noon today, General Hancock, who was charged with the execution of the sentences, proceeded to the penitentiary, and in company with Major General Hartranft visited the cell of each prisoner and informed each what verdict had been rendered. No one was present at this interview, but the two Generals and the turnkey.

Mrs. Surratt,

On learning her fate, was extremely depressed, and wept bitterly. She was alone, her daughter having left her a short time before, not knowing the sentence was to be announced to her mother today.

Payne.

Seem to regard it as a foregone conclusion and manifested little or no emotion. He has evidently unnerved himself to meet his death with firm resolution.

Atzerott

Was violently agitated and almost paralyzed with fear. He evidently hoped for a different result, but it is difficult to see how he could have expected it to have been otherwise.

Harold

Listened to the reading of the order in his case with boyish indifference, but soon after became impressed with the solemnity of his situation and appeared more serious, asking that his sisters might be allowed to visit him.

Payne asked for a Baptist Clergyman.

Payne asked that Dr. Stracker, a Baptist Clergyman of Baltimore, be sent for, which was done, and that gentleman arrived here this evening, as in attendance upon the prisoner.

Mary Surratt's Spiritual Advisors.

Mrs. Surratt asked that father's Walter and Wiget, Catholic Priest of Baltimore, be sent for. Her wish was immediately complied with, and both the clergyman arrived this evening, and were admitted to her cell.

Rev. Dr. Butler Attends Atzerott.

Atzerott could name no clergyman he wished to attend him; but upon General Hartranft naming Rev., Mr. Butler, a Lutheran clergyman of Washington City, the prisoner desired he might be sent for, and he was in attendance upon the prisoner early this afternoon.

The Hour of Execution.

The four prisoners will be hung tomorrow, between 10 and 2 o'clock, probably about 12.

Who Will be Admitted.

The execution will be conducted privately, no one being admitted except officers and soldiers connected with the prison, relatives, and friends of the prisoners, witnesses, and attaches of the press.

General Hancock was personally engaged this afternoon and issuing tickets of admission, and no one will be admitted without a ticket, and no ticket can be transferred. A register is, with the name of every person to whom a ticket is issued, and no other person will be allowed to use it.

Harold Sisters Visit Him.

Five of Harold sisters visited him this afternoon at the prison, and the scene was truly distressing. After they left him, they wept bitterly, in the entrance room downstairs. Two are grown ladies and the others young misses. But they all seemed to realize the dreadful situation of their brother.

One of them brought a small basket of cakes and little delicacies for the prisoner, which was left in charge of General Hartanft to be examined before being given to him. One of the elder sisters sat down and wrote a note to her brother, which was also left in charge of General Hartanft to give Arnold.

The Scaffold.

Is being built this afternoon, in the south yard of the prison, and will be large enough to execute all at one time. The coffins and burial clothes are being prepared this afternoon and evening at the arsenal.

A False Rumor.

An impression appears to be throughout the city that Mrs. Surratt will not be executed, that the President will commute her sentence to imprisonment.

In less than an hour after the findings had been announced this rumor was on the street, and it was asserted that many who had been most strenuous in asking for severe punishment upon the conspirators were willing to unite in an effort to have the sentence in Mrs. Surratt's case changed to imprisonment. This rumor was widespread, but had no foundation, in fact, the wish was evidently father to the thought.

No Executive Clemency.

Harold sisters called at the White House this afternoon, pleading for mercy, and father Walker and Mr. Aiken, one of Mrs. Surratt's counsel, also called on behalf of Mrs. Surratt, but the President declined to see any of them and referred them all to Judge Holt. It would seem to be the determination of the President to decline interfering in the matter, and there is no doubt, but all those condemned to death will be executed tomorrow, Mrs. Surratt among the number. Aiken says he has some after discovered testimony to offer, favorable to her case. But it is not probable the President will relent tomorrow.

Vermont Watchman and State Journal

Friday, July 14, 1865

DETAILS OF THE EXECUTION.

WASHINGTON, July 7.

This morning Judge Wylie granted the application of the counsel of Mrs. Surratt for a writ of habeas corpus *commanding Major General Hancock to produce the body Mrs. Surratt before the court. The writ was returnable at 10 o'clock, nearly 2 hours after that time, General Hancock entered the court, accompanied by Attorney General Speed, who apologized for parent delay in making return by the General, as it was unavoidable. He then proceeded to read the return, in which General Hancock said the body of Mrs. Surratt was in his possession, under by virtue of an order of President Johnson, for purpose expressed, which read as follows;*

Executive office, July 6, 1865. Two Maj. Gen. W. S. Hancock commanding,

I, Andrew Johnson, President of the United States, do hereby declare the writ of habeas corpus has been hereto for suspended in such cases as this, and I do hereby specifically suspend this writ and direct that you proceed to execute the order hereto forgiven upon the judgment of the Military Commission and you will give this order in return to this writ.

Signed Andrew Johnson, President.

The court remarked that no further steps would be taken in the matter. Attorney-General Speed briefly rejoined commenting upon the distinction between civil and military jurisdictions, showing the utter impossibility of fighting battles, carrying on war, maintaining the government in time of war, by process of law.

DETAILS OF THE EXECUTION

The all-absorbing topic of conversation this morning is the execution of the assassination conspirators. The city seems to wear the aspect of a holiday, appearing in strange contrast with the solemnity of the occasion. Numbers of people have been coming in on the early trains as sightseers to witness an event so singular for America. Crowds have all the morning been curiously observing the residence of Mrs. Surratt, while General Hancock's headquarters had been besieged for passes by an excited throng, rushing by the guard and bursting into his room after defeating their object by overwhelming haste.

Atzerott this morning is completely unnerved, exhibiting a picture of the most abject fear. Mrs. Surratt also is in a distressing condition, and has been fainting at intervals during the morning. Her daughter, Miss Anna Surratt, is excitedly waiting about the door of the President's house, trying to obtain an interview with him, tearfully and entreating every passing stranger to help her save her mother. Arnold's two sisters are also at the White House, exerting every means to obtain a mitigation of his sentence.

The execution of the four condemned conspirators, Payne, Atzerott, Arnold, and Mrs. Surratt, took place at precisely 1:22 o'clock in the presence of about 1000 spectators, all of whom (with the exception of about 250 or 300) were officers and soldiers.

At an early hour, many people were seen flocking toward the arsenal grounds, but only those could enter who had passes signed by General Hancock.

Four regiments of soldiers were in attendance – one outside the arsenal grounds, two just outside the yard, and one in the prison yard and on the walls.

At 11:30 o'clock this morning, large weights are put upon the scaffold, and the traps dropped to try them. They were found quite efficient.

The scaffold was constructed with two drops or traps – each one for two of the conspirators condemned to be executed.

From a beam above hung four ropes of different lengths, or according to the stature of the criminals – the longest being for Payne. The drops had a fall of 5 feet.

About 2 rods from the scaffold were four new-made graves, and near them rough pine board coffins.

As the hour of execution approached, the number of guards on the walls were increased until they stood in close order, elbow to elbow. Every precaution was taken to make the execution sure and quiet.

At one o'clock, four chairs are placed upon the scaffold for the four criminals. As the preparations approached completion, the spectators became more anxious, and everyone was on tiptoes to see or hear anything pertaining to the execution.

At a little past, one o'clock a regiment was drawn up, (inside the yard) forming two sides of the square; and about five minutes before the prisoners were led to the scaffold, a double line of guards was placed between the prison door and the gallows, which was about 2 rods distant. This part of the program completed; the wretched criminals were conducted to the scaffold.

Mrs. Surratt came out leaning on the arms of Col. McCall and a private soldier at the melancholy procession. She was followed by her spiritual advisors. As soon as her eyes caught sight of the gallows, she partially fainted, but was upheld by the strong arms of her attendants. She soon recovered herself, however, and although weak from illness, ascended the scaffold with apparently a firm step.

Payne, escorted on each side by an officer, followed. His gait was erect, and his demeanor did not exhibit the slightest of fear. He looked on the instrument of death with a steady eye, and without the slightest tremor visible in his athletic frame. He appeared to regard the scene with the utmost indifference until he reached the platform, when his manner changed and he momentarily gave way to his feelings, but soon recovered himself, and, until the cap was drawn over his eyes, maintained a stoic indifference. His spiritual advisor delivered the last prayer for him, which seem to affect him more than anything else, and his eyes were moist with tears, which he vainly strove to suppress.

Atzerott came upon the scaffold, the picture of despair. Harold's appearance was that of silly fear. The latter walked somewhat more firm, and was more composed than the other. His lips were constantly moving in prayer, following the whispered words of the clergyman. Atzerott occasionally did the same, but when unoccupied for a moment, consciousness of his position appeared on the ashen face and quivering, fallen jaw, which showed how terrible death appeared to his craven soul.

Mrs. Surratt was attended by fathers Walter and Wiget, Catholic Priest. The others were each attended by ministers of their own choice.

After being seated, General Hartranft proceeded to read the findings of the court – first that of Harold; second of as a Atzerott; third of Payne; and lastly that of Mrs. Surratt, who held a cross it her hands and was in very close communion with her spiritual attendants. The prisoners seemed muttering their prayers during the reading of their sentences. One of the priests then administered the last rites of the church to Mrs. Surratt.

Payne's advisor stepped forward and said that the prisoner Lewis Payne requested him to say that he (Payne) desired to thank all the officers and soldiers who had charge of him; that he had not received an unkind word or look from any one of them all. His spiritual attended then offered prayer in his behalf, asking that his sins might be forgiven him, and that an easy passage out of this world might be granted him. Similar prayers are offered for each of the other prisoners.

The prayers being over the prisoners were placed on the trap, and the nooses adjusted. At this moment, Atzerott seemed so overcome that he was almost unable to rise. While the ropes were being adjusted to the prisoners necks, Atzerott attempted to speak and said: "Gentlemen, beware!" After the cap was drawn over his head, he said: "Goodbye, gentlemen, who are before me now; may we all meet in the other world."

The others – Mrs. Surratt and Harold – had nothing to say, and at 1:20 o'clock, the drop fell. Payne and Harold struggled for about five minutes, Atzerott very little. Mrs. Surratt's neck was broken by the fall, and she died without struggle.

AUTHOR'S COMMENTARY

In 1883, Ulysses S. Grant, former General of the Army and President, recalled the day President Lincoln was assassinated.

Burlingame Herald

Saturday, April 21, 1883

Grant on Lincoln's Assassination

Correspondence of the Boston Traveler: General Grant, in a recent conversation, said: "the darkest day of my life was the day I heard of Lincoln's assassination. I did not know what it meant. Here was the rebellion put down in the field and starting up again in the gutters; we had thought it as a war, now we had to fight it as assassination. Lincoln was killed on the evening of 14 April. I was busy sending out orders to stop recruiting, the purchase of supplies, and to muster out the Army.

Lincoln had promised to go to the theater, and wanted me to go with him. While I was with the president, a note came from Mrs. Grant saying that she must leave Washington that night. She wanted to go to Burlington to see her children. Some incident of a trifling nature and made her resolve to leave that evening. I was glad to have it so, as I did not want to go to the theater. So I made my excuse to Lincoln, and at the proper hour, we started for the train.

As we were driving along Pennsylvania Avenue, a horseman drove past us on a gallop, and back around our carriage, looking into it. Mrs. Grant said: "There is the man who sat near us at lunch today, with some other men, and tried to overhear our conversation. He was so rude that we left the dining room. Here he is now riding after us." I thought it was only curiosity, but learned afterward that the horseman was Booth. It seemed that I was to have been attacked, and Mrs. Grant's sudden resolve to leave changed the plan. A few days after, I received an anonymous letter from a man saying that he had been detailed to kill me, that he rode on my train as far as Havre de Grace, and as my car was locked, he failed to get in. He thanked God that he had failed. I remember that the conductor locked our car, but how true the letter was, I cannot say. I learned of the assassination as I was passing through Philadelphia. I turned around, took a special train, and came on to Washington. It was "the gloomiest day of my life."

SHORT CRIME STORIES

Crooks, Cons, and Killers

AUTHOR'S COMMENTARY

A staple of newspaper reporting has been the short "filler" story. The "fillers" needed to meet a few standards while unintentionally providing us a glimpse into the contemporary society of the 1800s. The editor asked, why is this story worthy of inclusion? Would it interest our readers? And most importantly, will the "filler" help sell newspapers? Then, as today, printed media employs the identical standard for selecting stories—large or small. Will the story sell newspapers?

In the simplest terms, short stories provided filler material for leftover open space on each page. And, if it grabs the attention of the reader, it has served its purpose.

Today, with the need to fill airtime and considering the speed of the electronic media, many of these short stories would generate national and international attention within hours, if not minutes. Consider the following headlines: *Negro Rapist, Kills Her Lover and Rival, A Life of Crime Ended, A Rueben and a Shining "Gold" Brick,* and *"The Deadly Blue Gum Negro."*

In today's world, all would be considered shocking headlines. Yet, in the 1800s and early 1900s, they were not viewed as sensational or shocking. It was merely a matter of everyday life, which was considered interesting, but not worth donating a large amount of printed space.

The short stories also illustrate a sampling of crimes from the period. In many instances, the identical crimes are committed today. Others have given way to the ever-expanding new crimes of today.

Unfortunately, as "fillers," there are no follow up stories. We will never know if justice was eventually served.

Fort Wayne Daily News

Saturday, August 31, 1895

NEGRO RAPIST

An Angry Mob Looking for Him With a Rope

MANCHESTER, MO., Aug. 31. – John Wesley, a negro who has just completed a five-year term in the penitentiary for an attempted criminal assault upon a girl, made another unsuccessful attempt last night about 11 o'clock. The intended victim was Mrs. Rosaline Marmion, an aged widow of Manchester. A posse with the rope has been searching for the negro since midnight, and if captured, he will be strung up.

Fort Wayne Daily News

Saturday, August 31, 1895

Kills Her Lover and Her Rival— Tragedy at Quincy, Ill.

QUINCY, Ill., Aug. 31. – Henry Boling and Rosa Swearingen were shot last night by Dora Heilwagon. Boling had been paying attention to both the women. Last night he took the Swearingen woman buggy riding. Ms. Heilwagon followed in another buggy, and overtaking the pair a short distance outside of the city emptied a revolver at them. She then drove off and has not been arrested. Boling and his companion will die.

Dora Heilwagon surrendered to the police after driving all night in the woods.

Chicago Tribune

Friday, July 17, 1885

A LIFE OF CRIME ENDED.

JOSEPH TAYLOR, THREE TIMES A MURDERER AND FOR YEARS A CONVICT, IS HANGED AT LAST IN PHILIDELPHIA.

PHILADEPHIA, Pa., July 16. –(Special) – Joseph Taylor, one of the most vindictive and dangerous criminals with whom Pennsylvania courts ever had to deal, was hanged today at Moyamensing Prison for the murder of his jailer. Taylor boasted of killing three men and of stabbing or shooting 17 others.

He refused to see or hear a clergyman after his trial and conviction until last night, when his courage gave way. He wept on the scaffold and died after a hard struggle. At the postmortem examination, it was found that his brain, though unusually small (weighing but 43 ¼ ounces), showed no signs whatever of disease. Prof. Parker of the University Pennsylvania pronounced, upon examination, that it's conformation tallied exactly with that of the "criminal brain" – that is to say, it is more like the brain of a monkey than that of a man. The eyes were removed for examination, something which has not before been done in the history of medical jurisprudence in this country.

(Taylor was a most brutal and incorrigible convict, he had been subjected to solitary confinement for ten years and for five his food was passed into him through grated doors. He served five terms in prison, and began his career by stabbing a comrade at the age of 15. Between his last two long terms of imprisonment, he enjoyed 12 hours of liberty. The chaplain of the prison never entered his cell but once, and then Taylor nearly killed him. The last man who undertook to tame him was Keeper Doran, who was brained by Taylor with the leg of an iron bed the moment he entered the cell. It was for this crime that Taylor was hanged.)

AUTHOR'S COMMENTARY

During my research, I located many articles addressing the folklore of the "Blue Gum Negro." It is not the bite of a black man; it is a bite from any ethnicity which can cause deadly infections. It was years before the invention of antibiotics, and a human bite or any wound breaking the skin could result in a fatal infection.

As stated by the Cleveland Clinic, *"Wounds that break the skin can be especially dangerous because of the variety and concentration of bacteria and viruses in saliva. Human bites have more than 50 types of bacteria. Such bites are thought to have a higher rate of infection than dog or cat* bites. About one-third of all hand infections are caused by human bite injuries".

The Newcastle Weekly Courant

Saturday, May 28, 1891

"DEADLY BLUE GUM NEGRO."

There has always been a suspicion throughout the South that the bite of a "blue gum negro" was as poisonous as that of a rattlesnake. While this has been the superstition, there have been doubts about the existence of a "blue gum negro." Many people know of other people who have seen the so-called poisonous negro, but few have ever been found to have actually seen such a person.

The fact that such an individual really exists, and that his bite is poisonous, has been fully established among the people along the Saline River, south of Warren, Arkansas. For several years there has lived a family of negroes in a cabin on the bank of the river, who have eked out the usual poor negro existence by fishing and hunting, the same as hundreds of other families have been doing for years in the same neighborhood.

The family has never been noted for any peculiarity, but recently there has grown a young man who developed certain vicious tendencies which were foreign to those of his family. He has been in constant trouble with his neighbors and with the authorities on account of certain thieving and fighting tendencies. He got to be looked upon as a "bad nigger," and was a sort of desperado who was shunned by all right-minded people of his race.

Recently he got into a fight with another "bad nigger" who lived in another neighborhood, and whom he met at a dance near there. In the fight, he bit his opponent through the hand, with the result that the bitten man became deathly sick in a few minutes, and in about three hours, died from the poison in the wound. Afterward, when the negro was arrested, he bit two of the constables, and both died within four hours of receiving the wound.

This strange incident caused an examination to be made, and it was discovered that the negro was a veritable "blue gum negro," and the fact that the three deaths followed so surely and suddenly after the bite convinced the people that the man was not safe to be left alive, and the result was that the night following the deaths he was taken from the gaol and hanged to a tree.

The Press

Friday, June 22, 1894

SAME OLD STORY

Two Crooks, a Reuben and a Shining "Gold" Brick.

Henry Holker, a wealthy farmer residing near Hopkins, Missouri, was sitting on his porch the other afternoon when three stylishly dressed man drove up. They engaged him in conversation and finally offered to purchase his farm at a high figure. They told him they were Colorado miners and had just returned with plenty of gold.

To prove the assertion, they displayed a valise filled with what appeared to be gold bricks. A trade was soon fixed up, Holker agreeing to take the gold bricks in payment. Then the swindlers discovered that the bricks would overpay the amount by $5,000. Holker went to the bank at Hopkins and drew that amount in cash, which he turned over to the swindlers, who then left for Marysville to draw up the transfer. Holker took the bricks to Hopkins, where he discovered he had been duped. A reward of $500 is offered for the swindlers.

The Press

Friday, June 22, 1894

Father and Brother Avenge a Girl's Alleged Wrongs.

Chicago is greatly excited over a crime which was committed in one of the principal streets the other night. Archibald McKillop, a streetcar conductor, was shot dead by Richard and Orlando Keatley, father and brother of Miss Emily Keatley, to whom McKillop had been engaged.

It seems that the murdered man had been paying marked attention to Miss Keatley for upwards of two years. She was a cashier in a large commercial establishment and became acquainted with the conductor on her trips to and from the business.

It soon ripened into love, and in a year they were engaged to be married. The event was postponed several times at McKillop's request. Finally, they were to be married Saturday evening, June 9. At the last moment, however,

McKillop refused to take the girl as his wife. This so angered her father and brother that they resolved to take his life.

On the following night, he was decoyed from his home by the Keatley's and asked if he would consent to a marriage, upon refusal both emptied the revolvers into his body, leaving him dead on the pavement. They were subsequently arrested on suspicion and finally confessed the deed.

They plead the betrayal of the young woman in justification of their crime. The Keatley's are well connected. The son is a prominent Chicago lawyer. The friends of McKillop are investigating the matter and will push the prosecution of the Keatley's if they find that Miss. Keatley was not what an expected bride should be.

Lincoln Journal Star

Saturday, May 13, 1916

MAYBE PRACTICAL JOKE OR A GROTESQUE MURDER

CHICAGO, May 13. – Authorities today sought to solve a mystery that may reveal Cook County's most grotesque murder or the practical joke of medical students. The body of a man, stabbed 13 times, shot three times and bound and gagged, was found in the Des Plaines River late yesterday by Mr. and Mrs. Walker Motter, who were picking flowers. At the morgue, a strange discovery was made that the body, which apparently had been in the river for several months, had been embalmed.

One police theory was that medical students had thoroughly mutilated a cadaver and tossed it in the river.

The Brooklyn Daily Eagle

Thursday, November 12, 1874

The Maddening Effects of Murder

Murders are multiplying. They are not only multiplying in numbers, but are increasing in atrocity. The Eagle of last evening contained a narrative of another murder whose description would make any man's hair stand on each particular end. It occurred on board the ship Neptune, of the Black Ball Line. Two men had set up on Stephen A. Smith, the boatswain of the crew, cutaway half his face, exposing the jawbone, with the ragged edge of raw flesh clinging to it in threads. They had cut off his left hand, and, the gangrene setting in, the arm rotted to the shoulder, and they had hacked his body with their knives. The man is at the Long Island College Hospital but no care, no skill is likely to affect his recovery.

This morning at 10 o'clock, Udderzook was hung in Westchester, Pennsylvania. Udderzook murdered a man in the woods, cut off the head of the victim, and most wanton mutilation, left the head in one place and transported the ghastly trunk to another.

In Paris, a few weeks since, a man shot his wife, cut her body in pieces, and strewed them on the floors of several rooms.

Two other cases of grotesque murder lately occurred in London.

Murder, alas, was never a very scarce crime among men since the days of Cain; but this fondness for mutilation, for its own horrible sake, apart from the motives that inspired the murder itself, has in it something strange. It is explainable only on the theory that the committal of the murder, the site of the first blood that wells from the victim, crazes the murderer.

We vehemently believe that if the truth were known, in many cases where insanity has been proven to exist and has been accepted as a reason for acquittal, the insanity was the result, not the cause of the murder. Accepting, for illustration's sake, the theory of Goodrich's murder by Kate Stoddart. It is very easy to believe that Kate was saying when she killed Goodrich, and that the site of what she had done bereft of reason.

Dickens seemed to have an appreciation of this effect on a murderer when he described the flight of Sykes after the murder of Nancy, the hiding of Jonas Chuzzlewit after the murder of Tigg. The character of both men is described as utterly changed.

Cunning remains in both, but in both, the reasoning faculty is fairly disorganized. It is impossible on any other theory to account for the useless barbarity lavished by murderers on the dead. A man, after committing murder remaining perfectly sane, would have no idea but that of escape or concealment. Webster was saying when he mutilated Parkman. The mutilation there was not a mutilation committed for its own sake, but to help conceal the fatal results of the first blow. But this man in Paris, cutting his wife into mincemeat and strewing her about the house, could not have been sane. Yet the examination shows conclusively that he was sane up to the very moment of the murder, though insane immediately after it.

The murder itself crazed him – the site of the blood. It is worthy to remark that these mutilations are always committed after murders were blood has been shed to take a life. A prisoner whose victim dies and bloodied has never been known to mutilate its body and these horrible ways.

Of course, there is no possible way of preventing mutilation of the sort, and we have no suggestion to offer thereon. We simply desire to call attention to the frequent maddening effect of murderers accompanied by bloodshed as an example of the frequent insanity of murderers, known in the past to have been perfectly healthy mind. It is only in its application to the frequent plea of insanity that we refer to it. The plea of insanity at the time of the murder has often been based on the alleged manner of the murder. Such extreme atrocities, I needed to affect death, have been pleaded as evidence of madness. It is not well, in such cases, to inquire whether the atrocities did not follow a murder planned in sound mind, but subsequently brutified by the madness which the murder itself awoke?

Lewiston Daily Teller

Friday, December 10, 1880

BEECHER'S BURGLARY

Beecher's Church in Brooklyn is now the center of a network of telephone wires running out to thousands of public and private partners. The object is that all can hear the great preacher miles away from the church in their own private homes. The rental of the wires net him over $200,000 per year from private families. Of late, he preaches to a transient congregation, his regular congregation listened at home.

Recently a number of burglars entered the church by night and were engaged in stripping the church of its golden ornaments, while the telephone carried their conversation to the homes of the whole congregation, and as the men were absent, the church was soon surrounded by the women, and the five burglars were caught.

AUTHOR'S COMMENTARY

As a police officer, I testified in scores of criminal cases and heard dozens of ridiculous excuses proffered by defense attorneys hoping to sway a naive jury for acquittal. The excuses ranged from semi-truthful to utterly absurd, and at times, they were hilarious. However, the defense attorney in the following story proved to be typical for the 1800s and today. They will say anything if it will result in their client being found not guilty.

In this case, the woman's back story is fascinating. She was known as Mrs. Virginia Seymour, Dr. Emma Burleigh, and Mrs. McCarty. During the Civil War, she was arrested several times by Union troops as a rebel spy while smuggling quinine and other supplies across the Potomac River to the Confederate Forces. During each arrest, she was dressed as a man and used the name Johnny McCarty. It would seem her punishment for aiding the rebel forces would have brought swift and unforgiving justice under Article 88 of the War Department Adjutant General Order in 1863, the punishment listed for spying was death by hanging. According to records, not all spies were executed; some were exchanged for prisoners of war.

However, every time she was arrested, the Commanding General holding her for trial before a military tribunal received an urgent order from the Secretary of War to immediately release her. Undoubtedly, those orders puzzled the General since hanging spies was considered standard punishment. But it would not confuse anyone with an understanding of Washington, D.C., then and now. This lovely lady was the mistress of many of the leading Union politicians in Washington. She was also known to blackmail the men she "serviced".

In the following incident, the man she meant to shoot was Mr. Milton Thompson. He was one of the many men she had been blackmailing. When he cut off the funds, she tracked him down and started shooting. He survived, but Mr. Henry Hall, an innocent man, was killed by an errant shot and another man wounded.

Before this shooting, she operated an illegal and "secretive" abortion clinic on Clinton Ave. in Washington, D.C. It was believed, and probably true, that some of the young women obtaining abortions were the mistresses of various married high-profile Washington politicians. Operating the illegal clinic did result in criminal charges. However, being the mistress of powerful, nationally-known politicians, the charges quickly and quietly vanished.

Also, late at night, she secretly "serviced" many politicians in her home on Clinton Ave and at various Washington, D.C. hotels. Without question, she was an enterprising woman. Today, anyone with a working knowledge of Washington's politicians understands nothing has changed.

According to the Vermont Journal of Saturday, May 25, 1872, after the jury deliberated for an hour, she was found not guilty of shooting and killing Henry H. Hall. The paper commented, *"This result of acquittal was, of course, to be expected. The wonder is that she was indicted and tried for the crime of murder. That she will finally go free, or at the most receive, but slight punishment for her brutal assault seems quite probable. The sort of females to which this person belongs seem to be regarded with special compassion by juries and judges, and it is now a pretty* serious question whether female assassins in this country are not a "privileged class."

During the 1800s, like today, it pays to have powerful politicians in your pocket, or as in this case, in your bed.

The Tiffin Tribune

Thursday, February 22, 1872

The Defense Attorney and The Washington, D.C. Mistress

The nation never lived with a more funny criminal practice than these United States; and of all its funny things here is the best: Mrs. McCarty shot at a man in Utica, N.Y., and missed him, wounded a second and killed a third. Upon trial she pled insanity, and here is what followed.

Court—"Does the counsel claim that the accused was insane before and is still insane?"

Counsel—"Yes; as far as it is necessary to exculpate the accused from legal accountability for the crime."

PHOTOS

Jack the Ripper, Illustration

Elizabeth Stride, Jack the Ripper victim

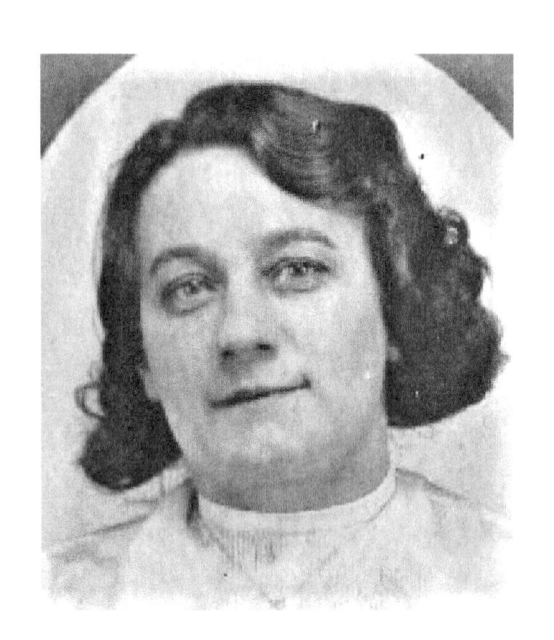

Anna Maria Zwanziger

Lizzie Halliday, serial killer

Billy the Kid

Butch Cassidy

The Sundance Kid

Jesse James

Tribucio Vazquez

President Lincoln

Lincoln in coffin

John Wilkes Booth

Lewis Powell, Lincoln conspirator

David Herold, Lincoln conspirator

George Atzerodt, Lincoln conspirator

Mary Surratt

Lincoln's conspirators hung

*For More News About Mike Rothmiller,
Signup For Our Newsletter:*

http://wbp.bz/newsletter

Word-of-mouth is critical to an author's long-term success. If you appreciated this book please leave a review on the Amazon sales page:

http://wbp.bz/tcc2a

**AVAILABLE FROM MIKE ROTHMILLER
AND WILDBLUE PRESS!**

TRUE CRIME CHRONICLES: Volume
One by MIKE ROTHMILLER

http://wbp.bz/tcc1

AVAILABLE FROM SUSAN HALL AND WILDBLUE PRESS!

THE WORLD ENCYCLOPEDIA OF SERIAL KILLERS: VOLUME ONE by SUSAN HALL

http://wbp.bz/tweoska

AVAILABLE FROM ALICE KAY HILL AND WILDBLUE PRESS!

UNDER A FULL MOON by ALICE KAY HILL

http://wbp.bz/underafullmoona

WILDBLUE PRESS

See even more at:
http://wbp.bz/tc

More True Crime You'll Love From WildBlue Press

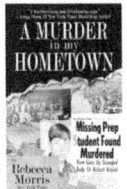

A MURDER IN MY HOMETOWN by Rebecca Morris
Nearly 50 years after the murder of seventeen year old Dick Kitchel, Rebecca Morris returned to her hometown to write about how the murder changed a town, a school, and the lives of his friends.

wbp.bz/hometowna

BETRAYAL IN BLUE by Burl Barer & Frank C. Girardot Jr.
Adapted from Ken Eurell's shocking personal memoir, plus hundreds of hours of exclusive interviews with the major players, including former international drug lord, Adam Diaz, and Dori Eurell, revealing the truth behind what you won't see in the hit documentary THE SEVEN FIVE.

wbp.bz/biba

SIDETRACKED by Richard Cahill
A murder investigation is complicated by the entrance of the Reverend Al Sharpton who insists that a racist killer is responsible. Amid a growing media circus, investigators must overcome the outside forces that repeatedly sidetrack their best efforts.

wbp.bz/sidetrackeda

BETTER OFF DEAD by Michael Fleeman
A frustrated, unhappy wife. Her much younger, attentive lover. A husband who degrades and ignores her. The stage is set for a love-triangle murder that shatters family illusions and lays bare a quiet family community's secret world of sex, sin and swinging.

wbp.bz/boda